Joy and Sadness in Children's Sports

written and edited by

Rainer Martens

HUMAN KINETICS PUBLISHERS
CHAMPAIGN, ILLINOIS

ISBN 0-931250-10-2.

Copyright © 1978 by Rainer Martens. All rights reserved. Except for use in a review, the reproduction or utilization of this work in any form or by any electronic, mechanical, or other means, now known or hereafter invented, including xerography, photocopying, and recording, and in any information storage and retrieval system is forbidden without the written permission of the publisher. Printed in the United States of America.

HUMAN KINETICS PUBLISHERS
BOX 5076   CHAMPAIGN, IL 61820

to my *parents* —
who helped me know
the joy of sports.

Preface

Sports mean a great deal to me. They played an important part in my childhood. They are important in my adulthood. I am convinced that my early participation in Cub Scout baseball, rag-tag football, and midget basketball enriched my life immeasurably. Sports have brought me much happiness and taught me many useful lessons. I cannot prove it to others, but I believe it to be so.

I want today's children to be enriched by sports, to learn the lessons I found helpful, to know the joy of sports that I have known. I want them to discover the natural "highs" found in sports rather than those they can purchase on the street. I want them to know the beauty of skilled human motion rather than the ugliness of uncoordinated movement. Through sport I want them to acquire respect for authenticity and individuality, to discover courage and perseverance, and to experience the harmony of body and emotions.

I do not, however, view sports as a panacea. Sports will not solve all the problems of children; they may even create some. Sports can help children enjoy their childhood and facilitate their transition into adulthood, but this help is not guaranteed by mere participation. Louis Alley recently stated in the *Phi Delta Kappan* that sports "should be thought of as a two-edged sword, capable of cutting in opposite directions. The direction the sword cuts depends on those who swing it, not on the sword itself." Adults are swinging the two-edged sword in children's sports programs, and this book examines the direction in which they are cutting.

Joy and Sadness in Children's Sports is a biased book, for I am a proponent of children's sports. The book emphasizes the joy of sports, but it also examines those events that create sadness. Hopefully this will help us learn how to swing the sword in the right direction.

The focus of the book is on nonschool sports, but many of the issues are pertinent to school sports programs as well. Our examination begins when children first enter sport, which in some cases is incredibly young, and continues to about 14 years of age. The book is not comprehensive. It is uneven in its depth of treatment for different topics, reflecting the unevenness in our knowledge and concern about various issues in children's sports.

The book was prepared for those adults who care about children's sports—whether they are parents, volunteer coaches, or professionals. Concerned parents and dedicated coaches will find much to contemplate as they read this book. Sports administrators, both school and nonschool, will find a wealth of information in these pages. Physical educators and recreators also should find this anthology stimulating. It is my hope that this book may help adults increase the joy and decrease the sadness in sports both for children and for themselves.

Over the past 2 years my research associate, Julie Simon, has identified an extensive body of literature on children's sports. From this literature I selected 36 articles to appear in the book on the basis of three simple criteria: pertinence, succinctness, and quality of writing. Initially I intended to provide only brief introductory and closing comments to each part and section; however, as the book developed, I found myself writing substantially more. My comments throughout are intended to serve several purposes. First, they try to bring some cohesion to the readings. Second, they summarize some of the pertinent research on the issue when such research exists. Third, they raise points of concern when others have not done so. And fourth, they express my opinion about issues in children's sports.

To those authors and publishers who permitted me to reproduce their articles, I am indebted (literally in some cases). My thanks to Mary Ann Carmack and Jack Halbert for providing helpful remarks about the manuscript. I also wish to acknowledge my secretary, Mrs. Dolores Sawtelle, for her help in preparing the manuscript. A special thanks goes to Julie Simon who spent many hours identifying and locating the literature on children's sports and who also provided helpful comments on an earlier draft. And to my wife Marilyn, who is "me," I thank you for being you.

Rainer Martens
Champaign, Illinois
April 1978

Contents

PART FIVE
More Joy and Less Sadness   *345*

PART ONE

The Controversy

Mark Davis hates sports. He doesn't play them or watch them, and he forbids his son to play in organized sports programs. Mark's aversion for sports is not without cause—his experiences in sports as a youngster were entirely negative. Awkward at age 11 because of a rapid growth spurt, Mark was rejected each time he attempted to join a team. He tried out for the Sprinkle Plumbing baseball team, but the coach told him that he just wasn't good enough to play with his friends. What he needed, the coach said, was to play in the farm league so he could develop his hitting, fielding, and throwing skills. So to the farm league he went, but the only things he developed were patience and a few holes in the bottom of his britches from sitting on the bench for most of the season.

Mark gave up baseball, but thought that with his newly acquired height perhaps basketball would be his sport. After only 4 weeks of playing with a community league team, Mark quit. The coach, a young college student, constantly criticized Mark, poking fun at his awkwardness. The other kids on the team were quick to pick up on the coach's example. "What's wrong, butterfingers?", "Come on, clodhopper!", "Hey, clumsy!" were the words of encouragement that he heard from his teammates. Humiliated and discouraged, Mark never again sought to participate in organized sports programs.

☆ ☆ ☆

Dale Peterson lives in New York City. His vocation is firefighting; his avocation is wrestling. For the last 10 years Dale has spent most of his free time as a wrestling coach for about 40 8- to 14-year-old boys. His enthusiasm for wrestling is transfused to his young grapplers through his spirited efforts to build self-respect and confidence while constantly striving to make practice and matches FUN. Few coaches have been more revered by their proteges than Dale Peterson. He is totally devoted to kids' wrestling because he believes his life was transformed by the sport and a coach—a coach who took the trouble to care.

As a youngster Dale had almost no parental guidance, receiving most of his direction from a local street gang. Crime and drugs occupied his life until he met Bob O'Connor. Bob, who also was a fireman, persuaded a reluctant Dale to attend a Boys' Club wrestling practice. Dale's life changed markedly from that day on. Wrestling provided Dale with the identity he had sought through the street gang; he found a new model of leadership. As his wrestling skills grew, he gained the self-respect and confidence that he now strives to build in the youngsters he so proudly coaches.

Sports had profoundly different effects on Mark Davis and Dale Peterson. One was unfortunately negative and the other inspiringly positive. One was a story of sadness and the other a story of joy. But WHY? In *Joy and Sadness in Children's Sports* we search for answers to this question for the millions of children who have been both "turned on" and "turned off" when participating in sports.

In Part One we identify the major issues in children's sports. We will see that the controversy about children's sports is far from being a simple black and white issue as many would have us believe. We begin with a brief history of the rise of children's sports programs in this country and discuss the significance our society ascribes to them. Then the major issues pertaining to children's sports programs are identified through a series of articles written by either proponents or opponents of these sports programs.

SECTION A

A Prelude

The Emergence of Children's Sports

General George W. Wingate and Dr. Luther H. Gulick had the radical thought that in addition to reading, writing, and arithmetic, the New York City school curriculum should include organized sports for boys. They tried their unconventional idea in 1903 by forming the Public Schools Athletic League, thereby inaugurating the first adult-organized youth sports program in the United States. Beginning with little more than 300 enthusiastic boys, the program grew to over 150,000 youngsters in just 7 years. When supporters hailed it as the "greatest athletic organization the world ever saw," little did they know how children's sports programs would continue to grow. Today 17 million boys and girls participate in over 50 sports organized by schools and a host of community and national youth agencies.

Sports rose to rapid prominence in the schools of America during the first 30 years of this century. By the middle 1930's, however, educators were becoming alarmed at the overemphasis on winning and the associated physical and emotional strain of championship play. Eventually educators began denouncing the very sports programs they had created, advocating replacement by a broad-based physical education program for all youngsters. Understandably, such criticism of school-sponsored sports was not well-received by a public who only recently had acquired sufficient leisure time to engage regularly in sports. So, as schools eliminated sports programs, the public turned to a number of community agencies to obtain what they wanted. YMCA's, Boys' Clubs, Boy Scouts and Girl Scouts, local service clubs, religious organizations, and local park and recreation programs quickly met the demand. These organizations saw sports as a vehicle for providing a useful service to the community by fighting delinquency and teaching youngsters discipline and sportsmanship.

The concerns of educators about highly organized sports were not unjustified, but their attempt to dissolve these programs was a gigantic blunder. Unquestionably, well-conducted physical education programs are beneficial for children. It was, however, an unfortunate misjudgment for educators to assume that the limited physical education programs in the schools would satisfy the sports appetite of youngsters and their parents. As more and more elementary and junior high schools eliminated or curtailed interschool sports programs, nonschool agencies developed increasingly larger and more diverse sports programs. Ironically, educators suddenly found themselves no longer leading the movement they had begun. Instead of trained professionals guiding the sports programs of children, well-meaning but untrained volunteers assumed leadership roles. Sadly, educators were left on the sidelines shouting their unheeded warnings and criticisms.

In the 1940's physicians joined educators in voicing their concern about the safety and value of adult-organized children's sports. The American Medical Association and the American Academy of Pediatrics along with the American Association for Health, Physical Education, and Recreation, the National Education Association, and the Department of Elementary School Principals issued a policy statement which emphatically opposed

1. Highly organized competition of a varsity pattern for children of elementary and junior high school age.

2. Tackle football for children below the ninth grade.
3. Boxing for children of any age.

These recommendations, however, were only partially heeded by elementary and junior high schools. Boxing disappeared and tackle football was curtailed somewhat, but all interschool sports competition was not eliminated. A survey completed in 1962 revealed that of 528 school districts sampled, 193 or 37% offered some form of interschool sports competition. Of those schools with a K-6 structure, only 26% offered interschool sports competition, but 64% of the K-8 schools did so.[1]

Today a healthy change in attitudes is occurring among both physicians and educators as they recognize that children's sports programs are here to stay. These professionals—many of whom are past participants of children's sports programs— are now working more constructively with directors of these programs rather than criticizing from the sidelines.

Ironically, it was the unpropitious policy statements of the past which stimulated the growth of *nonschool* programs. From the late 1930's through the 1960's, when physicians and educators were most critical of children's sports programs, all of the major nonschool children's sports organizations were born. For example, Carl Stotz began Little League baseball in 1939, not with the intent of launching a national organization, but in response to the overwhelming interest generated by the baseball league he started in Williamsport, Pennsylvania (see Arthur Daley's *30,000 Little Big Leaguers* for a more complete history of Little League baseball). By 1952 Little League baseball had grown to one-half million boys and by 1977 to 2.26 million boys *and* girls. And yet that number comprises only about 50% of the youth who play organized baseball in this country. During the same period tackle football grew from less than 50,000 participants to over 1.5 million. Pop Warner football, which officially incorporated in 1959 and is the largest nationally organized tackle football program, currently has 240,000 youngsters participating.

As our culture's most popular sports, baseball and football have always attracted the largest number of young participants, but many other sports are now emerging on the scene. Today national organizations exist for just about every sport from archery to wrestling. Under the rubric of sport, kids are riding motorcycles, skateboards, surfboards, and even broncos. They hit golf balls, tennis balls, ping pong balls, and racquetballs. They compete on dirt, grass, ice, hardwood floors, and a host of new synthetic surfaces. They race horses, bicycles, go-carts, and of course each other.

Youngsters not only are entering sports in greater numbers, they are entering sports at an earlier age. If parents are so inclined, they may permit their son or daughter to enter competitive swimming at the age of 3, to play ice hockey or race go-carts at the age of 4, to compete in baseball, bowling, soccer, or tennis at the age of 6, or to race motorcycles and bicylces at the age of 8. For most of these sports, the 4- to 8-year-old can compete to earn not only a national title, but cash prizes, medals, and trophies which often stand taller than the recipients.

The media, which has contributed so much to the sports mania in this nation, is increasingly publicizing young people's sports events. Television coverage of high school sports and other youth sports such as the AAU Junior Olympics is becoming more extensive. A popular magazine devoted to youth sports, the *Young Athlete*, has completed two successful years; and the *Weekend Coach*, a journal devoted solely to helping the volunteer coach, is also emerging as a promising new publication.

Today young people have more opportunities than ever to participate in sports of their choice. They have better playing facilities and equipment, more available information on how to play sports, and more adults willing to help organize programs and teach sports skills. In fact, it is estimated that nearly 2.5 million adults give voluntarily of their time and another half million are paid in part or full to help conduct children's sports programs.

The cost of conducting children's sports programs is enormous; but because nonschool sports rely on volunteer help, they are substantially less expensive than school sports for the number of children involved. School sports cost the public about 13 billion dollars annually and provide sports opportunities for about 4 million youngsters. Nonschool programs cost about 6 billion dollars for 17 million young participants.

Estimates of the number of boys and girls ages 6 to 16 years who are playing various nonschool sports are given in the table below. These estimates were compiled from information obtained from national youth sports agencies, projections made from an extensive youth sports survey in Michigan,[2] and other published figures. The total number of participants is higher than 17 million because many children play in more than one sport.

As shown in the table, sports are no longer the exclusive domain of boys. Girls are obtaining increasing opportunities in sports—through either voluntary or legislated programs. And today, certain sports are no longer limited to the affluent. Golf, tennis, and swimming, for example, are becoming accessible to an increasing number of American children.

Estimate of Participation in Nonschool Sports Among Children Ages 6–16 (in millions)

SPORT	BOYS	GIRLS	TOTAL
Baseball	4.20	0.79	4.99
Softball	1.97	2.41	4.38
Swimming	1.71	1.91	3.62
Bowling	2.07	1.51	3.58
Basketball	2.13	1.22	3.35
Football (tackle)	1.56	0.29	1.85
Tennis	0.88	0.95	1.83
Gymnastics	0.59	1.17	1.76
Football (flag)	1.11	0.36	1.47
Track and Field	0.76	0.54	1.30
Soccer	0.72	0.52	1.24
Other	1.24	0.79	2.03
TOTAL	18.94	12.46	30.41

Similarly, sports are no longer the prerogative of only the average and gifted, as children with a wide variety of handicaps are now finding opportunities to participate. For example, the Special Olympics, created by Eunice Schriver, gives mentally retarded children opportunities to experience the joy of sports. The International Committee of the Silent Sports provides the young deaf child with a variety of sports programs. Through the National Games for the Visually Impaired, blind youngsters are able to participate in wrestling, track, and swimming; and they can bowl competitively through programs sponsored by the American Blind Bowling Association.

The physically disabled also are finding more sports opportunities through the National Wheelchair Athletic Association, although programs are still insufficient for younger children.

Any activity which has grown as rapidly as children's sports, mostly through voluntary participation and leadership, must appeal to the basic interests of children and adults alike. In the next article we examine *The Significance of Children's Sports* for a closer look at this phenomenon in our society.

References

1. American Association for Health, Physical Education, and Recreation. *Desirable athletic competition for children of elementary school age.* Washington: Author, 1968.
2. *Joint legislative study on youth sports: Agency-sponsored sports-Phase I.* State of Michigan, November 1976.

The Significance of Children's Sports

The growth in children's sports has been phenomenal. The investment in time, energy, and money is huge. Sport themes pervade every cultural level of our society. Presidents and statesmen proclaim the virtues of sports in building a strong nation. Educators and clergymen issue edicts heralding the importance of sports in socializing our youngsters. To many, sports are not merely games; they are a religion. Indeed, the baptism to sports has become a significant rite of childhood.

We expect sports to develop motoric skills and physical fitness in our youngsters. We believe sports promote and convey the value of our society by teaching children how to compete and cooperate. Through sports we seek to inculcate moral behavior, leadership, and initiative. We want youngsters to develop positive self-concepts and to become independent through interdependent sports participation. Most importantly, we hope sports will help children develop healthy, strong identities so that they may have an opportunity to fully realize their potentialities.

A popular psychological theory suggests that sports and games may help children learn how to deal with the problems awaiting them in adult life. Sports and games are thought to give children an opportunity to resolve the psychological conflicts they encounter as they are growing up by exposing them to the emotional and cognitive polarities of these conflicts. For example, through sports children experience the emotional highs and lows associated with victory and defeat. Sports also confront children at times with the cognitive dilemma of having to choose between being honest or dishonest competitors.

The theory holds that sports and games provide a form of buffered learning, permitting children to be slowly integrated into adult life without suffering the harsh consequences associated with adult misbehavior. Thus, some psychologists and sociologists contend that sports attract youngsters because of this "unreality." However, although *games* may permit children to fantasize and to occupy themselves with unreality, it is doubtful that this is so with adult-organized children's *sports*. Sports are real to both the children and to the adults involved. Sports expose youngsters to competitive life, where the outcomes are as meaningful, if not more so, as the outcomes of other facets of their lives. The intense involvement of parents in children's sports certainly suggests that something more is taking place than fantasy through children's games.

Many parents and educators believe that sports are especially valuable in helping to teach moral behavior—to convey to youngsters the values of our society. Former professional football players Frank Gifford and Bart Starr, however, believe that today's youth are not learning the values that made Vince Lombardi and America great. They feel that kids are not as mentally tough, as committed to excellence, as determined to win; that they lack pride, loyalty, and dedication; and that they are unwilling to make self-sacrifices. Indeed, Gifford and Starr lament that too many children merely want to play for FUN!

Two rebels of the sports establishment have another view. Jack Scott and Dave Meggyesy see sport as a symbol of a society whose values are bankrupt. Michael Novak succinctly states Scott's and Meggyesy's views:

Organized sports are one of the bastions of the evil old order and must be stormed before the revolution of values in this society can take place. The goal of the new values is not success—accumulation of goods and all that this entails—but rather the development and cultivation of the person, his growth in awareness and inner peace. The means is not individual striving but rather group participation and cooperation, communal sharing and mutual engagement with experimental culture forms—all of which lead not to class-consciousness but to increasing openness and acceptance of others. The manner is not puritanical but sensual: gratification is immediate, suppression and discipline give way to free expression, and optimistic pragmatism is replaced by a utopianism that, to be sure, is somewhat pessimistic and nihilistic.[1]

I doubt whether youngsters have lost all the values which Gifford and Starr believe they have. In fact, young people today may have sports in better perspective than do their elders. I also doubt whether sports will be an important instrument for changing the values of our society as Scott and Meggyesy suggest. Instead I believe sports reflect our society and its present values. These values are not appreciably different from those values of the past. Our society continues to reward excellence, to emphasize achievement, and to value hard work. If, as a society, we are not happy with the values conveyed through sports, we will first need to change the values in the larger society. Just as the tail does not wag the dog, sports have not and are not changing the values of America.

Children, of course, can be socialized successfully into adulthood without the benefit of sports. They can and do learn our society's values for success, achievement, and conformity to normative codes of behavior through a wide variety of non-sport activities. But sports possess the potential to make some special contributions to children's development. These special contributions emanate from the intrinsic appeal of sports. The physical essense of sports, the intense emotion associated with competition, the decisiveness of direct comparisons with peers, all appeal exquisitely to the quintessence of youth. The feeling of commitment—the perception of involvement in a competitive test worthy of their best effort—motivates youngsters to master a sport.

James Coleman has observed that many children have inadequate opportunities to develop the capacity to engage in an
activity with intense, concentrated involvement. In *Youth:
Transition to Adulthood* he writes that "the most personally
satisfying experiences, as well as the greatest achievements of
man, arise from such concentration, not because of external
pressure, but from an inner motivation which propels the person and focuses his or her attention."[2] I believe that sports are
one of the few activities in which children find ample opportunity to develop this type of concentrated involvement. Because of both the intrinsic and extrinsic appeal of sports, children discover them to be worthy of such commitment more so
than many other activities.

Sports also make a special contribution by teaching children
to appreciate their bodies and the wondrous things they can
do. The joy in a child's face when successfully hitting a ball for
the first time—the inner satisfaction of mastering a complex
skill—is beyond description. And this alone is sufficient to
make sports a worthwhile pursuit. But mastery of sports skills
also may contribute substantially to the development of positive self-concepts. To children, skill in sports is a highly prized
attribute which is often accompanied by considerable peer
status. The pride of accomplishment and the associated admiration from friends goes a long way toward developing the
youngster's self-image of being a worthy person.

Sports make yet another contribution to the development of
children. Throughout most of their youth, kids are cast in the
role of being dependent on others, whereas others are seldom
dependent on them. Sports are noteworthy because they provide excellent opportunities for youngsters to have others
dependent upon their actions. This responsibility training
through cooperative efforts is an important dimension of the
childrearing process.

If sports are able to provide even some of these benefits,
they stand alongside the home, school, and church in contributing to the socialization of children. Yet the potential benefits
of sports are not guaranteed by mere participation. In the
hands of the unknowing sports can systematically strip a child
of his enthusiasm for movement, stifle his imagination and
creativity, and destroy his feeling of self-worth.

On the other hand, sports can produce children who enjoy

movement, who strive for excellence, but can realistically evaluate their abilities. They can produce youngsters who do not fear failure in order to achieve success and who grow with both praise and constructive criticism. But sports can only produce such children when the adults who guide youngsters possess these attributes themselves. Too often children's joy of sports is obliterated by adults who seek glory through victory. These adults have forgotten that the prerequisites to the desirable long-term outcomes of children's sports are the immediate joy, fun, and exhilaration of playing. Undoubtedly, the greatest challenge in children's sports programs today is to meet the need for quality adult leadership in order to help youngsters achieve the full benefits of sports.

References

1. Novak, M. *The joy of sports.* New York: Basic Books, 1976, p. 215.
2. Coleman, J. S. *Youth: Transition to adulthood.* Chicago: University of Chicago Press, 1974, p. 4.

SECTION B

The Pros and Cons

With more Americans involved in children's sports than ever before, more are concerned about the *quality* of this involvement than ever before. Parents, educators, physicians—all those interested in the welfare of children—are posing such formidable questions as these:

1. Are sports good for our children's physical and psychological health?
2. Is there too much pressure to win?
3. Will the demise of children's sports be parents who vicariously live their athletic yesteryears through their young athletes?
4. Are young athletes over-coached by under-qualified adults?
5. Is there any fun left in kids' sports?

Five excellent articles follow which look at these questions and others, examining the pros and cons—the harmful and beneficial effects—of children's sports programs.

In the first selection Arthur Daley describes the beginnings of Little League baseball, the first national nonschool children's sports organization. Daley explains why Little League baseball not only appeals to young boys but also to adults. Written in 1951 when the American trinity was God, Country, and Little League, Daley showers the organization with praise.

> *I trust in God*
> *I love my country and will respect its laws*
> *I will play fair and strive to win*
> *But win or lose, I will always do my best.*

So reads the Little League pledge which epitomizes the sanctimonious view of Little League in those early days. But those innocent days came to a halt in the middle 1950's when a coup was led by Peter McGovern to oust Carl Stotz from the directorship of the organization which Stotz had founded. Martin Ralbovsky, in *Little League Baseball: Where Boy Meets Coach for the First Time*, recounts the details of this coup and attacks Little League for its objectives and financial operations.

We might logically assume that professional baseball players, by the nature of their experience, would be advocates of Little League. But this is not always true. Robin Roberts, a former pitching great for the Philadelphia Phillies is strongly opposed to Little League:

> I still don't know what those . . . gentlemen in Williamsport had in mind when they organized Little League baseball. I'm sure they didn't want parents arguing with their children about kids' games. I'm sure they didn't want to have family meals disrupted for three months every year. I'm sure they didn't want young athletes hurting their arms pitching under pressure at such a young age. I'm sure they didn't want young boys who don't have much athletic ability made to feel that something is wrong with them because they can't play baseball. I'm sure they didn't want a group of coaches drafting the players each year for different teams. I'm sure they didn't want unqualified men working with the young players. I'm sure they didn't realize how normal it is for an 8-year-old boy to be scared of a thrown or batted baseball. For the life of me, I can't figure out what they had in mind.[1]

But Little League baseball also has many proponents among past and present professional baseball players. Bob Feller, a former pitching star for the Cleveland Indians, teams up with Hal Lebovitz, a Cleveland sportswriter, to present many of the proponents' arguments in the third article.

Next a California sociologist, Jonathan Brower, gives his impression of kids' baseball based on his 200 hours of watching 350 boys play 70 baseball games. In a hostile essay, Brower concludes that the league's organization and games are really for the pleasure and benefit of adults. The boys, he contends, are like pawns in a chess game.

In the final article our focus shifts from kids' baseball to midget football and the ever-present parental concern about physical injury. John Underwood, the nationally renowned writer for *Sports Illustrated*, takes a very critical look at the consequences of midget gridiron battles. "Kids play football because they enjoy it. But adults want kids to play little league football for a lot of other reasons—and that's where all the trouble starts," according to Underwood.

In these articles the rhetoric is superb, the differences in opinion enormous, but the factual evidence meager. The opinions of the authors are based on hearsay and casual observation, not on systematically acquired evidence. When reading each article, the date and author's background should be kept in mind in order to fairly evaluate his position. And although the sports discussed in these readings are confined to baseball and football, most of the observations are not limited to these sports.

Reference

1. Roberts, R. Strike out little league. *Newsweek*, July 21, 1975, p. 11.

30,000 Little Big Leaguers

by **Arthur Daley**, *former sportswriter for the* New York Times. *He won a pulitzer Prize in 1956 for his outstanding sports coverage and commentary.*

The Little League began as a community project in Williamsport, Pa., in 1939. It was not much more than a supervised sandlot proposition. But it stepped out in more formal manner a year later with three 4-team leagues, and then virtually hung in a state of suspended animation during the war.

But—oh, brother!—how it was to grow!!!

Never for an instant was any attempt made to use high-pressure methods in forcing its expansion—and there still isn't, either. It is the spontaneous character of this movement that is both its most astonishing feature and its greatest charm. Like Topsy, "It jes' growed."

The appeal of the Little League idea is almost irresistible. Each Little League is an entity in itself, locally financed, locally supported, locally governed, and locally supplied with personnel. What is more, the entire movement is strictly nonprofit.

Abridged from *American Magazine*, April 1951, pp. 42–43; 134–136.

There is an over-all league headquarters in Williamsport, its birthplace, but connection between the whole and the component parts is very much on the tenuous side. Not much more is required for being franchised than observance of the Little League rules and formula—a 4-team league, uniformed players in the proper age group and with the proper distribution of talent, a playing field that is, roughly, two-thirds of the dimensions of big-league baseball, smaller bats, balls, and other equipment, and, lastly, adequate supervision by grownups.

The Little League was born because an imaginative young man named Carl Stotz once dreamed a small boy's dream. When he was a tiny youngster in Williamsport he wanted to play baseball. Great was his disappointment during those early years, however, to discover that the bigger boys, the teenagers, unceremoniously gave the little kids the brush-off when they were choosing up sides or picking their teams. Once in a while a little fellow would get a break as a last-minute fill-in, but it was never more than that.

So Stotz made the firm resolve that he'd some day have his own baseball team "when I get rich." He isn't rich in dollars yet. But he is rich in accomplishment.

The vague, formless idea he'd had as a boy took shape when he saw a couple of favorite nephews forlornly sitting on the side lines while bigger, older, and more talented youngsters made use of the diamond. What the little fellows needed, he reasoned, was competition in their own age group, with field and other equipment trimmed down to their size.

Thus did the Little League movement begin. With some like-minded friends, Stotz, who was then a minor executive in a bottling plant, started the project. It was only a community affair then, but it was so generically sound that it spread to adjoining towns and then to adjoining states, until it raced with the speed and consuming avariciousness of a prairie fire. And Stotz soon learned that he had created something of a Frankenstein monster.

He was flooded with inquiries and he didn't have either the time or the money to handle them. By way of adding to the dilemma, the Little League "World Series" had grown too big for him and for Williamsport.

And along came a financial "angel" in the nick of time. It was the United States Rubber Company, which offered to pay all

"World Series" expenses. Then, in 1949, it agreed to assume the tab for national headquarters, along with a salary for Stotz as a full-time commissioner.

This, by the way, is the only hint of commercialism to the entire project. It wasn't planned that way and the rubber company has never sought to capitalize on it. It has remained in the background as much as possible, regarding its contribution as a public service, just as the Ford Motor Company regards its support of the American Legion baseball program for the teen-agers.

Stotz embarked on his hobby-made business none too soon. In its original, haphazard form the Little League had grown much too big for its britches. It desperately needed a national organization and it desperately needed an enthusiast like Stotz to head it.

He is a tireless worker, touring the country from one end to the other in order to spread the gospel. He speaks by invitation only and arranges his schedule so that he can make one or two stops a day. At these talks one of the first questions generally popped at Stotz is the ageless one: How much?

There is nothing mysterious about finances. Each of 4 sponsors is required—perhaps "requested" is the softer word—to put up $200, a total of $800 for each league. This pays for 48 uniforms, 5 dozen balls, 2 dozen bats, 4 sets of catcher's outfits, a home plate rubber, a pitcher's rubber, bases, and a scorebook, everything but the scorebook coming in miniature sizes.

Since the Little League has nothing to sell but its principles, Stotz suggests local merchants supply whatever equipment is necessary, the only requirements being that they meet specifications. This also has two strong psychological advantages: First of all, it enlists local merchants as Little League boosters. Secondly, it eliminates any possibility of the charge that the Little League prefers one dealer or manufacturer over another.

Ironically enough, this even applies to the U.S. Rubber Co., which makes a type of rubber-soled sneaker that the Little Leaguers use. It doesn't rate the position of favorite, but has to scramble for business in the same fashion as a complete outsider.

The total cost of a 4-team circuit, by the way, will average approximately $725. The balance of the $75 goes into a pool for improving the field and adding grandstands, fences, dugouts, scoreboards, or whatever else is wanted.

As originally conceived, not a cent went to national head-quarters. There was a nominal $10 franchise fee as an evidence of good faith, but the fee was returned at the end of the first season of operation. However, expenses zoomed so alarmingly as the movement mushroomed to giant size that the Board of Directors—one of the public-spirited members of the board, for example, is Ford Frick, president of the National League—was forced to alter procedures in order to break even financially.

A year ago it voted to return only half of the franchise fee, but now annually charges a flat $10 per year for each franchise, new or old. No one yet has begrudged it.

The secret of the success of the Little League movement—not one league ever failed—is the ingenious scheme devised by Stotz to give it balance. That is the player pool.

At the formation of any Little League, 4 managers are assigned to teams. These managers, by the way, are not necessarily chosen for their knowledge of the inner strategies of the game. They are picked on a basis of character, because they are dealing with youngsters in their most impressionable years. It's much more important that they exert the proper influence on the boys than be able to order a hit-and-run play at the right time.

Once the managers are named, the call is issued for candidates to engage in preseason "spring training," a tryout period which enables the managers to study the boys and grade them according to their abilities. As soon as the rating is done, each manager is assigned 36,000 credits—it's like having $36,000 of play money—and an impartial "Player's Agent" auctions off the midget maulers.

A manager is permitted to bid as high as he wishes for any player. But if he plunges too heavily on a miniature Joe DiMaggio or Bob Lemon, he would have to take "minor leaguers" to fill out the rest of his squad. Once credits are all used up, names are drawn from a hat until each squad has 12 "regulars" and 6 "reserves." Each squad, by the way, is limited to 5 players who are the maximum 12 years of age, and it must include at least 3 who are 10 or younger.

All players thus "purchased" become the permanent property of their "owners" for the rest of their Little League careers, a system not unlike organized ball's "reserve clause." They can be traded or even bought outright—if the buyer has sufficient credits to swing the deal.

The player auction is kept completely secret—and for good reasons. A kid picked first might get a swelled head or delusions of grandeur. One chosen last might be branded by an inferiority complex. So there is no first or last. A boy doesn't know whether he cost 20,000 credits or was picked for free merely to fill out the squad.

The players' pool has another distinct advantage: It becomes a community melting pot. The rich boy from the hills plays alongside the lad from the wrong side of the railroad tracks. Youngsters tend to travel in cliques or "gangs." But the pool cuts across all lines. Although an effort is made to keep brothers together on the same team, pals are more likely than not to be separated.

What is more, each league generally has so much balance as a result of the hand-picked distribution of talent that one team is not likely to dominate the competition, as frequently happens in ordinary sandlot play. The tail-enders in the Little League thus don't lose interest nor does monotonous winning satiate the leaders, the fundamental flaws in the average small-boy league.

With the passing of each year adults have grown increasingly aware of what a strong deterrent to juvenile delinquency the Little League is. It has received the enthusiastic endorsement of J. Edgar Hoover, the head of the Federal Bureau of Investigation, and has endorsements by the gross from high and low police officials the country over. Significant, too, is the fact that there probably are more police-department sponsors than any other.

"It's undoubtedly true," admits Commissioner Stotz, "but I don't like to go around waving the American flag. I'm delighted that it's worked out that way. However, I'm only interested in presenting the Little League on its merits and in accordance with the principles motivating us when we started it. Purely and simply, it's baseball for boys."

Nothing can quite match sports as a wholesome outlet for the sheer animal energies of youth. But the Little League has an extra gimmick for making the boys behave. It wasn't consciously intended to operate that way. But it has, nonetheless.

That is the baseball uniform. In some happy fashion that he still can't explain, Stotz hit on the idea of garbing his Little Leaguers, not in T-shirts and peaked caps, but in regular uniforms just like Babe Ruth used to wear. They cater in the full to child psychology. Boys have an almost irresistible urge from babyhood to dress up—like cowboys, Indians, firemen, policemen, or anyone else who requires a uniform.

In every community the baseball uniform has become a badge of distinction. The kids love to wear the uniforms, and the mothers grow to appreciate them even more. A mother who used to get the "Aw, gee," response to her request to little Johnny to trot down to the store for a loaf of bread, finds that he is very proud to go on the same mission when he is wearing his Little League uniform.

There even have been instances of Little Leaguers who are so enamored with the baseball suits that they have even worn them to bed, too delighted with them to take them off for anything as prosaic as pajamas.

Twilight is the preferred time for games, and that generally means a considerable juggle of meal schedules by most mothers. Strangely enough, few if any of them ever object, even though it occasionally means feeding the family in shifts.

But the whole family is forced—albeit willingly—to have a share in Little League play. One day Jack Doyle, a contractor, of Hartford, kept peering down the road for the boy bringing him his evening newspaper. Along came a girl in pigtails, struggling with a bundle of papers.

"Where's your brother?" asked Doyle.

"Playing Little League ball," said the girl cheerfully, "and I'm delivering his papers for him."

The fathers break into the act in scores of ways. Young Owen McNally, of Hartford, refused to go to the seashore with his family one summer. Mighty stubborn about it, too. He just couldn't. It would interfere with Little League games.

"I'll make a deal with you, Owen," said his understanding father, who is general foreman of an aircraft factory. "You go to the shore with your mother and the rest of the family. Then I promise I'll drive you back here for every game." It was a 50-

mile trip each way. But it was done. Thus was another great family crisis met and conquered.

Frank Wamester, manager of a team in Middletown, Conn., was delayed at the plant where he is superintendent one night, the night of an important game. He phoned his wife, Betty.

"Don't worry, Frank," she told him. "I'll manage the team for you."

She made like Casey Stengel. She won the game.

For many years the major leagues have been worrying about the fact that their sources of supply have been drying up. The newer generation doesn't play hard-ball baseball the way the older one did. It would be truly ironic if an idea which began as a simple community project in Williamsport would prove to be their eventual salvation, reawakening interest in our great American game.

No phase of sport in the history of this country has ever caught on with the contagious enthusiasm of the Little League. Nor is there any way of calculating where it will stop, or even if it will stop. The kids love it, and so do the parents. That's a combination impossible to beat.

Little League Baseball:
Where Boy Meets Coach for the First Time

by **Martin Ralbovsky,** *former sportswriter for the* New York Times *and author of several sports books, including* Destiny's Darlings.

Ah, Little League baseball. It is as much a part of the American tapestry as apple pie a la mode, Norman Rockwell paintings of little girls in pigtails eating drippy ice cream cones, and fireworks on July 4th. For thirty-five years it has been packaged as the ultimate haven for American boys between pablum and puberty; the late J. Edgar Hoover, who was a member of the Little League Board of Directors, once said that Little League baseball was the greatest deterrent to crime that America had ever seen. "Keep Kids in Sports and out of Courts," the motto went.

Now, after having digested all of the palatable myths for all these years, it usually comes as a shock to people when they discover what the organization known as Little League Baseball, Incorporated, really is: It is, among other things, a federally chartered corporation that operates in concert with the

Abridged from Chapter V of *Lords of the Locker Room,* New York: Peter H. Wyden Publishers, 1974. Reprinted by permission of David McKay Co., Inc.

United States government to promote Americanism in thirty-one countries; it is a franchise business that trafficks in millions of tax-exempt dollars every year; it is a conglomerate that sells the rights to the official Little League trademark to hundreds of companies. In a nutshell, Little League is a hydra-headed enterprise devoted to (1) earning money, and (2) promoting America. Boys and baseball are merely the whipped-cream topping.

On July 16, 1964, Lyndon Baines Johnson signed Public Law 88-378. The law gave the organization known as Little League Baseball, Incorporated, with headquarters in South Williamsport, Pennsylvania, a federal charter of incorporation. Federal charters are as rare in the halls of Congress as the duckbilled platypus; only five have ever been granted, to organizations such as the American Red Cross. The Little League charter was the work of two prominent matchmakers, Emmanuel Celler, then a representative from New York, and William Cahill, then a member from New Jersey. Before reaching the President's desk, the charter had to pass through both houses of Congress—with unanimous approval. It did.

The charter, once granted, made all the money that found its way into the Little League headquarters building on Route 15 in South Williamsport tax-exempt. All Little League Baseball, Incorporated, had to do in return for the federal charter was two things: (1) tailor its mission to the wishes of the U.S. government, and (2) file an annual financial (and philosophical) report with the Judiciary Committee of the House of Representatives. So, for the past decade, the largest sports organization on the planet Earth (8,500 leagues in 31 countries) has been a quasi-governmental agency, but it has been such a well-kept secret that the only people who seem to know it are the people in the General Accounting Office in Washington who audit the Little League reports.

Now, if you happen to think that your neighborhood Little League in Syosset or Smithtown runs by itself, you are wrong. Each of the 8,500 Little Leagues pays approximately $68 a year (depending on the number of teams) for the privilege of calling itself "Little League." That's $578,000 off the top, every year, to the headquarters in South Williamsport. Each of the 8,500 Little Leagues, like each McDonald's hamburger stand, becomes a separate entity—under the headquarters' umbrella—once it has paid the franchise fee. But all of the leagues, like all of the hamburger stands, are ultimately ruled by a small group of invisible men who sit high atop the corporate ladder. (Several court decisions have already decreed that the term "Little League" is a corporate trademark and cannot be used for profit without financial reimbursement to the Little League headquarters.)

Next are the all-star-tournament game fees. Every year, after July 18, when the all-star teams begin playing in tournament competition (which culminates in the annual Little League World Series, during the last week of August in the ten-thousand seat Howard J. Lamade Memorial Stadium in South Williamsport), collections from the spectators are taken at each game. From each collection, $5 is sent to the headquarters. Since 50,000 or so all-star tournament games are played (it's a single-elimination tournament) before a world champion is finally crowned, at the World Series, the headquarters in South Williamsport takes in approximately $250,000 from these games alone. Combined with the half-million dollars that it gets in franchise fees, the all-star tournament game fees raise the annual intake figure to over three-quarters of a million dollars—all of which the headquarters gets directly from the local leagues themselves. All of it, of course, is tax free.

Next is the business of subsidiary monies. For all of the millions of official Little League bats that are sold, the headquarters receives royalty fees in return for the use of the official Little League emblem. (In recent years, the Little League headquarters has encouraged the use of aluminum bats; in the next five years or so, most of the 8,500 leagues will make the conversion from wooden bats to aluminum ones. Result: Big profits for the bat manufacturers, big profits for the Little League Headquarters.) Royalty fees are also derived from such things as official Little League baseballs, official Little League batting cages, official Little League awards certificates, books, buttons, decals, desk sets, first-aid kits, gloves, batting helmets, leg protectors, pitching machines (which sell for as much as $650), public-address systems, cassette tape recorders and tapes, rulebooks, rubber-spiked shoes, snack-stand equipment, tumblers, women's-auxiliary jewelry, and athletic supporters.

The Little League headquarters also is in the summer-camp business (it operates several boys' camps in various parts of the country; $150 for ten days); the insurance business (with the American Casualty Company of Reading, Pennsylvania, as a partner, it offers "excess" policies to all of its players; when a boy is injured, Little League headquarters covers what his family's insurance policy does not); the real-estate business (Little League headquarters' property holdings are immense; in some cases, large tracts of land have been donated or willed to Little League baseball by civic-minded citizens. In the hamlet of South Williamsport alone, Little League headquarters has purchased forty-five acres of land, upon which sit its administrative building, its World Series stadium, and one of its summer camps.). It is also in the publishing business: Over one million Little League manuals are produced and sold throughout the world in various languages every year.

There is also the Little League Foundation. It has over $1 million at its disposal, for the "perpetuation of Little League baseball." The money was collected over several years during National Little League Week, which, significantly, always coincided with Flag Day (June 14). The money has been translated into marketable securities, common stocks, industrial bonds, and preferred stocks, almost all of which are in a custodial account in the Girard Trust Bank in Philadelphia. Exactly what the Little League Foundation is supposed to do with the money has never been spelled out (recurrent rumors that it is being invested in foreign real-estate have always been denied). But, according to the 1972 Little League Foundation financial report to Congress, as prepared by Price Waterhouse & Company, the Foundation had financial assets of $1,104,852.

In recent years, the headquarters of Little League baseball has moved to monopolize the entire field of boys' baseball. It has launched a Senior Little League, for boys thirteen to fifteen, and already has two thousand leagues in the fold; the Senior Little League World Series is played annually in Gary, Indiana. It also has a Big Little League for boys sixteen to eighteen; its World Series is played annually in Fort Lauderdale, Florida. All of which means that once the Little League headquarters wraps its tentacles around a boy at age nine, it will be able to hold on to him until age eighteen. Perhaps even more important, it will be able to hold on to his family for all of those years; the fathers and mothers of the players do all of the work in Little League baseball—they rake the fields, paint the fences, sell the soda and popcorn at concession stands, solicit the sponsors, etc. None of them is paid for his or her services; the only people who are paid in Little League baseball are the headquarters staff in South Williamsport. Everybody else is a "volunteer."

The man who has run the entire organization since 1955 is Peter McGovern. For twenty-one years he was the president of Little League Baseball, Incorporated, and the chairman of its board of directors. According to the 1971 financial report filed with Congress, McGovern's salary was $25,000 a year, plus expenses. Creighton Hale, the president since October 1973, had been executive director since 1956; in the latter job, he earned $18,750 plus expenses. Robert Stirrat, the public-relations director, earned $16,062 plus expenses. There are approximately sixty other people employed full-time in the red-brick headquarters building, which is the nerve center into which five other regional headquarters complexes are plugged. The others are in St. Petersburg, Florida; San Bernardino, California; Chicago; Waco, Texas; and Ottawa, Ontario. McGovern ran Little League baseball single-handedly from 1955 to 1973; it was in 1955 that he succeeded in ousting the founder, Carl Stotz, after a long and bitter federal-court battle.

Stotz, who was then commissioner of Little League baseball, had filed suit against McGovern to prevent him from turning the program into a big business. Stotz wanted to keep it the way he had envisioned it originally: a grassroots organization for boys and baseball. At one point in the dispute, the Williamsport sheriff actually padlocked the doors of the Little League headquarters to prevent McGovern from leaving town with the cash assets and setting up a new headquarters somewhere else. But when Stotz was finally removed from the scene, McGovern left the United States Rubber Company, where he had been an executive, and took control of Little League himself. (United States Rubber, now Uniroyal, had sent McGovern to Williamsport originally to look after its investment in the rubber-spiked shoes that Little League players wear.) Carl Stotz, who is now a tax collector in Williamsport, said that he hasn't seen a Little League all-star baseball game in eighteen years.

The dispute between Stotz and McGovern created sensational and uncomplimentary headlines in newspapers throughout the country. In all of the law suits, the name-calling, the allegations and counter allegations, Little League baseball lost its innocence. People who had previously looked upon Little League baseball as being nothing more than a charming caricature of the major leagues began looking upon it as the big business it was rapidly becoming. But Carl Stotz did not relinquish his original ideals without a fight; if Little League baseball was going to become a big business, it was not going to accomplish the transition without some resistance. Carl Stotz's official complaint was this: The Little League board of directors was being stacked by McGovern to include people who did not know anything about boys and baseball (but who were, presumably, philosophical allies of McGovern's). That meant that all of the people on the grassroots level, the people who were really the backbone of the organization, were being left without adequate representation on the board of directors. Carl Stotz filed a $300,000 suit against McGovern in a federal court in Lewisburg, Pennsylvania.

Carl Stotz withdrew his legal proceedings, he said, when it became evident to him that the judge would rule against him and he would lose his case. For a while he toyed with the idea of forming his own Little League organization—to be called "The Original Little League"—and encouraged defections from the McGovern-controlled organization. But a federal judge issued a restraining order against Stotz that said, in effect, that Stotz was to have nothing to do with boys and baseball—under the penalty of legal action. So, he abandoned the idea and hasn't been heard from since.

Don't Knock Little Leagues

by **Bob Feller**, *former pitching great for the Cleveland Indians and father of three boys, with* **Hal Lebovitz**, *sports editor for the* Cleveland Plain Dealer.

My father had a favorite saying: "You find the most clubs under the best apple trees." He meant, of course, that whenever something is good there always will be people trying to knock it.

This seems especially true of Little League baseball. While the program continues to grow, bringing fun and benefits to so many youngsters, there are rumblings that the competition it offers produces too much emotional strain for young minds and too much physical stress for young bodies. It's argued that kids break down and sob themselves to sleep after a losing game; that ten- to twelve-year-old bones can't withstand the pounding of a six-inning game on a cut-down field; that Little League breaks up family life because a boy has to spend so much time with his team.

Abridged from *Collier's*, August 3, 1956, pp. 78-81. Reprinted with permission of the author.

I disagree strongly with these attacks—as a Little League father as well as a Little League fan. I owe about everything I have to baseball, but I would not support Little League for an instant if I thought it could harm my youngsters. The Feller family, however, is genuinely grateful for the positive contribution our home-town program is making in the healthy development of our children. That's why I don't like to hear anyone knock Little Leagues.

I have three sons. Stevie is ten. He's a shortstop on a Little League team called, appropriately enough, the "Indians." Marty is eight. He was bat boy for Steve's squad last year and now is pitching in our junior Little League organization. Brucie is five. He's replaced Marty as bat boy and it won't be long before he will be the fourth Feller active in the local Little League. I say fourth, because I'm proud to be president of the Chagrin Valley Little League, which covers two small suburban communities on the eastern side of Cleveland: Gates Mills, where we live, and adjacent Hunting Valley.

The Little League came into our community life last year. My wife, Virginia, and I feel it's one of the best things that ever happened to Stevie and Marty—and we believe the same will hold true for young Bruce. Many of the other parents in our town have expressed themselves similarly about their sons. And some of our neighbors who have no children at all, or whose boys are now in college, say Little League baseball has been the most heart-warming, positive influence on our community in many years.

I first became aware of Little League through my job in the big leagues. As a Cleveland pitcher, I'm frequently called on to make visits and speeches to parents' and boys' groups. I was impressed with the keen interest of the youngsters and the zeal of the adults at the Little League gatherings. I looked at the bright, healthy faces of those happy kids and couldn't help saying to myself: "I wish my sons could get into something like this."

Being known to my friends as a planner, I began a thorough study of the pros and cons of the program. I discussed them with several doctors at the Mayo Clinic who have sons participating in Little League, with educators, and finally with the Reverend John R. Pattie, the minister of our church. The more I investigated, the more enthusiastic I became.

My enthusiasm has been contagious. Last year, when we first organized our Chagrin Valley Little League, about 85 boys participated. Now we have more than 200. Our group has expanded both above and below the standard Little League age limits. For those like Marty, under nine, we have the Midget League. And we have started a Babe Ruth League for boys over twelve. Our commissioner is Al Narstedt, a village policeman, and Lester Smith, the chief of police, is umpire in chief.

The growth of interest in our community is typical of what is happening throughout the nation. More than a half million boys now are playing with teams affiliated with the national Little League headquarters at Williamsport, Pennsylvania, and there are at least an equal number not officially affiliated.

These Little Leagues not only foster friendships, develop co-ordination and good health habits in the boys, but they break down social barriers and make for a more closely knit community. In our league, for example, we have the banker's son, the industrialist's son, the gardener's son, the grocer's son, the fireman's son and the ballplayer's son. No one pays any attention to how much money the boy's father has, or his social standing. Rich or poor, he's judged on how he performs in open competition. Where else is there a more practical training ground for democracy?

There is a new neighborliness, too, among the adults. Getting together at the ball games is almost as easy for the grown-ups as for the youngsters; we simply let the kids show the way. And almost as much fun as the games themselves is the custom we've established of meeting afterward at the nearby soda fountain. All the boys, winners and losers, and their dads, managers and coaches congregate over chocolate sodas, milk shakes and banana splits. I find these get-togethers more satisfying than the country club. In helping provide them, the Little League is fostering the healthiest kind of father-son relationship.

In baseball, a father and son can meet on a common ground from which bloom companionship, respect and real love. No one knows this better than I do. To me, my father was the greatest man who ever lived. I like to think that I'm trying to do for my boys what he did for me.

I want to emphasize this point: my dad never forced baseball on me. He never once mentioned it as a possible career for me. We played baseball together because it was fun. That I became a big-leaguer was purely a bonus—a most wonderful one, I admit.

The greatest tribute I can pay the Little League program is that I'm sure that if my father were alive he'd be just as active in it as he could be. This is not to say that the leagues are 100 per cent perfect. There are parents who push unwilling or un-athletic boys into Little League play and try to shame them forward; others who berate their youngsters for any mistake on the diamond. It is up to the rest of us to keep such driving, frustrated adults from running, and ruining, our leagues.

I am not conceding, however, that Little Leaguers are too young for competition. I just can't go along with the theorists who insist that too much stress is placed in Little League ball on winning and that a permanent emotional scar is left on a youngster when his team loses.

If this were true, competition would have to be eliminated at birth. Aren't children competing for attention almost from the moment they are born? Don't they compete when they make their first trip to the sandbox to see who makes the best mud pie, or in the second- and third-grade spelldowns?

Baseball is a contest. The object is to win and I don't believe it is normal or desirable to accept a defeat with a shrug.

Understand, I'm not trying to encourage emotional out-bursts. But I don't believe that strong desire to succeed is so unhealthy. I remember seeing one Little Leaguer cry last year. But he got over it and by the time we went to the drug-store afterward there were no salty tears diluting his choco-late soda. In fact, he had two. He's learned to live with a set-back. I've always felt that persons who jump out of windows when their plans go wrong never really experienced defeat before.

It's not my aim to make professional athletes out of my sons. The boys have other interests—music, scouting, fishing and science—which we foster as much as we do ballplaying. If they should want to try baseball as a career, I won't stop them. But I won't encourage them either unless I become certain they have sufficient talent.

Virginia and I are out to give our youngsters a happy childhood that still will prepare them for the ups and downs of life. The Little League is only one avenue for reaching this goal. But from personal experience we are sold that it's a valuable one.

Little League Baseballism:
Adult Dominance in a "Child's Game"

by **Jonathan J. Brower,** *professor of sociology at California State University, Fullerton.*

What is this insanity of highly organized and competitive sport for children? Laws exist to protect children at work and school, but their "play" as governed by adults goes unchecked. Is organized sport for children all that benign if not harmful?

As a sociologist, I recently spent ten months doing an in-depth study of one Southern California baseball league for 8½ to 15 year old boys. I attended both Board of Directors and general league meetings and watched over 200 hours of games and practices. I talked with and observed coaches and managers, parents, umpires, park directors, and of course, players. It was my intent to learn if the rules, procedures and history of the league had a significant impact on the behavior of its youthful participants.

This article was presented at the Pacific Sociological Association meeting, April 1975, in Victoria, B.C. and is reprinted with permission of the author.

The park league program that I studied consisted of the ten teams of the Coast League, made up of 8½, 9, and 10 year olds, the Little League's ten teams for 11 and 12 year olds, and the Junior League's eight teams comprised of 13 and 14 year olds. (The Little League division was not part of Little League Inc. with national headquarters in Williamsport, Pennsylvania. Nevertheless, in most respects this park league resembled the national organization.) The inept, awkward players did not readily filter into the higher leagues as easily as did the competent ones. The worst players found no pleasure or fulfillment and the "handwriting was on the wall." Poor athletes and their parents often "voluntarily" left the league and organized baseball, their exodus unofficially and subtly encouraged by the organization.

On paper, the 18 man Board of Directors, made up of managers and coaches, had the collective responsibility for setting league policy, ruling over protests and arranging the season's activities. In actuality, however, things were generally run by a small knot of board members who initiated policy and activity. This often led to arguments on the field and in the meetings from those outside of the impenetrable walls of the clique.

Registration and try-outs began in mid-January and lasted to early March. It was during this time that the adult "games" first became visible to me. Gucci-accessorized parents flashed impressive money rolls while those who were obviously unable to flaunt riches tried to outshine others in a different manner. A common way was for Mommy and Daddy to demonstrate worth through their kids. One mother, speaking of her child as a valuable athletic commodity, boasted, "Jeff is nuts about golf and baseball. The golf pro wanted him to take lessons, says he's a natural. But my son says you can't mix the two, each has a different swing. So it's baseball for now!"

Association with attractive mothers was often a fringe benefit for managers and coaches at sign-up time. When a seductive-looking mother, filling out a registration form, indicated her marital status was "divorced," one of the managers commented on this fact. Several of the other men, in a semi-joking manner, expressed hope that the boy would play for their team and the mother play for their affection. As one verbal man put it, "She looks like a good _____!"

A manager with whom I established an early rapport noticed me listening to the men express their sexual fantasies. "This is not just idle chatter," he confided. "Managers and coaches occasionally do have affairs with mothers. But even when matters do not reach this level, a lot of flirting and tintillizing behavior goes on. The physical attractiveness and availability of a mother could be a factor in drafting a player, regardless of his ability. More fathers come to games if the mothers are attractive. And managers want to enlist help for their team from the ranks of the fathers. It's all very logical."

Although all the children were guaranteed of making a team, try-outs were necessary to ascertain their playing ability. Ratings were based on throwing, fielding, running, and in some cases, hitting. Talents varied greatly. There proved to be a few superb athletes, many good ones, and a sizeable number of poor but eager players.

Try-outs came at a time when the kids were neither psychologically nor physically attuned to baseball. Still basketball season, many of the more able baseball candidates were spending their sports time on the courts. Timing and co-ordination for baseball were at a low ebb. The poorer players, while not involved with basketball, were also not ready for baseball since they had few athletic skills of any kind.

To perform on the diamond the "right way," as in most male-oriented athletic events, a high degree of masculine bravado was expected. Professionals hit by a pitch often travel to first base without any unmanly display of discomfort. The kids, well-schooled in the ways of baseball and knowing that the people rating them liked this gutsy display when pain strikes, tried to emulate this type of behavior at try-outs. Few players, however, could stay planted in the path of a fast approaching grounder, and shouts of "Stay in front of the ball so if you miss it your body will stop it!" echoed throughout the park. These ball-shy players were not measuring up to adult expectations.

As I watched try-outs I found myself surprised by pointed, open hostilities and cruel on-the-field kidding between children. More disturbing, though, was to see this occurring between children and adults. In the guise of joking, the adults razzed and teased, but defined it as harmless and friendly. Their views, unfortunately, were not always shared by the recipients of the so-called humor.

Top players, supposedly the most ego secure because of their high social status, were prime targets for masqueraded adult hostility. Yet it may not have been only because the men felt that the better players could take it while the poorer ones were most vulnerable. It might also have been that better athletes tapped more deeply buried adult hostilities. Possibly, on an unconscious level, stars were athletic ego threats to aging managers and coaches. Consciously, however, they wanted these wizards on their teams to insure victories. This kind of ambivalence can create discomfort in most people.

During the third week of try-outs, the reputed super star of Little League arrived. He was 12 years old, stood close to six feet and was considerably overweight. The paces he was sent through were a mere formality since everyone knew that he was the best in the league. When he came to bat, however, he was taunted by some of the fielders for his portliness. The razzing was cruel, but it did not seem unusual as I have often heard this type of verbal peer devastation.

But when one of the board members conducting the try-outs grinned and told the oversized player, "I'm going to work you so hard you'll lose 15 pounds!" I was distressed by his brutal reference to weight. It was hard to believe that an adult working with kids could lack such sensitivity. Yet, it would be inaccurate to characterize this man as an ogre. In another situation he had genuinely reassuring words for a troubled boy and his mother. This same person, in a span of 30 minutes, displayed two contradictory types of behavior!

Actual practice began in March, less than a week after the teams were chosen. Everybody was eager to start. Managers and coaches now had the overwhelming task of molding their heterogeneous teams into effective, smooth running units. To do this with seasoned professionals is extremely grueling and with youngsters it can be close to an insurmountable job. Frustrations were constant for managers, who wanted competitively superior teams, as well as for players, who could not fulfil the adult wishes. The men held expectations far too advanced for the average unmotivated child baseball player.

Paradoxically, the youngsters appeared eager to play. The majority of them had voluntarily joined the league. The key to the puzzle came in the meaning of the term "play." For the kids, to "play ball" was to do baseball in a game context; practice sessions were not what they wanted. Managers and coaches, on the other hand, expected their charges to be zealous for practice as well as for games. To do both with enthusiasm was to want to "play" by the standards of the adult leaders.

"You have to keep your mind on baseball when you're at practice," one manager told his day dreaming 9 year-old-right fielder. The boy stood still with his head hanging down and his eyes staring at the ground.

"Keep your head up!" barked the manager. "I won't yell at you. Do you want to play ball? If so, you'll have to stay out there and hustle."

The chastised fielder returned to his position and went through the repertoire of movements indicative of a "responsible" ball player. Immediately after practice he sprinted off with a teammate to climb a tree. Their joy in what they considered play was plainly evident by excited talk and laughter. Unencumbered by adult and team pressure, they were free and exuberant.

Childhood ought to bring the freedom to plunge into wholesome fun in leisure hours. Kids in organized sport, however, are in too important an activity for their "bosses" to let them do in their off hours what might be detrimental to the victory output. Managers customarily insisted their athletes avoid the beach, swimming, or other vigorous activities on game day.

In addition to demanding undivided attention and enthusiasm, adult leaders constantly urged professional performance from sandlot talent. "Fire that ball!" was a persistent command during practice. To the coaches' dissatisfaction, the boys continually lobbed the ball in a high arch to distant players. That is, distant in terms of pre-adolescent's physical ability but close in the eyes of the adults. To throw a baseball fast and accurately in a straight line, for say 60 feet, is not a commonplace skill. Such a throw for most required an all-out effort. Leaders who continually demanded "good" throws produced sore, tired arms and a feeling of powerlessness in their players. When the kids did throw hard, they also threw wildly. The package deal of speed plus accuracy was nearly impossible for these baseball neophytes.

Additional conflicts arose over the players' fears of getting hit by the ball during batting and fielding. To stand at the plate, face the pitcher and the in-coming sphere, produced timidity and anxiety if not primitive terror. Many hitters stood too far from home plate while waiting for the pitch. It would be great to connect, but not at the expense of "beaning." Managers, demonstrating their preferred stance, hounded, "Stand up there! Dig in! Don't be afraid of the ball! It won't hurt you!"

One coach, in a desperate effort to convince a "cowardly" hitter that the ball really would not hurt him, stood about five feet from him and with an underhanded motion, threw a ball softly at his mid-section. After the gentle impact he said, "See, it doesn't hurt. Now be a man!"

As soon as the coach was out of ear-shot, the reluctant batter turned to a teammate and said, "What does he think I am? No way does a lob feel like a pitch! He's _____!"

Timid fielders created further frustrations. The adults knew that games were not won by side-stepping grounders and fly-balls. They threatened and hollered for their players to "Get and stay in front of the ball!" Still, the youngsters' instincts for self-preservation prevailed. Because the ball-shy kids received regular reminders that their performances were inferior, they felt no pride or accomplishment. The men, disgruntled and discouraged with their negative baseball talent, threw temper tamtrums by shouting at players and, occasionally, flinging bats and other equipment at backstops and fences.

There was no doubt about it! Preseason training was the time to establish the winning habit. "Striving to win is important," a manager told me. "We're not park directors here to produce good times for the kids. We're here to teach baseball and competition!"

Another told his players, "I play straight baseball when games are close. We play to win! It's fun to experiment and try out new things, but only when we're way out front." Then he added, "You have fun when you win. When you're here to play don't think of anything else but baseball."

Parents, too, got caught up in the win ethic. One father proudly told a friend. "My kid doesn't care about sportsmanship. He says winning is what's important."

Victory in practice games, managers maintained, establishes a winning attitude. This meant a desire to win in whatever way possible without overt cheating. Overt cheating involves dishonest or unfair tactics that the rules of baseball explicitly prohibit. But if an umpire makes a mistake that is to the advantage of the team, baseball and "sporting" tradition holds it is not "cheating" for that team to withhold knowledge that the call is incorrect. An example of this type of questionable brand of "sportsmanship" occurred during a practice game. A Coast League manager wanted to take advantage of the umpire's incorrect call of strike three (when it was strike two) on the opposing batter. A well-intentioned teammate's father started to inform the umpire of the error. The manager quickly told the man, "Cool it! Don't help the other team! What's wrong with *you*?" The father, suddenly put on the defensive, half apologized and half avoided the irate managaer.

What effect does this type of acceptable dishonesty have on the kids who witness it? It gives them a glimmer of the hypocrisy and moral double-talk of their elders. To perpetrate it as they grow older is expected and condoned; to refuse to tolerate such morally bankrupt behavior is considered idealistic but impractical at best and downright deviant at worst.

Regular season play began in late April. "From here on in," as one manager bluntly put it, "the name of the game is win. We play for keeps." And hopefully, the preceding weeks of preparation and practice had produced the competitive atmosphere that the league would manifest for the next three months. Managers and coaches wanted to show results for their efforts. They hoped that they had brought the kids as far along in baseball as possible. To prove this to themselves and others meant only one thing—no defeats or fewer of them than any other team.

This thirst for victory and its accompanying competitiveness was far stronger among managers and coaches than players. The kids would offer help to other teams. Adult leaders frowned on this inter-team cooperation because they did not want assistance given to those who they would be fighting for the league championship.

Mothers and fathers often differed between themselves as to the importance of winning. Generally, fathers fostered competitiveness while mothers appeared less intent on having their kids win. A favorite strategy used by the kids during games was to avoid the parent with whom they did not agree concerning the importance of winning and the necessity of aggressive play.

One of the prime reasons that winning becomes so essential is that competitive athletics, as a rule, has no built in controls to lessen the blow of individual or team failure. Rationalizations abound, but they leave nagging doubts. In a situation where just making the team is a difficult task, bench warmers may be happy just being there, but only for a while. Soon these kids want to get in on the action. They wish to be treated as objects as valuable as the stars. Despite the good intentions of many adult leaders, the effects of high pressure baseball were to stigmatize youngsters when they messed-up a play.

Parents, too, voiced dissatisfaction when their offspring played poorly. Often this was done sub-vocally but with subtle cues that the kids could easily read.

Striking out, making an error on the field, running the bases poorly happened over and over to the lesser talents, for all to witness. Managers, coaches, and parents yelled "helpful" suggestions and made angry remarks. Such a broadcast could prove devastating to fragile egos. To many of these kids, to be incompetent at the game was to be a failure as a person. And they didn't like everyone around to see and hear that they were not O.K.

To compound matters, there was no opportunity for boys to voice complaints of any kind to the grown-ups who controlled the team. Kids who wanted to play knew that they had to listen and follow orders issued by managers and coaches, who often assumed a Vince Lombardian authoritarian manner. Strenuous physical activities such as running laps, windsprints, and calisthenics were popular methods of punishments for keeping young athletes in line. Sadly, this anachronistic ploy has been in vogue among coaches for decades. True, it is effective in getting players to obey, but it also teaches a distaste for running and calisthenics since they are being used as punishment. Unlike many other activities, running for enjoyment and health can be a part of one's life into old age. To teach these young players to despise it in this way is to help them become likely candidates for the typical sedentary adult way of life in America.

Not all league friction was between the two generations. Adults in conflict with each other—men on the same and opposing teams, umpires pitted against parents and managers, parents in the stands—was a persistent reality. Occasional fist fights and more frequent shoving matches between opposing managers took place during the heat of competition, as did some ugly scenes in which managers violently argued with and made threats toward umpires. Parents were not to be outdone. Whether "protecting" their offspring from the kid's own or opposing manager, or fighting, verbally or physically, with parents of vocal and different perspectives as to what was taking place on the field, parents often enough made a scene and embarrassed their kids in the process. Kids wanted, but rarely got, parents at the park who are seen and not heard! The atmosphere of competition seemed to foster unavoidable and at times ugly confrontations.

Umpires, also drawn into the fracas, had the toughest job in the league because baseball traditionally legitimizes hostile attitudes and actions toward them. These part-time employees of the park had other full-time jobs. While they had gone to umpiring school, they were clearly not of major league caliber. The sole umpire for each game, stationed behind home plate, was bound to make some errors in calls at second and third bases. Yet managers, coaches and parents rarely took this into consideration when they argued and shouted about bad calls. And it was not unusual for debates over these calls to continue days and even weeks after they occurred!

Managers charged umps during games by standing at close range to them and yelling and stamping their feet in the classic Leo Durocher-Billy Martin pose. Players, however, prohibited from swearing, were forced to behave in a more humane way. And even though their leaders were expected to politely discuss matters with the umpires, they took liberties as adult leaders and employers of the umpires.

One ump flatly stated, "Knowing from where my money is coming, I have to accept degrading behavior."

It was required, too, of the umpire to set behavioral limits and keep the game under control. Since these limits were never precisely defined, it was impossible for all to agree on the quantity of histrionics and loss of control that should be tolerated by the umpire. Even if such limits were identified by specific and precise criteria, it seems pathetic that the league's governing body needed to hire men who could keep them under control.

And then there was mom and dad. When the stands rocked with parental harrassment at the umpires, it usually was a case of collective behavior or group contagion. Since spectators were rarely in a good position to view the disputed call, they did not know why they were yelling except that others were doing it too! Few were well-versed in the park's baseball ground rules and so they blindly followed the lead of a disgruntled manager who had initiated the ferment.

"Parents in the stands, that's what it's all about," lamented one manager. "They are the cause of so much shit!" When I spoke with parents about league matters, many told me they felt free to talk with managers about gripes they might have concerning their sons. But they often did not speak-out and the result was a build-up of more hostility and resentment toward managers. One mother, for example, told me that she would assert herself and talk to the manager about having her son stop pitching because of the potential damage to his arm and the emotional responsibility that goes with that position. Rather than do this, however, she tried to convince her son that he might be better suited for another position. After hearing his mother's persuasive presentation, the young pitcher started to doubt his ability on the mound. During the next game he proved quite ineffective. Later, he related his conversation with his mother to the manager. Then, the mother received the manager's ill-will because she had put doubts into the boy's head. The boy, in turn, was chastised by his manager for letting his mother psyche him out!

In feeble defense of all these goings-on, league baseball supporters claim, "Age group sports greatly aid the physical fitness of the participating athletes." From an orthopedic and physiological perspective such an argument appears quite tenuous. Sport is not spontaneous play. Sport demands maticulous preparation and physical and mental efforts which extend past the bounds of interest in the activity; injured athletes push on in order to fulfill their obligations. This extension of physical effort past the benefits of physical fitness also existed in the youth sport program which I studied.

Sore-armed players were not a rarity. I often heard youngsters complain of pains in their throwing arms, but minimize this discomfort to the manager so they could stay in the game. The macho element of sport did not allow for giving-in to low key, nagging pain.

Most carefully guarded was the physical well-being of superior players. They, more than the other team members, could determine the outcome of a particular game. When a star was injured sliding into home plate, the rest of the team— players and adults—rushed out to ascertain the extent of the injury. Talk concerning his sprained ankle revolved around the difference it would make on the team's won-lost record.

Hot, summer days left players parched, but folklore and the "suffer ethic" encouraged most managers and coaches to caution, "Don't drink during games. Just rinse your mouth out!" Several managers felt this advice was ridiculous and told their colleagues so, but to no avail. The majority of men had been conditioned to swallow the old myth that the intake of fluids during physical exercise is harmful.

Marathon runners, from novice to Olympic caliber, drink all kinds of concoctions during their 26.22 mile grind, and they feel, and physiological research supports it, the benefits from liquid refreshment. Frank Shorter, 1972 Olympic marathon gold medalist, drank Coca Cola at each aid station on his victorious run. Surely, if fluid intake does not hinder the performance of athletes in a grueling marathon, it seems improbable that it would interfere with the routine of such a relatively non-taxing event as baseball.

The pitfalls of this league are common to most highly organized and competitive youth leagues. To the American consciousness, baseball, basketball, and football are the high status, primary sports. Generally speaking, the men running youth leagues centered around these sports are sedentary sports fanatics who would like to work and play in the world of athletics, but are unable to do so. Age group youth sports afford them a viable alternative where their fantasies of athletic prowess can be played out in a seemingly real setting.

Taking the Fun Out of a Game

by **John Underwood,** *nationally renowned writer for* Sports Illustrated.

The little league football season is in full swing, and we are reassured by its advocates and commercial sponsors that it is good stuff, keeping kids off the streets and out of the clutches of juvenile authorities. Also teaching them discipline, teamwork, respect for authority (*i.e.*, coaches), zone defenses, veer and winged-T offenses and the value of making more effective use of their little bodies—forearms, heads, elbows and other weapons.

Little league football, being more costly to operate, did not catch on as quickly as Little League baseball (the latter is capitalized, courtesy of the Congress of the U.S.), but once it did it spread like tidewater across the country. Now, apparently, there is no stopping it. From the lofty hamlets of Colorado to the red-neck towns of Mississippi, in spacious Montana and

Abridged from an article of the same title. Reprinted by permission of *Sports Illustrated* from the November 17, 1975 issue, pp. 86-98. Copyright 1975 Time Inc.

spaced-out Manhattan, 8- and 10-year-olds, wearing globular helmets that sometimes spin on their heads at impact, go to war against other 8- and 10-year-olds, often bewildered but always stylish in eight pounds of vinyl, polyurethane and viscose tailoring, at $100 per costume. Miniature cheerleaders bounce up and down like fish on a line, cheering indiscriminately (it is difficult at that age to tell offense from defense). Sometimes bands play.

Little league moms and pops, bursting with pride that their youngsters have been detoured from lives of crime, crowd the sidelines to encourage them, the veins sticking out on their necks. Grown-up officials in striped shirts blow their whistles in a cacophony of authority and tower over the action like Gulliver over the Lilliputians. Coaches scream and yell at the pint-size warriors and sometimes tell the officials a thing or two as well, in the best tradition of American athletic encouragement. "I've been asked if I sometimes think I'm Vince Lombardi," says one kids' league coach in Boston. "I say that sometimes I think I'm Lombardi and other times I think I'm Knute Rockne."

Little league football runs along very well-organized lines, like Little League baseball, but it comes in a greater variety of packaging. Most popular is the Pop Warner League, credited with launching the whole business in 1929 when Joseph Tomlin, a Philadelphia stockbroker, formed the league and named it after the old Carlisle coach, Glenn Scobie (Pop) Warner. Warner must have made a big impression on Tomlin because he also named his son after him (Glenn, not Pop).

The Pop Warners have lost a little of their luster and a few of their members in recent years because, for one thing, some nitpickers in California couldn't get answers to the question of where their registration money was going. They requested a financial statement and were refused. Nevertheless, the Pop Warners still account for 5,700 teams (about 175,000 young people) in 39 states and Mexico, and make up the only national group. Other local and regional leagues such as Football United International, American Youth Football and Khoury League have sprung up like pizza parlors across the country and are structured along similar lines, usually requiring a franchise for the league, and proof of birth and registration fees of $10 to $30 for players. Those whose parents do not pony up get their unconditional release.

League makeup does vary. If a parent has the nerve, he can shove Junior into the Dallas recreation department's football program at five, providing he is potty-trained, but usually a boy must reach the ripe old age of seven before he is strapped and cushioned and sent to battle. Leagues are divided by age (7- and 8-year-olds, 9- and 10-year-olds, on to 15) or by grades in school; and by weight (40- to 70-pound "tiny tots," 50-to-80-pound "junior peewees," on up to 150-pound "giant bantams" —nomenclature differs regionally).

The kids must wear suspension helmets, face guards, mouth-pieces, hip and kidney pads, cleats (or sneakers) and thigh and knee guards. For the most part they play their games on regulation fields, with paid adult officials. Injuries are said to be minimal; some coaches would have you think they are non-existent. The figures are indeed impressive—one broken bone in 17 years of play in Pop Warner ball in Boston, etc. Certainly, trussed up the way they are, and incapable at seven or so of delivering many foot-pounds of force per square inch, the kids are relatively safe. The only danger would seem to be muscle and eye strain from lugging home and studying the thick pro-type playbooks some pro-minded coaches dispense.

The animal clubs—Elks, Lions *et al.*—put money into the act, as do dry-cleaning establishments, mortuaries, taco emporia and pest-control firms. Around Boston, Pop Warner has franchises in 40 communities, each operating on an annual budget of about $17,000. There are 2,448 players on 115 teams in the Minneapolis Park Board lineup. In the Detroit area 200 teams play in three counties. In Southern California exact figures are not kept, but estimates range from 800 to 1,000 teams, or about 30,000 players. Outside Kansas City, Johnson County, Kans. has a 40-acre complex on which 11 games can be played simultaneously, two under lights at night. As many as 10,000 fans may turn out for the Saturday program, to say nothing of 1,500 girl cheerleaders. Houston has 11 separate booster clubs soliciting donations, publishing game programs and conducting dances and raffles to maintain two stadiums. Individual clubs sell advertising space on the fences, and seven adults are assigned to take up collections and maintain order at each game. In Illinois, kids' league banquets are said to be more elaborate than those of many high school or college teams. Trophies and gifts are passed out like supermarket flyers. The boys' pictures appear on the place mats. "It's too much," says the athletic director at a high school in Elgin, who also says he sometimes wonders what it's all about.

There have, of course, been many salubrious side effects of the kids' league phenomenon, according to its advocates. *The New York Times* reported some years ago that delinquency was truly on the wane in Westchester County because of the lessons being learned on the playing fields of Scarsdale. Dean Rusk was seen there, coaching his son in the kicking of a football. Entire communities have mobilized around their little Packers or Redskins. In Levittown, on Long Island, community spirit seized and uplifted (by prop jet) 25 parents who escorted their 12-year-old heroes to a Daytona Beach "bowl" game. Travel money was gleaned from door-to-door candy sales and by putting the touch on local merchants.

Teams have been sent to other midget bowls—to the Steeler in Fontana, Calif.; the Junior Liberty in Memphis; the Junior Orange in Miami; the Auto in Grosse Pointe, Mich.; the Carnation Milk, Santa Claus, Sunshine, Piggy Bank and Mighty Mite bowls elsewhere. Several years ago a Pop Warner team from Marin County, Calif. was flown, with parents, to the Honolulu Bowl, at a cost of $10,000. The money was raised by public subscription, much to the consternation of some stick-in-the-muds who reasoned that the money could have financed three more teams, or 105 boys, in regional competition. The junketeers didn't help matters by allocating $500 to an all-parents cocktail party.

Detractors of midget football have not been heard from much lately, but there are still some around. They include George Welsh, the Navy coach and ex-All-America quarterback, who said right out the other day that he was "absolutely opposed" to it. Welsh thinks organized football is too tough a game, physically, mentally and emotionally, for 8- and 9-year-old children, and that they become mired in it too early. "A kid becomes a tackle at eight and he stays a tackle the rest of his life," Welsh says. "How could that be much fun? At his age he should be learning *all* the skills. He should learn to throw and catch and run with the ball."

Pickup games would be better, Welsh believes, because

football presents unique problems in this respect. A Little League baseball player, no matter what his position, gets to throw, catch, hit and run bases. All basketball players get to dribble, pass and shoot the ball. Football—formal, 11-men-to-a-side, blood-and-guts football—could be played with a pecan waffle as far as offensive tackles or guards are concerned. They wouldn't have to know the difference. This truth is not lost on the kids, though some do prefer to hide in a position that will not draw much attention (or criticism). And perhpas there are others who view it as did 12-year-old George Kinkead of St. Paul, who was put at offensive guard a couple of seasons ago and came home in tears. "They got me playing the position that pays the least," he wailed.

Larry Csonka went out to watch a boys' team practice one afternoon in Fort Lauderdale and was appalled. Csonka is not a man who recoils from spilled blood, his or anybody else's, but he was horrified by little league football. "The coaches didn't know much about what they were doing," he said. "They just yelled a lot. They acted like they imagined Lombardi or Shula would act. Why, they had those 8-year-olds running *gassers* [postpractice wind sprints], for crying out loud."

Csonka will not let his two sons play in the kids' leagues. "Take a little kid, put him under the pressure of a big championship game before his parents and his entire world, and it can be very bad for him," he said. "Especially if he loses. The whole country loves football, and so do I. But parents don't stop to consider all the things that can go wrong for a young fellow pushed into that kind of pressure. For one thing, he can come home with a handful of teeth. Worse, he can come home soured on athletics for life."

The problem of the jaded peewee athlete is no laughing matter to Jim Nelson, who has been coaching for 26 years at a small Missouri college. Nelson yearns for the good old days, "not because we did everything right, but because we had fun. Nobody watched us play, and the fact that we played anyway proves we had fun. Now you see kids who've played little league five or six years. By the time they get to high school they've already been to bowl games and all-star games and had all that attention. What's left? It's too bad, because they need football more at the high school level. Not many sixth-graders are exposed to liquor and cars and drugs. High school kids are. They need an interest like football."

The burned-out football player is not unusual, of course, but when Minnesota Viking Center Scott Anderson quit training camp last summer he pointed out that he'd been playing organized football since he was eight and had had a bellyful. It doesn't have to take that long. Gerald Astor, writing in *The New York Times Magazine*, told of a Ridgefield, Conn. 10-year-old with "star potential" who quit because he tired of practicing "every day after school" and of "never having time for myself." And of a 13-year-old who was alienated from his peers by a coach in Westchester who objected to the boy's dad dragging him home to supper at 6:15, since it was 45 minutes before quitting time. "The coach thinks football is the only thing in the world," said the boy. He retired at 13.

A more widely shared complaint against kids' football, one that applies to any regimented kids' sport, is that it brings the virtues of adulthood down upon all those little heads. It is argued that too many parents and coaches are bequeathing to children the same dogged intensities that make them the cocktail-party bores they are today. It is also claimed that many parents eagerly clog the sidelines to hurl profanity at coaches, players and officials. A California psychiatrist once took a tape recorder to a little league football game and set it up near the stands. "You've never heard such vile, vicious language," he said. "With clenched fists and livid faces those parents goaded their children with nasty needling [and] yelled at the referee as if he were a criminal!"

Such gung-ho parents flock to the kids' leagues. Or become coaches. In Scarsdale, Gerald Astor wrote, one coach addressed an errant young warrior as "you stupid bastard." Others simply call their irresolute players "stupid," "slowpoke," "dumbass" or, when things are really bad, "crybaby."

As a result, even the less outgoing adults sometimes feel coerced into joining the fun, to protect their interests. Says a little league mom in south Florida, "If you want your kid to play, and not get yelled at too much, you volunteer. Your husband becomes an assistant coach. You become a sideline regular. You run car pools and work refreshment stands. You never get supper on before 8 p.m., and you develop sciatica sitting on foldup parade stools." Another mother, taking a more direct route, wound up in divorce court after her friendly persuasion made too noticeable an impact on the head coach. The coach said he knew he was hooked when he made her boy —who "ran like a cow on ice"—a starting halfback.

Within what has been described as this "rat's nest of psychological horrors," it is not unusual for a child to have his parent and/or coach falsify his birth certificate to get him into a favored division, one in which he might excel. Or submit to starvation diets to make a weight. One coach in Florida says that he sees these kids "flying around so high on diet pills they can barely tell you their names."

A parent can ruin his son early, according to one Kansas City child psychiatrist, "by making him feel like a scrunge for not playing football" when the son might be more inclined toward the piccolo. But the coach deserves as much credit; and coach and father may be one and the same. Chuck Ortmann, the former Michigan All-America who quit as chairman of a league in Glen Ellyn, Ill. in which strife and debate over recruiting violations had long been rampant (a fist to the lip of a league official ended one discussion), believes that if kids' football does not turn boys into men, it certainly turns men into boys. "They want to win at any cost," he says. "They tell their players, 'Go out there and break that guy's arm.' They won't even let all their kids play. Forty on a team, but only 11 or 14 play much."

One poignant protest from a little league mom appeared in a recent letter to *The Miami Herald*. Her son's coach screamed at referees, screamed into the faces of the boys and, worst of all, allowed only 12 of his 18 players to play. She wrote, "The other boys sat on the bench for the second week in a row, not being allowed in for even one play. These are 11-year-olds who give up every night of the week to practice, come home late, tired, dirty, hungry, but with the thought it will be worth it when they play on Saturday. Ha." In Minneapolis, adults running one "midget" division silenced this kind of insubordination by waiving the must-play rule for 12- and 13-year-olds. By that age, said a suburban little league official, the inferior players "know it's not their sport."

With so much riding on the outcome—bowl bids, adult egos, bragging rights at the local pub—it was predictable that violence would creep into kids' football, and last month in Kissimmee, Fla. a mob of adults attacked four coaches of a winning team of 12-year-olds with clubs and pipes, sending one coach to the hospital. A cry from the crowd, "He's dead!" apparently satisfied the mob and it withdrew just before the police arrived. The coach was not dead, only unconscious for four hours. One little league pop in Miami got into a fistfight with a coach who wasn't playing his son at his idea of the right position. A coach in Palm Beach strode to the center of the field after a particularly heartbreaking loss and extended his hand to the star player of the rival team, then punched him in the stomach, knocking him down. When he realized what he had done, the coach did not wait to be suspended. He quit.

Such incidents have caused massive end sweeps into the nearest circuit court, where big-league litigation is the next thing the little fellows are taught. The Optimist Athletic Conference has twice been to court in Miami in recent months, once when an entire 250-player group was expelled and again when a coach was suspended for threatening a commissioner. The teams won reinstatement; the coach did not.

In 1963 *The New York Times* used the word "grotesque" to describe a kids' bowl game it covered on Long Island, and *Life Magazine* pointed out that the American Academy of Pediatrics was opposed to little guys banging each other about because of the vulnerability of their epiphyses (the soft bone tips where growth originates). Deformities were said to be around the corner. *Life* added that the greater danger was psychological. "In sandlot ball you can always pick up and go home," it quoted a Big Ten physician as saying, "but in this game you must remain in competition. You must make your blocks and tackles. This can make a boy wary of competitive sports— either because of sheer boredom or because he's afraid."

It would seem the campaign against boredom is one that coaches must wage relentlessly in kids' leagues. When the trains pass, the kids stop and watch; when the planes go over, they stare. "Let a fire truck go by and it's Looney Tunes," says Dickie Maegle, a star halfback at Rice in the '50s now coaching little leaguers in Houston. "Suddenly they're out of it. I've seen 'em so excited at kickoff, with the crowds yelling and bands playing, that the kicker completely missed the ball. I've seen 'em running for a touchdown when their pants fell to their knees. I've seen crepe paper draped down from the cross bar and when the kids tried to run through, they fell down."

Maegle is one of those muddled thinkers who do not object to this kind of foolishness. He thinks kids ought to be allowed to act like kids. So does Galen Fiss, an ex-Browns linebacker. The other day in Kansas City one of Fiss' linemen came out of the huddle hopping and skipping to the scrimmage line. "For an instant, our coaches were horrified," said Fiss. "That's not the way you're supposed to approach the line. Then we realized, he's a 10-year-old kid! That's his way of having fun."

Bob Cupp is a 35-year-old father of two, self-described as having a Charlie Brown head under a Buster Brown haircut. He lives in Tequesta, Fla., a punt and a pass up the waterway from Palm Beach. An all-sports star in high school, Cupp went to the University of Miami on a baseball scholarship, played quarterback on his service football team (coaching high school football on the side), became a professional golfer and then a golf-course designer. He is still a golf-course designer, for Jack Nicklaus, out of Nicklaus' Golden Bear offices in North Palm Beach. Cupp is also a professional illustrator, and he sings professionally as well as in the church choir.

Bob Cupp is one of those curious people who love small children, even their own. His only other weakness is that he enjoys coaching children, even other people's. He somehow finds time for this year round: kids' football, basketball and baseball. Cupp smiles and laughs a lot, as though he might know something about life that no one else knows.

He has been coaching little league football in both the Miami and Palm Beach areas for six years—his son Bobby, 11, was recently described in a local paper as a "grizzled veteran," which the Cupps thought was pretty hilarious—and has some revolutionary ideas about what ought to be done with kids' football, some of which he has put to the test. Cupp thinks that most coaches are not necessary, that referees are not necessary, and that parents are not necessary, except in a strict biological-familial sense. He also thinks every kid should get to touch the ball every game—throw it, catch it, run with it. But Cupp has learned to accept, or at least anticipate, the game as it is in the small time.

"We had a coach in one league who had access to diet pills," he says. "The kids could get them for nothing. You never saw such a hyper bunch. But one of 'em was a lost cause. He came to the weigh-in in his daddy's heavy rubber suit, his face red with sweat. He looked like a cherry sticking out of a duffel bag. When he took off his sweat suit, his poor fat little body was pink as a salmon, but he missed by four pounds.

"Parents will allow their kids to go through any torture to play. This fall the boy who'd been kingpin of the 80-pound league for two years tried to make the weight again. He dieted and dieted and still weighed 86. The coaches told him he was good enough to move up to the next division. His parents said no. The boy didn't think he was good enough. He quit. He couldn't face not being the star anymore.

"Coaches are as guilty as parents. One I know decided to give his team a little boost by injecting a stimulant—Benzedrine, Dexedrine, something—into the oranges he always fed them before a game. He used a hypodermic and kept upping the dosage. After the third or fourth game the players started complaining of headaches and throwing up. The coach later admitted to me what he'd done, but at the time everybody blamed the oranges.

"Most of the coaches I have seen, more than half, I'd guess, haven't even had high school experience. They teach a lot of things wrong, even fundamentals like stances and handoffs and blocks. They see something on TV, and even though they don't understand it they try to put it in. I had a guy try to use an end-in-motion on us. I pointed it out to the referee, and he laughed and threw his flag. The coach came running over. 'What the hell,' he said. 'The Cowboys do it, why can't we?' The ref explained that it wasn't the end the Cowboys had in motion, it was the flankerback.

"The sad thing is, the really qualified guy isn't always the best for kids. Can't always relate. We had one last year who had all the credentials and loved the game, but he was a wild man. He reduced his team to tears daily. I've seen him, and others, too, manhandle kids, pick them up and throw them around. He'd yell things at 'em like 'You're gonna block if I have to kick your ass all afternoon!' The kids were 8-year-olds. They'd just turn to jelly, walk off the field crying. Another coach criticized him one time for not playing some of his lesser kids. He said, 'Why should I play kids who look up at the sky and chew grass while everybody else is sucking up their guts in practice?' The other coach said, 'Maybe if the kids played more they wouldn't look at the sky so much.'

"We had a rule that the son of a father or legal guardian who is coaching has to play for his father or guardian. I looked up one day and a coach was trying to add somebody's grandmother to his coaching staff—a black woman with gray hair who happened to have three of the best players in the area living in her home. Two were brothers and one a cousin, all of them little O.J.s, just the right age. A gold mine. Grandma was their legal guardian. When the coach announced at the league meeting his plan to add her to his staff, the place went up in smoke. You never heard such carrying on. He finally withdrew his motion.

"This one really ticked me off. One of our less charitable coaches had a kid who was kinda lousy and the coach didn't want to play him. We have this must-play rule where every player is supposed to play a series every quarter. I let mine play longer so the poorer players can improve, but some don't think along those lines. Anyway, this guy worked out a scheme whereby he'd send the poor player, No. 50, say, in with, say No. 60. The woman who checks the substitutes—we call her the watchdog—checks off 50 and 60, coming in. Then as soon as 50 gets to the huddle he turns around and runs back off with the player 60 was sent in for.

"The watchdog wasn't asked to check who went out, only who went in. No. 50 never played. And nobody caught on till the fourth or fifth game, after his team had won four straight. The watchdog who spotted it couldn't believe her eyes. She asked the boy if he'd played at all. 'No,' he said, 'I just run in and out.'

"The league called a special meeting to decide whether to forfeit the team's games or suspend the coach, or both. The league president made a good case for throwing the coach out. Then the team's sponsor got up. He waved his checkbook over his head and announced that if the decision went against his team in any way, his sponsorship would be withdrawn. He was serious, too. The league needed sponsors. The question never came to a vote."

Another challenge, says Cupp, is those pretty young mamas who want junior to play quarterback or some other glamour position. "They're not always subtle about it—they can come on pretty strong. When I see it coming I always start talking about my wife and kids, but I've known it to get pretty rough for some guys. Mama comes around in a tight pair of pants and a halter and wants to engage in a philosophical discussion about football. At her place.

"Fathers try to influence you, too, but they have to do it the hard way. Some of them lug big coolers of beer around and stash them behind the stands on a hot day so the coach can sneak back for a short one now and then. A couple beers and the coach is calling for his kid, to put him in."

Cupp says he has not escaped the behavioral pattern of kids' league coaches in one respect; no one seems to be free of bad temper. "I let my whole team have it after a loss a few years ago because I thought they'd given up, the one thing I told them I wouldn't tolerate. I chewed 'em out pretty good. When I got home afterward my son handed me his jersey and said he was now an ex-linebacker. He said he couldn't play for a crazy man. I got the message.

"In another game, on the very first play, a coach sprang a sneak play on us and scored. One of those sideline passes without a huddle. The receiver was all by himself. A sandlot play, but legal, and great. I should have just laughed. Instead, I blew my top. Ran out on the field, complaining and yelling at the ref. A regular buffoon. My ego had been hurt, see. I'd been had. And I wound up getting my kids so riled up they just poured it on and won 39–6. The other coach hasn't spoken to me since, and I don't blame him."

Cupp believes that "coaches and their personalities, the way they relate or don't relate" is the crux of what is wrong with little league football. "Coaches don't get along, don't even try. It rubs off. The drive to win is so great the kids don't learn anything. The Lombardi philosophy is ridiculous at this level. Losing isn't death, winning isn't everything. The idea is to have fun. Period. If a kid isn't, if he's not enjoying it and quits, the coach should ask himself, 'Would he have quit if I'd done a better job?'

"Last year in our league I proposed a selection process to make our teams more nearly even. The idea was foreign to everybody, but my boys had won everything the year before, so the other coaches listened. We had a get-acquainted clinic, and all the coaches rated all the kids on a scale of one to 10.

Then we sat down with the commissioner, right out on the field, and drew for teams. And something happened to those coaches. We got along great the whole year. The league was tight, and I think we all had fun. I know my kids did. You'd see 'em during a game running back to the huddle and sliding in on their knee pads. It didn't look like the Dolphins, but it was fun.

"Our practices were chaos. Half the time I'd just tell 'em to go over there and play pickup. They should be playing more and practicing less, anyway—playing three or four games a week instead of seven or eight a season. Practicing one-on-one, hitting dummies—that's a drag. A kid wants to play. Lord knows, he's going to find less time for it later on."

Cupp believes that if everyone involved would step back and take a look at what is going on, most of these problems would be solved. Parents, he says, should stay home. At least in the lower levels of kids' football. "A preadolescent has a great need to please his parents, and his failures shouldn't be scrutinized. Just being watched puts pressure on a kid. Maybe by the time he reaches the ninth grade he can bear it. Maybe."

Fathers, suggests father/coach Cupp, should not coach. Not if their sons are in the league. "Fewer coaches would be better all around. At the youngest level one good coach could easily handle four teams. Two coaches at the most, providing encouragement, teaching a few techniques, refereeing the fights. Even officiating. Coaches could be impartial referees if the parents weren't breathing down their necks. And kids should get the idea that games can be played on the square without having to pay a policeman. A lot of our officials are just in it for the money, anyway.

"After kids advance to the older leagues, they still don't need more than two coaches per team. Qualified guys, though, who've played the game, who know at least enough not to teach them things that could hurt. The idea is to let a kid learn more on his own. Developing talent is really a kid's responsibility, not an adult's. A kid learns by playing, by imitating. The last thing they need is an unqualified coach messing them up."

The most radical of Cupp's proposals, his favorite and the one he knows is not going to get him elected little league coach of the year, is the one whereby every player gets a shot at glory by playing a position in which he actually handles the ball. Cupp says coaches laughed when he suggested the idea last fall. Later, "when we were running them out of the ball park," they quit laughing.

"I used to see stagnation set in when kids were relegated to a position like guard or tackle for the whole year. It was like a sentence. Before long, many of the linemen wouldn't even show up for practice. They were usually the smallest guys, anyway—that's the way it works in the little leagues—and what did they need with extra punishment? They were getting enough on Saturday. I couldn't blame 'em. They were typecast. One coach used to bring a roll of masking tape to practice and slap **guard** or **tackle** on the players' helmets, like a brand.

"Let's face it. Running the ball, throwing it, catching a pass, making touchdowns—those are the things kids think of as football. Sustained drives and quality blocking they may think about later, when they're in high school, but for now they don't and shouldn't have to. We're not a feeder system for the high school coaches."

A recent questionnaire gave league kids a choice of playing for a losing team or sitting on the bench for a winner, and they voted almost unanimously to play. "They'd rather play than sit any day," says Cupp. "Busting into the line with the ball can be an unforgettable experience for a fat little kid who will never get the chance again. Next year he may be a guard for good.

"So I worked out my rotation system this way. With my 15 players, I drew up three different offensive teams. Each player, every game, would have to play three positions: a ball-handling position such as halfback, quarterback, fullback, a receiver, and an interior lineman. The more talented players got two ball-handling positions, but every kid got a chance at at least one.

"Funny things happened. The parents objected, some of them. Some of the kids objected, too. One kid refused to play anything but center. He said he didn't want to goof up. But after a while even the prima donnas came to realize there was more to football than being the star and everybody else blocking.

"One coach, a good friend of mine, said what I was doing was impossible. 'You're nuts,' he said. He beat us pretty good the first time we tried it. Then, when we got rolling, we beat him 20–0. He said, 'Maybe you got something.'

"The thing is, it was fun for the kids, and fun for me. I can't tell you the kick I get seeing a kid discover the joys of football. When I was coaching the real little guys, the peewees, I'd see one show up on the first day, thigh pads hanging over his knees, knee pads around his shins, shoulder pads on backward with the underarm straps under his crotch. He didn't know a linebacker from a carburetor. He wasn't interested in 'sticking' anybody. He didn't even know what that was.

"And then when he ran his first sweep it was a problem just holding onto the ball. But he excited you with the possibilities. You watched him run, all wide-eyed and open-mouthed, with a smile on his face. It's a joy.

"The trick," says Bob Cupp, "is to keep him smiling."

Comments

Whom do we believe? Are the proponents right when they claim that children's sports programs contribute to the learning of democratic values, to fighting juvenile delinquency, and to developing a physically fit nation? Or are the opponents correct when they contend that sports teach kids how to fight and cheat, that they exclude those who could benefit most, and that they cripple and maim the young in the relentless pursuit of victory?

Indeed, parents must at least be reluctant, if not totally frightened, to permit their children to participate in adult-organized sports after reading such books as Martin Ralbovsky's *Lords of the Locker Room*. In this damning essay on children's sports programs, Ralbovsky charges that coaches are dictators who are fanatics about winning. He asserts that coaches encourage cheating, promote blind obedience and warped values, and reject the very youngsters who could benefit most from sports. He exhorts us to explain why "no group or individual has come forward to speak out on behalf of the civil rights of one of America's largest and most vulnerable minorities: young athletes." "Good grief," said the mother of a 10-year-old gymnast when hearing such allegations, "I didn't know that sports were so bad that someone needed to speak out!"

Studies investigating the attitudes of Americans toward children's sports have consistently found them to be highly positive. Thus I suspect the vast majority of Americans must agree with the thoughts of Mickey Herskowitz and Steve Perkins as stated in their book *The Greatest Little Game:*

> A standing gag claims that kid baseball is a very good thing, because it keeps the parents off the street. There

is a thread of truth to that, and critics of the program have pounced upon it. Over a period of years, in fact, it has become fashionable to knock kid baseball, to expose it as a corrupter of young egos, to repeat all manner of horror stories about eleven-year-olds warped by adult pressures and adult ambitions.

Certainly, the parents get in the way (that's why they're parents). Certainly, organized teams and leagues tend to regiment the youngsters and give them grown-up illusions. In no other nation are children so pampered and adults so vicariously thrilled. And with that said, another point cries to be made: The critics never seem to ask the kids. They *love* it. As kids always do, they find the fun and innocence in it. They thrive on the scale model big league world around them: ball park, bleachers, scoreboards, press boxes, p.a. systems. They cultivate the mannerisms . . . the tap of the bat to knock dirt off rubber-cleated shoes, hitching the belt, rubbing rosin on their hands.

The wonder of it is that anyone still bothers to attack organized kid baseball and what it represents. In terms of what else boys and girls today can get obsessed with— television, drugs, each other—it is clean, healthy and, yes, wonderfully old-fashioned.

And yet the critics can always seem to find a psychiatrist to decry the pressure it places on tender psyches and warn that to fail, to be excluded, can turn them into the kind of grownup who cries over empty gum wrappers.[1]

Herskowitz and Perkins contend that we should celebrate kids' baseball, not indict it. They believe "it is time to quit kicking the tires, and accept the fact that the product runs. Petulance and adult temper, you see, are not limited to the grandstands of kid baseball. Or the dugouts."[2]

Sensational journalism, biased viewpoints, and gross overgeneralizations plague the image of children's sports. Little League baseball in particular has felt the wrath of adverse publicity. The bitter fight between McGovern and Stotz was widely publicized by the press. The 1973 decision to ban all foreign teams from competing in the Little League World Series was scorned by many Americans who were told it was because American teams were unable to defeat teams from Mexico, Japan, and particularly Taiwan. (In 1977, under considerable pressure, Little League once again permitted foreign teams to compete in the World Series, but under a structure that insured at least one American team in the finals.) Little League's image was further tarnished by its legal battle to exclude girls from its program. The issues and the results of those court battles are discussed in Section C of Part Three.

Some of the negative publicity certainly was deserved— some was not. But here is the point. In spite of the problems of Little League as an organization, Little League baseball has provided enjoyment and leadership opportunities to millions of American children, and adults as well. That fact should not be forgotten.

Yes, most certainly, children's sports should be celebrated, not indicted. Yet we cannot bury our heads in the sand: There are problems that require our attention. Just as athletes strive for excellence within sports, we should strive for sports programs to be excellent. There are legitimate concerns about the over-emphasis on winning, about the competitive pressure and resulting anxiety, about the physical well-being of youngsters, and about children's feelings of self-worth. And in some sports there is even justifiable uneasiness about corruption and violence. But the overriding factor which supersedes all other concerns is the quality of adult leadership provided by the parents and coaches who guide these programs.

References

1. Herskowitz, M., & Perkins, S. *The greatest little game.* New York: Sheed and Ward, Inc., 1974, pp. ix-x.
2. *Ibid.*, p. x.

PART TWO

Understanding Competition

Washington, D.C. Two Silver Spring football coaches in the Capital Beltway League were disciplined for giving weight-reducing pills to certain players so they could be eligible for a weight category in which they had a better chance to *win*. The boys were 14 and under.

— Washington Post
November 1976

Toronto. Boys as young as 8 years were offered bonuses of skates and three-speed bicycles if they signed to play hockey for a specific minor league team. Coaches explained that the bonuses were offered by team sponsors who were anxious for their team to *win* because of the glory and publicity accompanying victory.

—Globe and Mail
March 1976

Washington, D.C. League officials discovered that Vera Brown, mother of Wendell P. Brown, altered her son's birth certificate so that the 17-year-old could play on a 14-year-old and under football team. She explained that her 5-foot-1, 116-pounder needed a chance to be a *winner*.

— Washington Post
November 1976

Louisville, Ky. When boys quit a local high school football team their name tapes were removed from their lockers and pasted on a conspicuous "Hall of Shame." The coach who started this practice explained that it was used as negative motivation and caused the school to leave the ranks of losers and become habitual *winners*.

—Sports Illustrated
February 1975

Hearing such stories we are compelled to ask: What causes adults to become irrationally competitive in the pursuit of victory in children's sports? Have Americans been fed such a continuous diet of competition that they no longer recognize cooperation on the menu? Scholars warn us that the demise of this nation will be caused by our irrational desire to be first and our contempt for anything less.

Several years ago Linden Nelson and Spencer Kagan[1] conducted a series of experiments in which they presented children with a set of games. If the children chose to cooperate with each other when playing, each child received a reward. If they chose to compete, neither child obtained a reward. After testing hundreds of children, Kagan and Nelson concluded that our competitive spirit has produced a society whose children are systematically irrational. Children repeatedly failed to get rewards for which they were striving because they *competed* rather than cooperated.

Others also are concerned about the over-emphasis on competition and winning. Thomas Tutko and William Bruns in *Winning is Everything and Other American Myths* warn us of this insidious and contagious disease.

> Obsessive as we have become in cultivating our spectator sports, I believe a much more destructive craze is the prevailing competitive ethic: Winning is everything. . . . You are nothing until you are Number One. . . . Don't tell us how you played the game; did you win? . . . Are you willing to pay the price to keep winning? This win-at-all costs mania long ago seized high-level collegiate sports (helping to bring about deficits in the athletic departments at nearly every major university), but even more unfortunate is the fact that it is steadily engulfing children's sports.[2]

Terry Orlick and Cal Botterill also lament the winning-is-everything ethic in *Every Kid Can Win*.

> Youngsters of five and six years of age are being informed that they are not good enough and are being cut from teams. Some are being dropped for a better player who can be picked up when the big games come up. Others are sitting on players' benches freezing or being bitten by mosquitoes with the distant hope that they

might get a chance to play and that it might be fun. Many are being discouraged by what can be interpreted as pro-style handling of players (e.g., abrasiveness, tremendous demands, lack of sensitivity, dehumanization, etc.). Still others are being discouraged by the hostility, cheating, aggression, and violence that become part of games when defeating the opponent becomes too important.

Above all, there are youngsters who are *disappointed*, perhaps for one of the many reasons stated, but most often because *it isn't any fun.* Level of ability should not be a prerequisite for participation or having fun in childhood. The star usually has all the confidence necessary, and it is the others who may benefit most from attention during the critical period of childhood. For a lot of kids, winning isn't everything—*being able to take part and have fun means much more.*[3]

Although many argue that our nation's people are irrationally competitive and insanely obsessed with winning, others believe that the competitive nature of the American people has made this nation great. Gerald Ford, for example, expressed this conviction in *Sports Illustrated:*

It has been said . . . that we are losing our competitive spirit in this country, the thing that made us great, the guts of the free enterprise system. I don't agree with that; the competitive urge is deep-rooted in the American character. . . . We have been asked to swallow a lot of home-cooked psychology in recent years that winning isn't all that important anymore, whether on the athletic field or in any other field, national and international. I don't buy that for a minute. It is not enough to just compete. Winning is very important. Maybe more important than ever.[4]

And the celebrated American author, James Michener, expressed similar sentiments in his recent book, *Sports in America:*

I am on the side of healthy competition. I love it. I seek it out. I prosper under its lash. I have always lived in a fiercely competitive world and have never shied away. I live in such a world now and I would find life quite dull without the challenge.

I find competition to be the rule of nature, tension to be the structure of the universe. I believe that normal competition is good for a human being and I am sure that flight from it hastens death. I am prepared to acknowledge every charge against fanatical competition, or senselessly prolonged tension, and I would not foist either upon young people. But I would not wish to avoid reasonable competition, for I like a world in which men and women test themselves against others or against abstract ideals. . . . I do not want to see my nation fall into desuetude because its citizens are unwilling to meet the challenges of our time.[5]

Obviously considerable disagreement prevails regarding the value of competition. The opponents condemn competition for fostering all the mental and social ills of society. Conversely, the advocates posit that competition strengthens the work ethic and has helped make this nation great. It is hard to understand how competition can be viewed both so negatively and so positively. Is there no compromise?

In Part Two we seek an answer to this question through a better understanding of compeatition and the significance of winning and losing in sports. We begin with *Winning is Everything!* written by Stephen Ward who presents a straightforward statement on the virtues of winning and the evils of losing. He believes that sports—even children's sports—are a great sorting machine, and those of lesser ability on a team should not be permitted to play at the risk of defeat. In contrast to the opinion of Ward, *Must We Always Keep Score?* is a condemnation of our adult zeal to turn all children's activities into competitive events for the sake of identifying a winner.

Carolyn Sherif, in *The Social Context of Competition*, provides a more comprehensive and analytical evaluation of the issue. Rather than arguing the effects of competition as being unqualifiedly good or bad, Sherif sagaciously demonstrates that the effects are determined by the social context in which competition occurs. Although this article is somewhat more academic than others in this volume, it is important reading for the serious student of children's sports. In *Reassessment of the Value of Competition*, Hollis Fait and John Billing also provide insightful commentary on competition, making a useful distinction between direct and indirect competition and discussing how competition may influence intrinsic motivation to participate in sports.

References

1. Nelson, L. L., & Kagan, S. Competition: The star spangled scramble. *Psychology Today*, September 1972, pp. 53-56; 90-91.
2. Tutko, T., & Bruns, W. *Winning is everything and other American myths.* New York: Macmillan, 1976, pp. vii-viii.
3. Orlick, T., & Botterill, C. *Every kid can win.* Chicago: Nelson-Hall, 1975, pp. 30-31.
4. Ford, G. R., & Underwood, J. In defense of the competitive urge. *Sports Illustrated*, July 8, 1974, p. 17.
5. Michener, J. A. *Sports in America.* New York: Random House, 1976, p. 424.

Winning is Everything!

by **Stephen D. Ward,** *practicing psychiatrist and former college football player and coach.*

Participation in sports is of value to boys. Learning to be a good sport and a gracious loser is neither good nor desirable. Among superior athletes, good sports and gracious losers are probably nonexistent—at least the variety of these generally recognized by some sports reporters, most spectators, and every playground and youth center organizer, boy scout leader and the like. Good athletes do respect and admire skill, strength and aggressiveness in opponents, and even occasionally can admire dirty play, if it is done with some degree of finesse. Strong objection, however, is always taken to dirty play aimed at producing physical damage.

Some last-ditch ego-saving devices are available to athletes involved in losing causes. In a team sport even though the

Abridged from "The Superior Athlete" in R. Slovenko and J. A. Knight (Eds.), *Motivations in Play, Games and Sports*, 1967, pp. 307-314. Reprinted with permission of the author and Charles C. Thomas, Publisher, Springfield, Illinois.

team might lose, the individual player can be quite comfortable and free of anxiety providing he has the conviction that he personally performed well. If it is inescapable that he has done poorly, fantasy will frequently come to his aid. He will defeat his opponent in another endeavor. A very common fantasy in a defeated football player is that he will meet his opposite number or the whole opposing team, singly or in groups outside the dressing room and literally mutilate them in hand-to-hand combat. Occasionally the fantasy does not suffice; it must be acted out, and the crowd is treated to an added attraction. The late Jim Tatum, former head football coach at Maryland and before that at North Carolina, was pretty close to the spirit of things when he said, "Winning is not the most important thing —it is the *only* thing."

It takes a brand of courage to take your chances in a contest before a crowd. Courage is what is learned in any competitive sport. It is a necessary ingredient for success in any field. Courage is not a gift given freely to a few by some lucky chance of heritage or genetics. It must be learned; it must be acquired, for we are all basically cowards.

Should participation in sports be encouraged? Even egghead intellectuals will agree that it should, or at least they will pay lip service to this with the provision that everything should be regulated and controlled. There is room for disagreement on how this should be done and at what age body-contact sports should be encouraged.

I am not a believer in the Little League philosophy that everyone who shows up should get to play, regardless of who wins. Athletic contests are the relics and vestiges of what in former times were tribe and life-preserving struggles. I think it is not too farfetched to parallel our present international political no-win philosophy with our Little League philosophy for juvenile sports. It is somehow or other not very nice any more to win. Leo Durocher summed it all up very neatly several years ago when he said, "Nice guys finish last." We are certainly very busy trying to be nice guys.

One hears claims that this or that number or percentage of professional baseball players got their first start in the Little League. I am inclined to feel that they made it to the big leagues in spite of, rather than because of, their experience in the Little League. Why delude a child into the belief that success can be achieved by merely presenting himself as an aspiring candidate for the rewards of life? Will his first employer have as gentle a regard as did his Little League manager for the possible psychic trauma that might be done by firing him?

The Little League philosophy fosters security-seeking dependency, acceptance of weakness and goals of mediocrity. It does not breed superior athletes or enterprising citizens.

It has been said that the British Empire was won on the playing fields of Eton. There are many today who would therefore curse those playing fields for having nurtured imperialism and all of its much maligned concomitants. Perhaps, too, a similar hypothesis could account for the disdain with which intellectuals in general hold athletes and athletics. Perhaps the individual confidence, spirit of enterprise and independence nurtured on our playing fields constitute a threat to our current crop of social, economic and philosophical planners.

If such be the case, let's get on with the game!

Must We Always Keep Score?

It isn't whether you win or lose,
But how you play the game!

That's what we tell our children. In school, in church, in the theater, and at home we tell them. Personal satisfaction is reward enough, we say. Learn to live for the joy of living, not for the collection of prizes. We say it, we sing it, we preach it. And then . . .

At _____ Elementary School, just before the Easter holidays, fifth- and sixth-graders gave a square-dance program, with parents and children of other grades as audience. The youngsters wore colorful costumes of Western flair and flavor, and it was as charming and delightful a performance as you're likely to see in a school anywhere. They danced with all the exuberance of healthy childhood, and, obviously, they were having a wonderful time. The audience had fun, too. It was young America, in the best tradition.

Editorial appearing in the *Reporter Dispatch*, White Plains, N.Y. prior to December, 1952. Reprinted with permission of the *Reporter Dispatch*.

But, at the end, a committee of judges announced the winners. One group of fifth-graders and one of sixth-graders were pronounced "best." And the other dancers went away forgetting the fun they'd had, remembering only, "We lost."

And what was really lost was the spirit, the spontaneity, the wholesome pleasure of the whole afternoon—the basic value of a program to which the music, art, English, and physical-education departments had all contributed. All had worked hard, shared, cooperated . . . and a few had been selected "winners."

In that same week at the County Center the third annual area cheerleading contest was held, in the name of recreation and physical education. Groups from 22 schools of the county participated. By the traditional standards of cheerleading, some of these groups went far afield and presented what looked very much like a musical-comedy routine. Each unit performed twice, then waited for the decision of the judges. Tension built up to the point of hysteria, and as winners were announced some youngsters squealed and clapped and grabbed each other in triumph . . . while others slumped in their seats and wept.

In defense of this kind of thing, it is said, "They've got to learn to take it." But is that what they're learning? Isn't it being made painfully clear to them that the important thing is not how they play the game, but whether they win or lose? If that were not so, there'd be no need to select winners. Each unit would give a demonstration while the others observed. All groups might benefit by comparing and sharing ideas and going home refreshed and with a sense of achievement.

There's hardly an activity in school in which a child participates that he isn't working toward some prize or reward, trying to beat the others, prove himself better than the rest. It's true that when he finally leaves school and enters the business or professional world he'll find himself working in a competitive atmosphere—but, he'll be far better able to compete successfully if, somewhere along the way, he has developed the habit of doing some things just for the sheer fun of it, regardless of the score.

An authority in child psychology, speaking to several PTA groups in the city this year, discussed pressures and tensions operating in modern society on adults and on children, too. It seems ironic that our school system, instead of working to counteract those pressures and tensions, in many instances actually helps to create them.

Have we become a nation so uninspired, so lacking in interest and enthusiasm that we must always work or play for a prize? Can't we ever just relax and play the game without even bothering to keep score?

The Social Context of Competition

by **Carolyn W. Sherif,** *eminent social psychologist at Pennsylvania State University.*

Most discussions of competition among children do not concern the strenuousness of activity; they concern the social-psychological effects of competition on the developing human personality. Furthermore, such discussions too frequently bog down in irreconcilable controversy after the first few words are spoken. The participants almost always start with preconceived judgments about the effects of competition that no amount of talk can alter. To some, competition is regarded as natural, healthy, and essential for building character. To others competition is regarded as harmful, psychologically injurious, and detrimental to cooperative activity, which is endowed with all manner of beneficial effects and seen as the highest state of human relations. The person who butts into such controversies with simple-minded observations (such as

Abridged from *Social Problems in Athletics*, D. Landers (Ed.). Champaign: University of Illinois Press, 1976, pp. 18-36. Reprinted with permission of the author and publisher.

the terrifying consequences for social life if everyone competed all of the time, or the obvious fact that cooperative activities are integral to anything from a good ball game to a
ghastly war) is regarded as a maverick who just does not get
the point.

The point of such controversies is, of course, that the proponents have axes to grind. Their arguments are tools to support schemes of social arrangements—political, economic, or
even recreational. Serious analysis of competitive processes
involving children has no place for such ax-grinding. First, bias
inevitably hampers viable research into a sorely neglected
problem of major importance in child development. Second, it
prevents planning for the most felicitous contexts for the
development of human personality. But do-or-die defenders of
competition or of cooperation are seldom as interested in such
plans as they are in defending their own assumptions.

Try to find an instance of competition that does not involve
cooperation with someone. Try to find an instance of cooperation, either within a group or with another group, that in-
volves no competitive activity. According to the dictionary,
competition stems from the Latin verb meaning "to seek together." In the most general sense, therefore, competition
implies its supposed obverse: cooperation.

Trying as best we can to proceed without prejudgments, our
task is to examine and to study the effects of competitive
processes by inquiring into the *social context* in which children
come together to seek, and then to examine, the effects of such
contexts on the psychological outcomes of competition.

An occupational hazard of being a professor is to gain the
comfortable feeling that a high-sounding definition of a problem solves the problem. At the risk of being so interpreted, a
characterization of competition is here proposed because it
seems conducive to our task, and because it will permit us to
integrate a variety of research findings related to that task.
*Competition consists of activities directed more or less con-
sistently toward meeting a standard or achieving a goal in
which performance by a person or by his group is compared
and evaluated relative to that of selected other persons or
groups.*

A few words of clarification will permit us to proceed to the
major points in this discussion. The clarification consists of

emphasizing two words in the characterization of competition. *Consistently* emphasizes patterns of activity that, with no more than occasional diversion, weave toward a standard or goal. *Selected other persons or groups* implies that consistent patterns of activity are not compared to or assessed by everybody, or by just anybody. By its very definition, competitive activity implies a social context involving *certain* other people and a selective process determining who they are or shall be.

Research bearing on the social context of competition and its effects will be summarized in the remainder of this paper. In brief, the themes of the successive sections are as follows:

1. Very young children cannot compete; competition develops during socialization in a specific social context.

2. Competitive processes and their outcomes vary according to the structure of standards and goals which, in turn, differs enormously from culture to culture, group to group, sex to sex, and even sport to sport.

3. Aspiration levels, achievement, success or failure and their psychological consequences depend upon the social context of the competitive process, the effective social context consisting both of the structure of standards and goals and of those persons and groups who count for the child.

4. Since they neglect the social context, most research models for studying effects of competition, particularly in sports, are inadequate and probably misleading.

5. Research specifically analyzing the social context of competition over time indicates that the psychological consequences for the child generalize far beyond the specific competitive activities themselves.

By analyzing the effective social context of competitive processes, alternative plans are suggested, conducive to the widest realization of human potentialities.

In discussing each of these themes, I shall be summarizing large bodies of specific research, without embroidering the discussion with copious footnotes and references. The reader with serious research interests may find ample documentation and references.[1,2]

Children Learn to Compete

Very young children cannot compete in the sense defined here. The capacity to direct behavior consistently toward an abstract standard for performance or a distant goal develops only with age and, as Piaget has suggested, through inter-action with peers. Through such interaction, especially with peers who lack the overwhelming power of adults to impose standards for behavior, the child develops the ability and the desire to attain some defined level of performance or to reach a goal that does not automatically follow a short-time sequence of action ("a cookie after you eat the spinach"). Competition in-volves goals that are remote in time, carry abstract reward value, and are only probably attainable.

This does not mean that little children don't play, run, throw balls, swim, wrestle, hit, kick, suffer disappointments, or bask in the warm glow of approval. Infants treat one another as objects, but soon learn games such as "I hand the toy to you and you hand it back, and I hand it to you," and so forth. Young children's play is solitary or side by side. Interaction has little to do with improving the actual performance underway. In fact, studies have shown that the presence of another child in an activity intended by adults to be competitive may actually lower performance level. The pleasure of each other's company takes precedence over sticking to the business at hand.

Of course, the young child will respond to praise and correc-tion in an activity that is enjoyable, such as throwing a ball or running. He responds when that praise or correction comes from an adult, older brother or sister, or playmate whose words, smiles, and frowns count a great deal in his young life. But in these early preschool years, behavior directed consist-ently toward attaining a standard or reaching a goal to be com-pared with the performance of others is only an occasional happening. You may have heard, as I did, young children play-ing a game in which the rules specify winning in terms of speed, time, accuracy, or the like. The winner announced "I won," whereupon another child joyously proclaimed "I won too." Then, with the pronouncement "We all won," the chil-dren turned to another concern—in this case, a devout hope that the ice cream man would soon be on their block.

Ordinarily, by about the age of six in our society, a child can and does compete. Still, the consistency of competitive behaviors varies enormously. Research has shown, for example, that middle-class children with schoolteacher and business parents compete consistently at an earlier age than children of working-class families.

Several implications emerge from this brief account of the development of competition among children. First, the capacity to direct behavior consistently toward abstract standards or remote, uncertain goals in which one's behavior is compared and evaluated relative to others develops with age. The crucial evidence supporting this conclusion stems from a body of research showing that not only consistently competitive behavior, but also consistently cooperative behavior, consistent helping behavior, consistent sympathetic actions at the distress of others, and—most unfortunately—consistent prejudicial hostility toward groups traditionally discriminated against in our society all emerge at about the same period in the child's development.

Second, the process of development occurs in a social context in which parents, siblings, and peers are very important in providing the medium for testing one's own performance and for learning the reciprocal nature of rules and standards. Recreation leaders and teachers are important—but all of these significant figures are surrounded, like it or not, by a cultural context that is at least equally significant for the child's development. How else are we to understand the earliest buds of competition in rivalry over who gets to be father or mother, in divisions into good guys and bad guys for bang-bang conflict when the good guys and bad guys are precisely those whom the children meet in storybooks and on television? Evidence indicates that the social context for competition is crucial; if so, it is utter nonsense to speak of "born winners and born losers." There are, and always will be, individual differences. But the winners and the losers are shaped in a variety of ways by their social context, at times obviously and at others more subtly. It is more accurate to state that winners and losers are made by their experiences in a social context of other people who, to a major degree, determine the targets for their efforts and the structure of standards and goals related to those efforts.

Finally, the social context in which competitive behavior develops affects not only its rate of development but also the targets for competition—that is, what is important to the child and what can be left to the birds. In this country, at a very early age boys learn that sports of various kinds are *the* avenue for recognition to a far greater extent than girls. As a result some boys are placed in untenable situations psychologically, and many girls simply fail to persist in sufficient physical activity to develop strong and healthy bodies. We need to inquire into the variations in the social context that may produce strikingly different outcomes in what is regarded as important for competition and the behavioral outcomes of the competitive process.

Differences in the Nature and Structure of Standards and Goals

Particularly in a society such as ours, it is important to recognize that the nature of activities deemed important enough to warrant competition and the structure of the relevant standards and goals differ from culture to culture, group to group, sex to sex, and even sport to sport. Too frequently we assume that what is worthy of competition (the "good life," in our terms—athletics to build body and character) is and should be a universal norm and ideal. In fact it is not. Consideration of such differences may reveal some failings in our own society and suggest guidelines in planning for needed changes.

It is commonplace to point out that societies differ enormously in the prizes they offer for different activities, including sports and recreation. What is not so obvious is that societies that prize physical activity and health need not place enormous value on organized competitive sports. In some societies, physical fitness is prized for everyone and may be encouraged through universal physical activity, including work as well as fun and games. In others, excellence in sports is prized but rewarded indirectly through extra time for practice, opportunity to instruct, while those most outstanding are expected to be self-effacing in directing their efforts to the general improvement of physical well-being rather than personal aggrandizement and public acclaim.

Let us look at our own society. Sports compose a major value complex that the child encounters at an early age, especially if he happens to be male. Furthermore, sport is defined as competition to win. For the individual, the aim is to make the first team and, at all costs, to be on the winning team. If the varsity is winning, there is consolation even in being second or third or fourth string. Barring any of these positions, it is the rare boy who does not become absorbed as spectator of amateur and professional athletics, which may well mean that his own physical activity is limited to walking to the school bus or riding a motorbike. In our own extensive research on informal groups of adolescent boys studied in their natural habitats between 1958 and 1970 in the southwestern and eastern United States, we found only one group of teenage boys with no visible interest in sports. These were sons of recent Mexican immigrants of peasant origin. Other Chicano youths in the same city were intensely interested in sports: with the hope of making a team, one group even entered a high school reputed for its magnificent athletic teams but located halfway across the city of San Antonio. While their relatively small stature precluded this goal, the youths actually stuck to that school through thick and thin, working to maintain passing grades and walking a couple of miles back and forth each day—all for the pride of identification with those glorious winners.

With girls it is different. After about the age of twelve, they quickly learn that actual participation in sports brings little glory. Their claim to fame comes through feminine attachment to the male team members, the booster clubs, or—thrill of all thrills—being a cheerleader. We will refer to girls again in the next section. Here it is sufficient to note that, in the past, their recognition in sports came chiefly from swimming, diving, ice skating, and other such graceful (hence lady-like) activities.

[The] larger issues [in sport] center around the extreme importance attributed to organized competitive sports and . . . the structure of the goals that create problems in personal development for large numbers of young people. At present, the goal structure is a win-lose (or, if you wish, zero-sum) game. The aim is to win, thereby utterly defeating the opponent. This goal structure is clear enough in organized team sports; it is equally clear in the path that the individual child must take to succeed. He (or occasionally she) must gain exclusive hegemony over all competitors for the available slots on the team.

To contend that the prevailing structure of goals is necessary, normal, or natural can be countered even within the sphere of sports and recreation activities. The win-lose, beat-everyone-out-for-the-best-slot complex may indeed be characteristic of much of American life. But it is not true in many sports activities—mountain climbing, fishing, jogging, backpacking, nature hiking, many water sports, some snow sports, modern and folk dancing, calisthenics, and a good many others. Enjoyment or even excellence in golf or tennis is not dependent on the win-lose law of the organized sports jungle.

I am concerned that more children become actively involved in sports and recreation activities for both health and pleasure. I resent the undeniable fact that somewhere early in my own development I ended up out of sports activities, feeling inadequte and therefore unworthy of trying. I would like to see sports and recreation activities a part of my life and the lives of our children. Let us learn from social-psychological research just what psychological processes are involved in the effects of competition among children.

Psychological Effects of Competition Depend on Its Social Context

Competitive activities refer to performance that is compared to standards set by certain other persons, and to the assessment of performance by certain other persons. These reference standards and persons, along with the structure of goals awarded to the competitors, are the effective social context of the competitive process.

The psychological effects of the competitive process can readily be inferred from the substantial body of literature on levels of aspiration and the experiences of success and failure. Experiencing success or failure is always relative to standards to which the child aspires. Like it or not, these standards are influenced decisively by significant adults, peers, and the images portrayed through the mass media of communication. Thus the child is seldom entirely free to establish a standard that fits his interests and abilities. He cannot remain immune to the judgments of parents, teachers, and peers in setting the level of his aspiration for performance.

Long ago William James defined the experiences of success or failure in relative terms, as the ratio between one's actual performance and his pretensions or aspirations in that field of activity. Much later Kurt Lewin, F. Hoppe, J. D. Frank, and others initiated research into the relationship between aspiration level and performance. Several findings from this substantial body of research have definite implications for the effects of competition.

First, in a given activity, there is a strong tendency to maintain the same level of aspiration regardless of actual performance. Experiences of failure are in a sense inevitable on those occasions when performance falls below the standard. This failure to adjust one's standards to actual performance (or, if you like, this rigidity of the aspiration level) is typical both of the performer and of others with personal investment in his performance. For example, in a study I conducted some years ago with children and their parents in a dart-throwing task, the parents tended to maintain a rigid aspiration level for their children, as did the children for themselves, regardless of actual performance.

Although this may not be true for the professional athlete, the child's aspiration is typically set at a level that has the peculiar and unfortunate effect of assuring the better performer more frequent experiences of success than the child whose performance is average or below. Typically, the more adequate performer sets his aspiration level slightly below his performance level and keeps it there. The average or less adequate performer, on the other hand, sets a standard considerably above his typical level of performance, thereby practically insuring a continuing sense of failure and frustration. Improvement in performance, therefore, has quite different psychological meaning for the child who is able and the child who has less aptitude.

The level at which standards of performance for an activity are set by adults or older children reflects a social norm that may or may not be realistic for the developmental level and skills of the child. Many years ago Dwight Chapman and John Volkmann, then later Leon Festinger and a number of other researchers, used carefully designed experiments to show what happens when performance is compared to that of a group too advanced or too low for the person's actual potentialities. Quite simply, if the person is told the expected level of performance for a group that he considers inferior in a specific activity, he raises the standard for his own performance. However, if the comparison group is one that he regards as superior to his own, his aspiration level is sharply lowered. An adult who holds up the performance level of the varsity high school team as a standard to sixth graders may inspire the exceptional few to work harder, but the majority will simply lower the level to which they aspire. Similarly, as Joe Paterno remarked in *Football My Way*, the standards of professional sports may instigate great efforts from the ambitious few, but for most players such standards simply remove the fun of sports by producing an aspiration level recognized as inferior, hence offering little joy when it is attained.

Thus far, the summary of research on aspiration levels and performance has been abstracted from recognition of actual attainments. Of course, this is not the case. As N. T. Feather has shown, consistent improvement in skill is tracked by consistent raising of the standard set for one's performance. Conversely, consistent trends toward decreasingly adequate performance are tracked by lowering of one's expectations. This may happen to even the best athlete when he begins to lose his stride. Much more significant for young children, however, is Feather's finding that the aspiration level tends to be maintained rigidly at a high level when the actual level of performance over time is fluctuating and least predictable. This state of affairs is highly probable for the young child, whose performance is likely to vary considerably from day to day or week to week, with the result that the child faces the continuing hazard of experiencing failure for reasons that are seldom clear to him or her.

The effects of continuing experiences of success or failure in young children have been documented, notably beginning with the research of Pauline Sears. The child who experiences success at a level approved and rewarded by significant adults and peers is able to tolerate an occasional failure or an "off day," recognizing it as such. But the child whose persistent experiences are defined as less than successful, or as failures, suffers considerably from a temporary drop and the resulting disapproval from persons significant in his or her eyes. Over time, the level of aspiration set for performance drops lower and lower, and pretensions may even vanish altogether. The child simply stops trying.

The outcomes summarized above certainly have import for the planning of sports and recreation programs. Currently, the great emphasis on interscholastic competition, varsity sports, and professionalism means that the vast majority of children are doomed to be very small frogs in enormous pools. Surely, for the developing human personality, it is important to create pools in which most children can have the experience of growing and gaining because they were not pressured to maintain a constantly rising aspiration level.

The problem suggested is compounded tenfold when we focus specifically on girls' sports and recreations. As girls approach adolescence, the double standard emerges with a vengeance. The little girl who is active and skilled may be called a tomboy, but she need not suffer unduly except from the scorn of boys who don't want a girl tagging around. If her skills are directed toward sports such as water ballet, ice skating, diving, or gymnastics, she can make it through early adolescence and beyond without detracting from what she and many of her peers and adults think of as feminine. But if these graceful and accepted feminine activities are not her forte, she faces a dilemma: be typed by peers as one of those athletic oddballs, or drop out. The vast majority choose the latter course, to the great misfortune of their health, physical development, and future enjoyment. They even develop (in the sense used by Matina Horner in her doctoral thesis) a *fear* of success. If you play tennis and like it, go ahead and play, but not too well —certainly not so well that you beat male opponents.

The girl who remains devoted and who persists during her adolescent years in improving her skills in "unfeminine" sports faces a situation analogous psychologically to that of the successful black athlete. (I emphasize the psychological effects, because the sociological causes and consequences are quite different.) By striving toward and attaining a high level of performance, she experiences success in one respect but faces failure in others—namely, in those spheres traditionally defined as feminine. For the successful black athlete, of course, this impossible feat of high self-esteem and sense of accomplishment in sports is accompanied by the denial of rights and privileges that should be available to any athlete of attainment. For the female athlete in "unfeminine" spheres, the denial is psychologically painful, but perhaps less important from an educational and sociological point of view than the statistically more frequent fact that girls simply lose interest in sports, drop out, or try hard not to succeed too well.

Prolonged Competition on Win-Lose Basis Generalizes Beyond the Game

In his writings on the "split-level American family" and on the goal structures that pit child against child, age group against age group, and social group against social group, Urie Bronfenbrenner of Cornell University has made it poignantly clear that we have neglected to take the broad view of the effects of competition on children. Both he and other social psychologists who have commented on childhood in general (in contrast to simply analyzing the child at home, or the child at school, or the child in sports as though the child's development were split into compartments) have illustrated some of their main points through a series of experiments directed by Muzafer Sherif.

In three separate experiments conducted in natural circumstances in summer camps, Sherif and his associates demonstrated that prolonged competition on a win-lose basis between groups of children had effects that extended far beyond the specific context of the games played. It should be emphasized that these experiments used sports as a medium for prolonged competition, not as the butt of criticism. The participants in each case were American boys about twelve years old to whom sports were already of central interest, along with camping and outdoor recreational activities. To compete in sports was not only a natural but also a highly desirable activity.

The camps were organized by research personnel and arranged over time so that the structure of goals between groups of boys were systematically changed to study, first, the effects of prolonged win-lose competition and, second, the change of those effects in more creative directions. For this reason I believe that they have definite implications for the possibilities of planning and programming in sports and recreational activities.

For reasons of theory and hypothesis testing, which need

not be our main concern here, the participants in each of the three experiments were carefully selected to be unacquainted with each other at the outset, well adjusted in school and on the playground, and members of stable middle-class families of similar religious and ethnic backgrounds. The choice of such a homogeneous bunch of typical, normal American boys permitted us to rule out explanations of the results of their interaction on such possible bases as their being already unduly frustrated, insecure, poor losers, or divided by striking differences in background when they came to the camp.

Since the research concerned group competition, the first stage (about a week in each case) focused on group formation. The selected participants were divided arbitrarily into two bunches, matched as closely as possible in terms of size, skills, and interest. The sole conditions for activities, most of which were actually chosen by the boys themselves, were that they focus on interaction within the developing groups and that they encourage activities requiring that all members participate actively in order to reach their goal, enjoy themselves, or whatever state of affairs described the satisfactory outcome of the activity. For example, to use a canoe left by their cabin, the boys had to figure out a way to transport it through the woods. Or, when very hungry, they were given food in bulk form—ground beef, uncut buns, a watermelon, unmixed powdered drinks—whose transformation into a meal required their division of labor and cooperation.

In each case two groups formed; each group had little contact with the other and, in the last experiment, neither group actually knew of the existence of another group in camp. The groups had distinctive organizations (leader-follower relations) and norms (customs, preferred territory, nicknames for members, and names for themselves). One group developed a complex of norms centering around tough, brave masculinity that flinched at no danger and willingly endured discomfort, while the other (closely matched initially on an individual-by-individual basis) developed its little culture in a fashion that forbade swearing, emphasized moral uplift, and encouraged regular prayer.

The goal structure in which these groups first met was transformed to a win-lose structure very naturally when they discovered each other's presence and asked to compete in organized sports. A tournament of games was organized to accede to this request and "make it more fun"; highly attractive prizes were available for the winning group. The tournament lasted for several days, including a variety of sports events selected by the boys plus a few (tent-pitching, cabin inspection, etc.) that permitted the research personnel to keep the cumulative scores of events close to the very end. This particular structure of highly desirable goals that one group could attain only at the expense of the other's loss had a number of effects that far exceeded the bounds of the sports competition itself.

As good American boys and experienced competitors, the games started in the spirit of good sportsmanship, graceful winning and losing. However, they quickly turned into vicious contests in which the sole aim was to win and in which the competitors became increasingly seen as a bunch of incorrigible cheats, quite outside the pale of that brand of humanity identified within one's group. (In the experiment mentioned, in which the culture of one group was toughness and the other of piety, this outcome applied equally to both groups, regardless of the difference in their norms for internal group behavior.)

The prolonged competition between groups had a decided impact on the leader-follower relations, norms, and focal concerns within each group. The daily concern was developing strategy and tactics to defeat the other group. Leaders or other high-status members who shrank from the intense forms of conflict that developed were replaced; erstwhile bullies who had been "put in their place" within their own groups now became heroes of combat.

Outside the athletic competition, and against adult rulings, raids and acts of aggression were organized by the boys themselves. Such acts included messing up the rival's cabin, painting derogatory slogans on the stolen blue jeans of the opponent's leader—"The Last of the Eagles"—and hoarding small green apples to be used "in case" of attack by the other group.

Upon the victory of one group in the tournament, boys in each group possessed attitudes of extreme prejudice and hostility, universally condemning the individual characters of members of their rival group. In fact, each wanted nothing at all to do with the other group.

Appeals to moral values ("love thy enemy") had no effect at

all at this point. In religious services organized separately by each group, the local minister conveyed such messages and appeals in forms which the boys appreciated and understood— but immediately afterward they turned to renewed cursing of their opponents.

Cohesiveness, solidarity, self-initiated responsibility, and democratic procedures greatly increased within each group during the conflict. However, the norms of brotherhood and supporting one's fellows which were so strikingly apparent within each group did not apply to the other group. Democratic procedure, loyalty, and friendship at home need not be transferred to the treatment of those not within the magic bounds of one's own group or team.

In the experiments, several changes in goal structure were tried in the attempt to change this dismal state of affairs. First, there was a series of events that were highly appealing to each group separately (common goals) and in which they had to participate together as equals. However, these contact situations involved no interdependence between the groups. Each could eat the greatly improved food, shoot July Fourth fireworks, use new sports equipment, see a movie, etc., side by side without so much as speaking to the other group. In fact, they did speak. While they conducted their affairs separately, they used these contact situations as opportunities for recriminations, for accusations of "who's to blame" for the existing state of affairs, for hurling invectives, and when food was present, for "garbage wars" that had to be stopped when the weapons changed from mashed potatoes and paper to forks and knives.

The change that was effective, over time, in altering the generalized state of hostility and aggression created from prolonged win-lose competition was the introduction of a series of goals, each profoundly appealing to each group but whose attainment required the participation and the resources of both groups. To distinguish these from merely "common" goals, they were termed "superordinate goals": goals urgently desired by each group but unattainable without cooperation. In the first study, this condition took the form of a "common enemy." A team from another camp competed with teams selected from both of the rival groups. The short-term effects of this common enemy were to induce cooperation for "our camp" to beat theirs. However, when the common enemy was gone, the two rivals quickly retreated to their own in-groups, still unwilling to cooperate in other activities across group lines. Further, had we continued the "common enemy" approach, we would have ended by merely enlarging the scope of the generalized effects of win-lose competition that had already occurred within our camp. In effect, we would have had a bigger war.

The superordinate goals that were effective were problem situations—an apparent breakdown in the water system at a time when outside help was not immediately available; how to get another movie when the camp was short on funds and neither group had enough canteen funds left to sponsor a movie alone; a stalled Mack truck that was the sole vehicle to go for food when everyone was hungry and which was far too large for one group to push or pull alone; food preparation at a time when everyone was very hungry, even though "separate but equal" facilities were available but less efficient; tent pitching when all were tired and when the poles and stakes had somehow gotten all mixed up.

Such superordinate goal structures did not have an immediate effect on the hostility between the groups. They induced immediate cooperation, which dissipated into separate exclusiveness once the goal had been achieved. It required a series of such goals over time for a genuine and lasting change in the relationships between the groups to occur. Such a series of superordinate goals was effective; the boys not only learned to cooperate with each other as groups, but also took initiative to do so on their own. Over time, their views of the other group's immorality and ruthlessness were altered. They learned to take turns in camp activities and actually initiated campfire entertainments in which each group alternated presenting the best and funniest of their talent.

Between the alternative structures of win-lose conflict and superordinate goals, there are many other possibilities. I offer the results of these experiments to stimulate thinking, planning and, I hope, revising of the programs of the sports and recreational competitions in which our children participate. The advantage of superordinate goals, when these are genuine for each group (not imposed by adults), is that other measures which have been tried, often vainly, to keep competitive outcomes within bounds are transformed. Information is exchanged across group lines; friendships can form; leaders of groups can initiate new programs and actions without fear of being called traitors by their own groups; the creative potentials of the groups are given the broadest possible scope.

Particularly with young children in community and school contexts, the full understanding of the meaning and the potentialities of superordinate goal structures has the possibility for building competitive sports programs in which children learn the sorts of responsibility, loyalty, skilled efforts, practice, and teamwork that we believe build character, while avoiding some of the generalized consequences that accrue from competition in actual life. If seriously translated into action, these desirable and potentially fruitful experiences for development toward adulthood could create situations in which everyone can win—if not a total victory, at least enough to lift self-esteem, skills, and experiences that may universally benefit the bodies and minds of our youth. I leave the creation of superordinate goal structures to those who know much more than I about sports and recreation. I am convinced, however, that their planning requires not sheer individual genius, but cooperation and competition among those charged with such planning to produce the most effective and viable programs. I am further convinced that many of those so charged would find great joy in the experience of trying.

References

1. Sherif, C. W. *Orientation in social psychology.* New York: Harper & Row, 1976.
2. Sherif, M., & Sherif, C. W. *Social psychology.* New York: Harper & Row, 1969.

Reassessment of the Value of Competition

by **Hollis F. Fait** *and* **John E. Billing,** *well-known physical education professors at the University of Connecticut.*

Competition has been defined by Slusher[1] as a "contention of interests," that is, it is a rivalry between opposing forces (man, animal or nature) in which the interests of both are not mutually obtainable. In sports and games, the contenders are, of course, individual players or teams who seek the same goal, to win the contest. Contention of this kind has been labeled direct competition. In contrast, competition against a record or one's own past achievements is indirect competition.

Direct competition by its very nature requires at least one competitor to fail for every one who is successful. Game theorists call this situation a "zero sum game," i.e., the sum of winners and losers is zero. In fact, most sport situations produce a negative sum game, in which the number of losers exceeds the

Abridged from *Issues in Physical Education and Sports,* G. H. McGlynn (Ed.). Palo Alto, California: Mayfield Publishing Co. (formerly National Press Books), 1974, pp. 15-22. Reprinted with permission of the authors and publisher.

number of winners. A zero or negative sum game is the inevitable outcome of any direct competition, but we in physical education and coaching make our own unique contribution to the creation of even larger numbers of losers. We construct elimination tournaments and plan championships at the conference, regional, sectional and finally national levels, always increasing the percentage of losers in comparison to winners. In classes we hold races, play competitive games, and conduct skill contests—all creating only one or a few winners and many losers.

Inevitably, direct competition in sports and games focuses strongly upon winning. In recent years winning has come to receive such heavy emphasis that it has obscured all other objectives. The "winning is everything" philosophy is reflected in the practice of judging all results by one criterion and in directing all effort, funds and talent to the one goal of victory. As a consequence, we are forced into, at best, a zero sum game.

Indirect competition, on the other hand, allows positive sum results. If a performance is measured against past performances, then success does not hinge upon another's failure: it is not necessary to beat someone else to be successful. It is within the realm of possibility for all to succeed, to reap the benefits of achieving. Obviously, positive sum conditions are highly desirable in an educational context.

Indirect competition should not be confused with cooperation. Competition denotes a struggle among a number of individuals to obtain values which are scarce, while cooperation can be defined as achievement of a goal that is only possible if another is also successful. In direct competition one individual or group opposes another, whereas in cooperation individuals are mutually reinforcing. Although cooperation is often cited as the antithesis of competition, this is not entirely true. In both cooperation and competition the ultimate outcome is affected by the participation of others. The success or failure of an individual in both cooperative and competitive situations relies heavily on the actions of others; their performance either enhances or detracts from the individual's success. Although indirect competition could involve cooperative effort, it is generally a self-directed endeavor that is not dependent upon the actions of others for success.

It should be noted here that competition is neither inherently good nor bad; it is simply one type of human behavior. With respect to education, it is good if it maximizes the acquisition of knowledge and skills; it is bad if it detracts from learning. If maximum development of *all* students is desired, direct competition, by its very nature, negates this goal.

Using direct competition in teaching sports and games is based on the assumption that competitive relationships are more stimulating and interesting and thus create higher motivation in students. This increased motivation, it is contended, produces rapid learning and good performances. But is this true for the habitual loser, or only for the continual winner? Have we not for too many years directed our sole attention to the winners and ignored the effects of competition upon the losers who, as we have seen, constitute at least half the participants? All physical education teachers have seen individuals who actively avoid competitive situations, who are frightened and withdraw from the challenge. Most of these are students who are not highly skilled and who have had a poor record of success. But might not the same person view his competition on the football field quite differently from competition in a mathematics class, where he has achieved success? Might his differing reactions be related to his relative competency in the two areas? Even casual observation leads to the conclusion that the effect of competition on motivation is situationally specific and reflects individual expectations of success or failure.

Rosenthal and Jacobsen[2] demonstrate that people make prophecies about many events and consciously or unconsciously operate to fulfill their prophecy. Common athletic parlance reflects this phenomenon: "You must think like a winner to be a winner"; the team "was beaten mentally"; "the game was lost before the players ever went out on the field." Coaches and players are well aware of the value of positive thinking and the necessity to prepare mentally for the competition.

When individuals expect to fail because of a history of past failures or because they know that only a small minority is allowed to succeed, a self-fulfilling prophecy of failure results, and in all but the rarest of instances is realized. If teachers are to help students develop the very necessary expectations of success, we must provide experiences which support a success prophecy. We must work against any situation which produces large numbers of failures and thus expectations of failure. Possibly then we can stop our unintentional, but nevertheless detrimental, division of students into winners and losers.

In education the major concern is learning. We need . . . a situation with the least possible amount of anxiety, in order to produce students who are free to question, try, experiment and gamble with little fear of failure. But such situations do not seem to exist in our schools today. Holt[3] claims that most children are scared most of the time in school. He is convinced they fail because they are afraid, bored, and confused. They are afraid, above all else, of failing. When physical educators use direct competition, in which significant numbers must inevitably fail, we induce many students to avoid failure rather than to seek success. For many students this is a reasonable tactic, since their chances of avoiding failure are better than their chances of succeeding. Although it might seem that a student would work hard to avoid failure, just as he does to ensure success, this is not the case. The student seeking to avoid failure never attempts anything of his own volition: he never volunteers, takes an extra trial, or ventures an idea or response to a question. In fact he may actively avoid participation, for he cannot fail if he does not attempt. Every teacher has observed many such students in both classroom and gymnasium. In the classroom they simply refuse to answer. In the gymnasium they may refuse to participate, become ill, complain of an injury, or hide in line to avoid their turn. When pressured into making an attempt, they respond with a half-hearted effort that shows the others they aren't trying, for it's not so bad to fail if you don't really try.

Staunch defenders of competition maintain it is significant training for life in our competitive society. Certainly there is value in experiencing both success and failure when striving for a goal, but it is extremely doubtful if those students with a steady diet of failure learn better how to compete; rather, they learn how to avoid failure through withdrawal, compensation, and rationalization. If one of our goals in physical education is to produce a populace which actively and enjoyably engages in sports and games throughout life, we must strive to prevent the development of these avoidance mechanisms by ensuring greater incidence of success for all students. This can be accomplished by structuring the learning environment to maximize success.

Many members of our profession have noted with alarm and despair the failure of students and adults to engage voluntarily in sports and fitness activities and, in response, continue to attempt to entice them into participation with prizes, awards, and so on. Some interesting findings are beginning to be reported concerning the influence of extrinsic and intrinsic motivators on voluntary participation. Although physical educators continue to use extrinsic rewards and punishments to motivate participation, many would concede the superiority of intrinsic motivation, recognizing it as less transitory and more conducive to permanent changes in behavior. To kindle a continuing interest in learning or activity, we must produce situations that are inherently interesting, challenging and gratifying. Surely motor activities meet these criteria for a large number of persons; yet these same persons do not engage regularly in or frequently select games and sports for leisure activities. Recent work by Deci[4] points to some possible ways in which we operate to decrease the intrinsic motivation of activities by linking the activity with extrinsic rewards. When subjects in the Deci study were supplied with extrinsic reasons (rewards or the threat of punishment) for engaging in a basically interesting act, the construction of the soma puzzle, their desire to participate in the act decreased when the external reasons for doing so were removed. However, given the same challenge and no external motivation, the subjects consistently evidenced a stronger desire to continue. It appears, then, that when a person engages in some behavior without the influence of extrinsic rewards, he justifies his behavior as "doing it because I like it." As soon as an extrinsic reward is imposed on the participant, he tends to link his behavior to it, "doing it for the reward." This shift from internal to external rewards has important consequences for the probability of participation once the external motivator is removed. When winning becomes the primary reason for competing, and when it becomes obvious to a competitor either in a specific game or a broad category of experiences, that winning is no longer possible, he logically declines to continue. Do extrinsic rewards decrease the perception of intrinsic value in an activity? It is likely that imposing external rewards shifts personal perception of the reason for participation toward the external and away from the internal. Later when extrinsic reasons are no longer present or potent, the individual is less disposed to find the intrinsic values sufficient to elicit participation. Thus, attempting to instill intrinsic values through extrinsic devices appears inherently contradictory. Should we not concentrate more in our teaching of motor activities on the pleasure of *doing* and less on the value of *winning* or the threat of *failing*?

If we wish to produce people who enjoy physical activity, we must redirect our emphasis from direct competition and winning to learning fostered by indirect competition. By judging performance and improvements in relation to past achievements, we raise self-development to the major criterion, allowing for multiple winners in a positive sum game. This will require a significant shift in our basic approach to and recognition of performance. We will need to reduce the number of direct competition situations, while we concentrate on producing intrinsic reward opportunities for all levels of performance. Success and gratification must be directed so as to emanate from continued participation and improvement, rather than from besting another.

References

1. Slusher, H. *Man, sport and existence*. Philadelphia: Lea & Febiger, 1967.
2. Rosenthal, R., & Jacobsen, L. *Pygmalion in the classroom*. New York: Holt, Rinehart & Winston, 1966.
3. Holt, J. *How children fail*. New York: Pitman, 1964.
4. Deci, E. Work—Who does not like it and why. *Psychology Today*, August 1972, pp. 57-58; 92.

Comments

I find the debate about the value of competition meaningless. Competition is neither good nor bad. It is a social process whereby individuals or groups compare themselves with others using some agreed upon criteria for evaluation. The environment in which a child competes—the social context as described by Sherif—determines whether the effect of the events encountered during the competitive process is positive or negative. Thus, depending on the circumstances, competition may result in either desirable or undesirable outcomes.

When the consequences are undesirable, the solution *is not* to abolish competition and replace it with cooperative games, as some have advocated. Children need to learn both competitive and cooperative behaviors, and as Sherif observed, both competition and cooperation are inherent aspects of sports. The solution is to change the circumstances. The value of competition depends on *how* the competition is conducted, *how* the events are interpreted, and *how* the emphasis is placed on the participation in relation to the outcome. There is nothing wrong with competing—with being intensely competitive, with wanting to win, with striving to best an opponent—so long as one maintains perspective about the relative significance of the participation and the outcome.

George Sauer, Jr., the former New York Jets receiver addresses this relationship in *Ramparts*:

> Opponents in sport are not enemies. They are not beasts venting a blood lust into acceptable channels. They are not what so many persons, acquiescing to myth, have said they are. If anything, athletic opponents are brothers in a universal sense. They compete in contests to express something about men in the face of challenge.

Opponents mutually enrich their challenges by presenting an intelligent unpredictability that is absent in sports without opponents . . . opponents reflect ultimately a co-operation in the form of competition. Even the words "compete" and "contest" imply a togetherness rather than separateness. Compete literally means to "seek together," and contest, to "bear witness together!" Opponents finally are seeking something together and together they are bearing witness to what man can become in the face of challenge. In this way, they serve each other with a means of testing their limits and testing their spirit, while at the same time providing a drama for a dynamic excellence of man.[1]

Children's sports programs need not be great sorting machines to label winners and losers. Young people should not fear failure in sports to such an extent that they are unwilling to risk participation to reap the satisfaction of achievement. When the pain of failure overshadows the sweetness of potential success, children's motivation to excel is choked rather than kindled.

The emergence of a healthy sense of identity is jeopardized by continual failure and by situations in which children sense that they are "less than others." Youngsters must learn that losing in sports is not failure, but that putting forth less than their best effort is. They must learn that being a poor player does not mean being a poor person. Too often the positive benefits of sports are subverted by the belief that, unless you are a winner, you can never be a truly happy or satisfied person. Success is not the score or the result of a race, but striving to achieve one's potential.

Edward Walsh writes:

To fail is to lose face. But ironically, in our lust for victory, we have lost an opportunity to learn valuable lessons taught only by losing. Like death and taxes, failure is a fact of life. Yet we Americans, weaned on winning, dare not stare at the Medusa of defeat, lest we become petrified like the ancient Greeks. Though postprandial orators wax eloquent over the thrill of victory, seldom is heard an encouraging word about learning from the agony of defeat.

Instead, we're fed that line from the Gospel according to Vince Lombardi: "Winning isn't everything, it's the only thing." Lombardi never said it quite that way, but, quoted or misquoted, the phrase still sticks like a fishbone in our collective consciousness. In contrast, how many people at sports dinners hear Berton Brayley's "Prayer of a Sportsman"? which says, "If I should lose, let me stand by the road and cheer as the winners go by."[2]

When a display of comradeship with an opponent is considered a sign of weakness, or when laughter is judged to be a lack of competitiveness, winning is out of perspective. When a coach instructs a weak hitter not to swing but to try for a walk, winning is out of perspective. When youngsters are given drugs, cajoled to cheat, and intimidated to excel, winning is out of perspective. When winning the game becomes more important than winning friends, respect, self-confidence, skill, health, and most of all self-worth, then *winning is out of perspective.*

And yet it would be tragic to bar children from sports because some adults have lost their perspective. We should not punish the youngsters by withholding from them the joy of sports; rather we should rid ourselves of the adults who cannot keep all facets of sports in perspective.

Children seek out competition as they mature. As they develop a certain level of skill in an activity, they want to know how they stand in comparison to others. Not all children of the same age or skill level, however, are prepared to compete at the same time. Forced competition—whether in sports or other activities, whether in the schools or elsewhere—eats at the mind and heart of the child who fails, and gives the wrong values to the child who succeeds. The overuse of competition to motivate children, where emphasis is always on evaluating one's performance against that of others, may destroy the intrinsic satisfaction derived from engaging in sports.

Competition can be healthy, winning should be important, and losing may be rewarding, but only when sports are kept in their proper perspective. James Michener echoes these words in the closing chapter of *Sports in America:*

Those who are not great athletes can derive a comparable benefit from reasonable competition, and the best is when the individual assesses the capacities allocated to him by his genetic inheritance and determines to use them to the best of his ability. . . . But for life to be meaningful, there must be competition, either external or internal; I therefore reject all recent philosophies based upon a theory of non-competition, because such theories run counter to the experience of nature, of the individual and of society. Destructive competition carried to neurotic levels, I cannot condone. Creative competition, which encourages the human being to be better than he or she might otherwise have been, I applaud.[3]

References

1. Scott, J. Sports. *Ramparts*, December 1971, p. 67.
2. Walsh, E. An American problem: How to live with defeat. *New York Times*, March 20, 1977, Section 5, p. 2.
3. Michener, J. A. *Sports in America*. New York: Random House, 1976, pp. 426-427.

PART THREE

Prominent Issues

With a better understanding of the competitive process we are now ready to tackle seven *Prominent Issues* in children's sports.

"Just let 'em play; leave 'em alone. Let 'em enjoy their childhood," argues an adversary of adult-organized children's sports.

"Hell, kids today will just sit around and watch TV if we don't organize sports programs for them" counters a proponent.

In Section A we consider the longstanding, frequently debated issue of whether it is better for children to play adult-organized sports or unorganized, sandlot-type games. We will see that arguments on both sides of this issue have merit.

"I'm sorry son, but we just can't use you this year. Why don't you come back next year and give it a try." These are the words of a football coach to a dejected 10-year-old boy. In Section B we investigate the child-destructive practice of eliminating kids from sports, either by "cutting" them or by driving them to cut themselves.

"Girls not allowed!" says the stern-faced Little League director.

"Oh, yeah? I'll get an injunction," rejoins a determined little girl.

And so it is today in girls' sports. With changing laws, no longer is it a question of whether or not girls will be allowed to play sports, but what sports they should play and whether they should compete with boys. These questions are examined in Section C.

Two boys skated side-by-side onto the ice as they warmed-up for their hockey game. One boy was 3 ft.-8 in. tall, weighed

62 lbs. (with his equipment on) and had not yet discovered what "peach fuzz" was. The other boy was 5 ft.-9 in. tall, weighed 149 lbs. (in the buff), and was using a razor three times a week. They were both 12 years old!

In Section D we discuss the problems arising from children competing against each other when they differ vastly in maturity. Various methods of "maturation matching" are examined in the search for a solution to this dilemma. We also offer some recommendations in this section regarding when children should begin competing in organized sports.

Occasionally we read about a child suffering a broken neck, sustaining a concussion, or even being killed when playing sports. We also hear and read alarming statistics, causing us to wonder whether we should permit our children to play certain sports. In Section E we look carefully at the risk of physical injury to participants in adult-organized children's sports. This section also contains suggestions for making children's sports safer.

Physical harm is not the only concern of young athletes' parents—many also worry about the psychological injuries that their children may sustain. Staunch critics of children's sports often claim that the "psychological stress" of sports mentally scars young children for life. In Section F we find out just how "uptight" youngsters actually become when competing in sports. We also learn about the causes of competitive anxiety and how to change the competitive environment to reduce the potential stress in children's sports.

Finally, in Section G, we evaluate the contribution of sports to children's moral development, presenting two tragic but true stories of cheating and violence. In addition, we attempt to resolve some of the confusion about what is and is not sportsmanlike behaviors. We also examine how children learn sportsmanlike behaviors and the role parents and coaches play in this learning process.

SECTION A

Sandlot Vs Organized Kids' Sports

I believe the youth league idea is great with some minor changes: Put an eight-foot board fence around the playing area and only let the kids inside; take away all uniforms and let the kids wear street clothes; let them choose teams by the one potato, two potato system; let them play until it gets dark or until the kid with the ball goes home.

—David Gey, Philadelphia[1]

We tend to "league" everything. I'd like to see a new league formed everyday by a bat toss or a free throw. This reduces the "us" and "them," friend and enemy feeling between competitors. And sometimes I feel that youth league sports provide a convenient and organized babysitting and day care center.

—Wynn Lembright, Philadelphia[2]

These are the views of two adults. Yet when a group of 35 high school athletes were interviewed about their participation in children's sports programs they indicated they enjoyed them. Sports for these recent graduates of children's sports programs were far more fun than the critics would have us believe. Most of these youngsters were appreciative of having an organized league with a coach, a schedule of games, facilities, and officials. They enjoyed the uniforms, lights, and post-season banquets. They felt a part of something and benefited from participating in the following ways:

"I learned how to play with a team and stick together, win or lose."
"I developed a desire to compete."

"I acquired a good attitude towards accepting defeat."
"I gained some important basic skills."
"I met and made friends with a lot of guys."
"I had the feeling of being somebody."[3]

In this section we look for an answer to the question: Is it better for children to compete in adult-organized sports programs or to play in unorganized, sandlot sports? In the first reading Edward Devereux, a leading advocate of sandlot sports, discusses the value of play and sports participation without adult intervention. In contrast, Edward Wynne describes perceptively how organized sports offer powerful incentives that motivate children to become voluntarily involved in purposeful activities.

References

1. FCA staff members look warily at youth league sports or "We never met an unorganized kid we didn't like." *The Christian Athlete*, December 1976, p. 14.
2. *Ibid.*, p. 15.
3. Don't worry about winning. *The Christian Athlete*, November 1976, p. 23.

Backyard Versus Little League Baseball: The Impoverishment of Children's Games

by **Edward C. Devereux**, *developmental psychologist at Cornell University.*

In this paper I shall focus on some consequences of young children's participation in highly competitive, adult-organized and promoted athletic programs such as Little League baseball, football, Pee Wee hockey, and interscholastic sports. My critique of Little League baseball and other such major sports programs for children will be based not so much upon what participation in such activities *does* for the children as upon what it does *not* do for them. I will argue that "Little Leaguism" is threatening to wipe out the spontaneous culture of free play and games among American children, and that it is therefore robbing our children not just of their childish fun but also of some of their most valuable learning experiences.

Abridged from *Social Problems in Athletics*, D. Landers (Ed.). Champaign, Ill.: University of Illinois Press, pp. 37-56. Reprinted with permission of the author and publisher.

On the Educational Functions of Play and Games

Why should we care about what has been happening to the recreational and spare-time activities of our children? In approaching an answer to this question, I would like to say just a bit about the functions of games and informal play activities in childhood and comment specifically about the kinds of learning which may occur in spontaneous, self-organized children's games. I will then go on to assess how organized, adult-sponsored competitive sports stack up against this model.

It has long been recognized that children's games and play activities represent miniature and playful models of a wide variety of cultural and social activities and concerns. To take a familiar example, the activities of little girls revolving about dolls and playing house undoubtedly serve some function in the process of anticipatory socialization to future roles as mothers and housekeepers. Similarly, in the games of boys, such elemental social themes as leading and following, of capturing and rescuing, chasing and eluding, attacking and defending, concealing and searching, are endlessly recombined in games of varying complexity in what Sutton-Smith[1] has called a syntax of play. For example, the chase-and-elude themes of tag are combined with the capture-and-rescue elements of relievo in the more complex game of prisoner's base. When the chase-and-elude themes of tag are combined with the attack-and-defend themes of dodge ball, we have the more complex game represented in football.

As Roberts and Sutton-Smith[2] have pointed out, games of different types represent microcosmic social structures in which various different styles of competing, winning, or losing are subtly encoded. Through their participation in a wide variety of different game types, in which the various elements of skill, chance, and strategy are variously recombined in gradually increasing complexity, children find an opportunity to experiment with different success styles and gain experience in a variety of cognitive and emotional processes which cannot yet be learned in full-scale cultural participation.

I would stress, at this point, that for game experiences to serve their socialization functions effectively, it is essential that children engage in a wide variety of different types of games, and at varying levels of complexity appropriate to their stage of development. If the American game culture is becoming overly constricted, will our coping styles and success strategies as adults also become constricted? Could it be, as some journalists have speculated, that America's inability to cope with the realities of world politics stems in part from the fact that our president, a football addict, is committed to a narrow-gauge game plan and success style which is grossly inadequate to deal with those of opponents who are skilled in such sophisticated games as chess and go?

Another feature of spontaneous games renders them especially effective in serving as "buffered learning experiences" for our children: the models they embody are miniaturized and rendered relatively safe by the recreational context in which they typically occur. As Lewin[3] noted, games tend to occur on a "plane of unreality," which renders them especially well suited as contexts in which to toy with potentially dangerous psychological and emotional problems. Thus Phillips[4] has observed that many children's games provide a miniature and relatively safe context for gaining useful experience in the mastery of anxiety. Consider in this connection the titillating joys of peek-a-boo, the universally popular game in which infants toy with the anxieties associated with mother absence, and the happy resolution achieved in the discovery that one can bring her back by uncovering one's eyes. In playful games, older children deliberately project themselves into situations involving risk, uncertainty, and insecurity, and the tensions generated by the conflicting valences of hope and fear. Particularly where some element of chance is involved, failure is less invidious and hence more easily bearable. Similarly, in games involving mock combat, aggression may be safely expressed because, as Menninger[5] pointed out, "one can hurt people without really hurting them" (p. 175)—and, of course, without too much danger of being really hurt in return.

I must stress in particular the point that children's games are effective as expressive models for gaining experience in the mastery of dangerous emotions very largely because of their miniature scale and their playful context. They are rendered safe by remaining on a plane of unreality, in which "reality consequences" do not have to be faced. I would like to go on to argue that "child's play," far from being a frivolous waste of time as it is so often pictured in our task-oriented, puritan culture, may in fact represent an optimum setting for children's learning.

To gain some perspective on this matter, consider what psychologists are saying about the kinds of conditions in which optimum learning may occur. In designing their famous computer-typewriter-teaching-machine, or "automatic reflexive environment," O. K. Moore and A. R. Anderson[6] were careful to take into account what they believe to be the essential features of a really good learning environment: it should be "agent-responsive"; it should provide immediate and directly relevant feedback; it should be "productive," that is, so structured that a wide variety of ramifying principles and interconnections can be learned; it should be "autotelic" or self-rewarding, i.e., related directly to the child's own spontaneous interests and motivations; and, finally, it should be responsive to the child's own initiatives in a way which will permit him to take a "reflexive view of himself." Otherwise put, the environment should be such that the child may alternate in the roles of active agent and patient, and at times may step back and view the whole setting from the viewpoint of an umpire.

If we take these principles seriously, it is easy to see why many children do not learn very much in traditionally structured school settings. In such traditional schools, the pupils are patients and the teacher is the active agent. The principles which are to be learned are explained, perhaps even demonstrated, by the teacher, rather than being discovered by the children themselves. Learning is defined as work, which implies that the children, left to follow their own motivations and interests freely, would rather be doing something else. The pacing of activities is rigidly controlled by the teacher, the school schedules, or the tyranny of the lesson plan. And the evaluative feedback, coming from the teacher rather than from the materials themselves, is often delayed, irrelevant, and peculiarly invidious.

These principles, so widely violated in the regular educational settings in which children are supposed to be learning, are all admirably incorporated in a spontaneous, self-organized and self-paced game of backyard baseball, and in many other children's games and play activities. Little League baseball— and other adult-organized and supervised sports—do a pretty good job of bankrupting most of the features of this, and other, learning models.

But before continuing with this line of argument, I would call your attention to another eminent child psychologist's observations about the functions of spontaneous, self-organized children's games. In his classic study of the moral development of children, Jean Piaget[7] noted that social rules, for the young child, originally appear as part of the external situation, defined and enforced by powerful adults. At an early stage of "moral realism," the child conforms because he must, to avoid punishment and to maintain the needed goodwill of his parents. But he feels no internalized moral commitment to these rules; he had no share in defining them, they often seem arbitrary or unnecessary, and they are often imposed in an arbitrary and punitive fashion. Piaget argued that children's experiences in informal games and play activities with their own age mates play an essential role in moving them beyond this stage of moral realism. In an informal game of marbles, for example, where there is no rule book and no adult rule-imposer or enforcer, and where the players know the rules only vaguely or have differences of opinion about what they really are, the children must finally face up to the realization that some kinds of rules really are necessary. They must decide for themselves what kinds of rules are fair, in order to keep the game going, and interesting, and fun for all; they must participate in establishing the rules and must learn how to enforce them. Experiences like this, Piaget theorized, play a vital role in helping the child grow to a more mature stage of moral development based on the principles of cooperation and consent.

Along somewhat similar lines, Parsons and Bales[8] have argued that the enormous power differentials between adults and children present serious obstacles to certain kinds of essential learning. For example, adult authority usually appears to young children to be heavily ascriptive in character; authority flows from the fact that one is a parent, a teacher, a coach, or simply an adult, possessed of awesome powers to punish or reward. But the relevance of this power is not always obvious. Within the peer group, where differences in power are on a much smaller scale, leadership is much more likely to be based on relevant, universalistic criteria. A child leader is accepted and followed only to the extent that he effectively expresses the children's own values and helps them to work or play together in self-satisfying ways. It is largely within the framework of informally organized peer groups, these authors reason, that the child learns to conceive of social relationships as being patterned on relevant, universalistic principles in which people must get along in common subjection to general rules.

Kohlberg[9] has pointed to yet another feature of unstructured children's play for the processes of moral development. If rules are rigidly fixed once and for all by parents, teachers, coaches, or rule books, the child may learn them and perhaps accept them, but he will not gain much experience in the development of mature moral judgment. According to Kohlberg, it is only with some real experience with dissonance, as when the rules are ambiguous or when there is some cross-pressure or opinion difference about which rules should apply, that children learn to understand how certain more general moral principles must be formulated to help them decide for themselves what they should do. Much of my own recent research has tended to support the notion that informal peer group experiences and their accompanying dissonance contribute to the development of moral autonomy in children[10] and that authoritarian control by adults has precisely the opposite effect.[11]

Backyard Versus Little League Baseball, Viewed as Learning Settings

In the light of what has been said thus far, I shall now comment on what I see as some crucial differences between an informal and spontaneous version of backyard baseball and the organized and adult-controlled Little League version of the same game. Let me grant at once that the latter form of the game is obviously much better equipped, better coached, and probably also a good deal safer. No doubt Little League children really do get better training in the official rules and strategies of our national sport, and better experience in the complex physical skills of ball handling, fielding, and so on. If the purpose of the game is to serve as an anticipatory socialization setting for developing future high school, college, and professional ball players, the Little League sport is clearly the winner.

But if we look at the matter in a more general educational

perspective, it appears that those gains are not achieved without serious cost. In educational terms, the crucial question must always be not what the boy is doing to the ball, but what the ball is doing to the boy. In Little League baseball this is often not the case. Almost inevitably, in a highly organized, competitive sport, the focus is on winning and the eye is on the ball. How often does the well-intentioned volunteer coach from the phys ed department really think about what kind of total experience his boys are having, including those who have warmed the bench all afternoon, or who were not selected for League competition?

Of that, more shortly. But first let me describe a typical variant of backyard baseball, as played in my own neighborhood some fifty years ago. We called it one-o-cat. There were no teams. With a minimum of five kids you could start up a game, though it was better with seven or eight; once the game got started, usually a few more kids would wander over to join in. Often these were kids of the wrong age or sex, but no matter: it was more fun with more kids, and the child population was a bit sparse back then. One base—usually a tree, or somebody's sweater or cap. Home plate, usually a flat stone. Two batters, a catcher, a pitcher, a first baseman. If other kids were available, you had some fielders, too. If someone had a catcher's mitt, we'd use a hard ball; otherwise a softball, tennis ball, or anything else. If someone had a face mask, the catcher would play right behind the batter; otherwise, way back. There was no umpire to call balls and strikes, so the pitcher was disciplined mostly by shouts of "put it over!" Fouls were balls that went to the right of the tree marking first base or to the left of a shrub on the other side; in other yards or fields, different foul markers would have to be agreed upon.

The rules of the game, as we vaguely understood or invented them, were fairly simple. Pitched balls not swung at didn't count either as balls or strikes. Three swings without a hit and you were out. In principle you could go on hitting fouls indefinitely, but after a while the other kids would complain and make you swing at a wild one. A caught fly put you out. A good hit could get you to the tree and back for a home run; a lesser hit could leave you stranded at first, to be hit in, maybe, by the other batter. Or you could be put out either at first base or at the home plate in the usual fashion. Since there were no fixed base lines, when a runner was caught between the first baseman and the catcher, a wild chase all over the yard frequently ensued. When you went out, you retired to right field and everybody moved up one notch, catcher to batter, pitcher to catcher, first baseman to pitcher, left fielder to first, etc. There were no teams and nobody really bothered to keep score, since the personnel of the game usually changed during the session anyway, as some kids had to go do their chores or as others joined in. The object seemed to be to stay at bat as long as you could, but during the afternoon every kid would have plenty of opportunities to play in every position, and no one was ever on the bench. If a few more kids showed up, the game was magically transformed to two-o-cat, now with three rotating batters and a second base somewhere near where third would have been; the runners now had to make the full triangular circuit in order to complete their run.

Maybe we didn't learn to be expert baseball players, but we did have a lot of fun. Moreover, in an indirect and incidental way, we learned a lot of other kinds of things which are probably more important for children between the ages of eight and twelve. Precisely because there was no official rule book and no adult or even other child designated as rule enforcer, we somehow had to improvise the whole thing; this entailed endless hassles about whether a ball was fair or foul, whether a runner was safe or out, or more generally, simply about what was fair. We gradually learned to understand the invisible boundary conditions of our relationships to each other. Don't be a poor sport or the other kids won't want you to play with them. Don't push your point so hard that the kid with the only catcher's mitt will quit the game. Pitch a bit more gently to the littler kids so they can have some fun, too; besides, you realize that you must keep them in the game because numbers are important. Learn how to get a game started and somehow keep it going, as long as the fun lasts. How to pace it. When to quit for a while to get a round of cokes or just to sit under a tree for a bit. How to recognize the subtle boundaries indicating that the game is really over—not an easy thing, since there are no innings, no winners or losers—and slide over into some other activity. "Let's play tag"—"Not it!" Perhaps after supper, a game of catch with your father, who might try to give you a few very non-professional pointers. Perhaps, for a few, excited accounts to the family of your success at bat that day and momentary dreams of later glory in the big leagues. But mostly on to the endless variety of other games, pastimes, and interests which could so engage a young boy on a summer afternoon or evening.

In terms of the learning models proposed by Roberts, Sutton-Smith, Moore, Piaget, Parsons, Kohlberg, and many others, it was all there. It was fun; the scale was small, and the risks were minimal; we felt free and relatively safe (at least psychologically); it was spontaneous, autotelic, and agent responsive; it was self-pacing and the feedback was continuous and relevant. The game was so structured that it required us to use our utmost ingenuity to discover and understand the hidden rules behind the rules—the general principles which make games fair, fun, and interesting, and which had to govern our complex relationships with each other; the recognition of the subtle differences in skills, including social skills, which gave added respect and informal authority to some; the ability to handle poor sports, incompetents, cry-babies, little kids, and girls, when the easy out of excluding them from the game entirely was somehow impractical. How to handle it when your own anger or frustrations welled up dangerously close to the point of tears. Although the formal structure of the game was based on a model of competition and physical skill, many of its most important lessons were in the social-emotional sector— how to keep the group sufficiently cohesive to get on with the play, and how to handle the tensions which arose within and between us.

All these are things which were happening to the boys when left to themselves in this informal game situation. And it seems to me that they are far more important than what was happening to the ball. By now the ball is lost, anyway, somewhere in the bushes over by left field. Perhaps someone will find it tomorrow. And besides, it's too hot for baseball now, and the kids have all gone skinny-dipping in the little pond down the road.

How does Little League baseball stack up against this model? Rather badly, in my opinion. The scale is no longer miniature and safe, what with scoreboards, coaches, umpires, parents, and a grandstand full of spectators all looking at you and evaluating your every move with a single, myopic criterion: Perform! Win! The risks of failure are large and wounding, and in the pyramidal structure of League competition, only a few can be winners; everybody else must be some kind of loser.

In Little League ball, the spontaneity is largely killed by schedules, rules, and adult supervision—a fixed time and place for each game, a set number of innings, a commitment to a whole season's schedule at the expense of alternative activities. Self-pacing? Obviously not. Fun? Yes, in a hard sort of way; but please, no fooling around or goofing off out there in right field; keep your eyes on the ball! Instant feedback? Yes, loud and clear from all sides, if you make a mistake; but mostly from adults, in terms of their criteria of proper baseball performance.

The major problem with Little League baseball, as I see it, is that the whole structure of the game is rigidly fixed once and for all. It's all there in the rule books and in the organization of the League and the game itself. It is all handed to the children, ready-made, together with the diamonds, bats, and uniforms. It is all so carefully supervised by adults, who are the teachers, coaches, rule-enforcers, decision-makers, and princpal rewarders and punishers, that there's almost nothing left for the children to do but play the game. Almost all the opportunities for incidental learning which occur in spontaneous self-organized and self-governed children's games have somehow been sacrificed on the altar of safety (physical only) and competence (in baseball only).

Competition and Little Leaguism in Contemporary America

No doubt there are some who will argue that ours is a tough, competitive society and that somehow, during the educational process, children must be readied for the rigorous competition of real life they will face later on. It is certainly true that competition has played a central role in American society, and for generations there were many, like Theodore Roosevelt, who thought of it as the backbone of American character and achievement. But at what cost to other values? More than thirty years ago the psychoanalyst Karen Horney, in her classic analysis of *The Neurotic Personality of Our Time*,[12] saw fit to devote an entire chapter to "neurotic competitiveness." But while Horney saw the problem clearly enough, most psycholo-

gists and educators of that generation did not. It is interesting
to note that among the twenty-three experimental studies of
competition reported by Murphy, Murphy, and Newcomb,[13]
the focus is almost invariably upon the effects of competition
on the performance of some task; not one of these studies dealt
with any measures of the effects of competition upon the subjects themselves!

But there undoubtedly are effects, among them the apparent inability of American children, reared in a competitive
style, to know when *not* to compete. This point was neatly
demonstrated in an experiment by Madsen and Shapira.[14] An
apparatus was so arranged that no child could get any reward
without cooperating with the other children. Mexican children
(and, in another study by Shapira and Madsen,[15] Israeli kibbutz
children) were quick to fall into a cooperative plan, to everybody's mutual advantage, but the American children continued
to compete even after it became quite obvious that no one
could win anything.

The time has surely come to reassess the heavy stress we
have placed on competition in our educational system, and in
our culture generally. In this connection it is interesting to
note that recent movements toward educational reform call for
a drastic reduction in the role of competition. More generally,
the new counterculture flourishing on our college campuses is
strongly anticompetitive in basic orientation. Somehow a
whole generation of fathers, still deeply involved in major
sports and other facets of the old American dream, has managed to rear a generation of sons, a very substantial segment
of whom will have no part of it.

What can be said, more specifically, of the effects of Little
League competition on children? I shall not take space here to
consider such measured physiological side-effects as the
famous Little League elbow, or the evidences of measured
galvanic skin responses of young boys before and after competition,[16] or the reported losses of sleep and appetite before or
following competition.[17] I have no reason to doubt that first-
rate child athletes, like the adult athletes studied by Ogilvie
and Tutko,[18] really are better built, better coordinated, and
have fairly well integrated, if somewhat aggressive, personalities, in comparison with less athletic peers. But the crucial
question must be whether participation in Little League

sports helps make them that way, or whether the reported differences are a result of the selection processes involved. In the adult study cited above, the authors believe that most observed differences result from the selection processes rather than from the character-molding experiences of athletic competition. Hale's[19] finding that the Little League players who made it to the Williamsport national competition had more, darker, and curlier pubic hair than non-playing age mates almost certainly reflects a selective factor rather than a consequence of ball playing.

Similarly, in Seymour's[20] study, it is clear that the major reported differences between the Little Leaguers and their class mates, documenting the superiority of the League players, all existed before the season began. On all the self-rating scales used in this study, moreover, the nonparticipants actually improved more than the participants, ending ahead of the participants in their post-season self-ratings of their feelings about "me and my school" and "me and my home." The nonparticipants also gained somewhat more than the participants in the teacher ratings on social consciousness, emotional adjustment, and responsibility. On the sociometric ratings, as expected, the athletes were the sociometric stars in their classrooms both before and after the season. The author does note, however, that on the post-season sociometric test, the Little League boys were somewhat less accepting of their peers, as measured by ratings they extended to others, than they had been before the season started. Perhaps these results represent a gentle forecast of the Ogilvie-Tutko[18] description of adult athletes: "Most athletes indicate low interest in receiving support and concern from others, low need to take care of others and low need for affiliation. Such a personality seems necessary to achieve victory over others" (pp. 61-62).

If some processes of selection are at work in sifting out the children who get to play in League or interscholastic competition (as they quite obviously are), and if both the adult and peer cultures shower these children with special attention and kudos (as they surely do), then responsible educators must have some concern about all the other children who are losers or nonparticipants in this one-dimensional competition. How sure are we that the values and character traits selected and carefully reinforced in Little League sports are really the best for wholesome child development? In a culture as fanatically dedicated to excellence in competitive sports as we have become in modern America, are we needlessly and cruelly punishing the children who are physically smaller or less mature, or less well coordinated or aggressive, who can't compete successfully and perhaps don't even want to? Many will no doubt turn into fine and productive adults—but only after a childhood in which they were never able to live up to the myopic values of the peer culture, or to the expectations of their sport-addicted fathers.

Don't misunderstand me. I am certainly not coming out against baseball as such, though for the reasons indicated I believe that the informal, backyard variants have far more learning values for children than the formally organized, adult-supervised version. My most fundamental opposition to Little League baseball is based not so much on what it does by way of either harm or good to the players, as it is on what Little Leagu*ism* is doing to the whole culture of childhood, to participants and nonparticipants alike, and to the schools, families, neighborhoods, and communities where Little Leaguism has taken root.

Look first at what has happened to organized sports in high schools, and the picture is perhaps clearer. In a high school of 2,000 students, only a relative handful get to participate even on the squads of any of the major teams. All the rest are consigned to the role of frenzied spectators at interscholastic meets, or, still worse, in many sport-minded communities, to being nonparticipant nonspectators, perceived by adults and peers alike as odd-balls or pariahs. As Coleman[21] showed, this group may in fact include some of the best students, but they get precious little reward for their academic efforts. The kids who do go out in earnest for a high school sport find that, to compete at all effectively against our fanatic standards of excellence, they have to make it almost a full-time job both in season and out, at the expense of virtually all other extracurricular and leisure activities. In one way, you're damned if you don't participate; in another way, you're damned if you do.

In Little League and other variations of organized interscholastic sports, we now see clear indications of the invasion of this sports culture into the much more precious and vulnerable world of little children. Like the bad currency in

Gresham's famous law, it is an inferior product which ends up driving out the good. Because of its peculiar fascination, more for the parents than for the children themselves, it nearly monopolizes the field and drives almost to bankruptcy the natural and spontaneous culture of play and games among American children.

Let me close with [a] quotaton from [Iona and Peter] Opies'[22] fascinating monograph [*Children's Games in Street and Playground*]:

> In the long run, nothing extinguishes self-organized play more effectively than does action to promote it. It is not only natural but beneficial that there should be a gulf between the generations in their choice of recreation. Those people are happiest who can most rely on their own resources; and it is to be wondered whether middle-class children in the United States will ever reach maturity "whose playtime has become almost as completely organized and supervised as their study" (Carl Withers). If children's games are tamed and made part of school curricula, if wastelands are turned into playing-fields for the benefit of those who conform and ape their elders, if children are given the idea that they cannot enjoy themselves without being provided with the "proper" equipment, we need blame only ourselves when we produce a generation who have lost their dignity, who are ever dissatisfied, and who descend for their sport to the easy excitement of rioting, or pilfering, or vandalism (p. 16).

A final word to physical education professionals is in order. My rather limited contacts with physical education teachers have persuaded me that many (perhaps most) of you are really on my side on the matter of promoting competitive sports among young children. The problem, as I see it, stems not from the physical education programs in our elementary schools and from those who teach in these settings. It stems far more from the parents and from the common culture in our sports-ridden communities.

What can you do about it? Not too much, I'm afraid. But I can think of at least three things I would hope that you might try. First, in training students who will work with young children, urge them to keep in mind that "It's not what the boy is doing to the ball, but what the ball is doing to the boy!" Or, to reverse the old cliché: "Keep your eye on the boy!"

Second, physical education instructors, as experts in this area, are in a strategic position to influence public opinion on this important matter. I hope that you, in your contacts with parents, teachers, school administrators, and community leaders generally, will continually stress the important role of spontaneous play and of unsupervised, self-organized games for young children, and the very real costs involved when we push our children into competitive sports too early.

Finally, I hope that physical education instructors who work with children will do whatever they can to reintroduce some of the wonderful traditional games which earlier generations of children found so rewarding, and which, in my opinion, are far more appropriate for the elementary school ages. The instant success of capture the flag, introduced to one of our schools by a student volunteer, indicates that perhaps it can be done. The kids simply didn't know what they had been missing.

But once a game has been taught and is beginning to catch on with the children, I'm afraid the rest of my message really is: "Get lost!" Let the kids handle it themselves.

References

1. Sutton-Smith, B. A syntax for play and games. In R. E. Herron and B. Sutton-Smith (Eds.), *Child's play.* New York: Wiley, 1971.
2. Roberts, J. M., & Sutton-Smith, B. Child training and game involvement. *Ethnology*, 1962, *1*, 166-185.
3. Lewin, K., Dembo, T., Festinger, L., & Sears, P. S. Level of aspiration. In J. M. Hunt (Ed.), *Personality and behavior disorders.* New York: Ronald Press, 1944.
4. Phillips, R. H. The nature and function of children's formal games. *Psychoanalytic Quarterly*, 1960, *29*, 200-207.
5. Menninger, K. *Love against hate.* New York: Harcourt, 1942.
6. Moore, O. K., & Anderson, A. R. Some principles for the design of clarifying educational environments. In D. Goslin (Ed.), *Handbook of socialization theory and research.* New York: Rand McNally, 1969.

7. Piaget, J. *The moral judgment of the child.* New York: Harcourt, 1932.

8. Parsons, R., & Bales, R. F. *Family, socialization and interaction process.* Glencoe, Ill.: Free Press, 1955.

9. Kohlberg, L. Development of moral character and moral ideology. In M. L. Hoffman and L. W. Hoffman (Eds.), *Review of Child Development Research* (Vol. 1). New York: Russell Sage Foundation, 1964.

10. Devereux, E. C. The role of peer group experience in moral development. In J. P. Hill (Ed.), *Minnesota Symposia on Child Psychology* (Vol. 4). Minneapolis: University of Minnesota Press, 1970.

11. Devereux, E. C. Authority and moral development among American and West German children. *Journal of Comparative Family Studies*, 1972, *3*, 99-124.

12. Horney, K. *The neurotic personality of our time.* New York: Norton, 1937.

13. Murphy, G., Murphy, L. B., & Newcomb, R. M. *Experimental social psychology.* New York: Harper, 1937.

14. Madsen, M. C., & Shapira, A. Cooperative and competitive behavior of urban Afro-American, Anglo-American, Mexican-American and Mexican village children. *Developmental Psychology*, 1970, *3*, 16-20.

15. Shapira, A., & Madsen, M. C. Cooperative and competitive behavior of kibbutz and urban children in Israel. *Child Development*, 1969, *40*, 609-617.

16. Skubic, E. Emotional responses of boys to Little League and Middle League competitive baseball. *Research Quarterly*, 1955, *26*, 342-352.

17. Skubic, E. Studies of Little League and Middle League baseball. *Research Quarterly*, 1956, *27*, 97-110.

18. Ogilvie, B. C., & Tutko, T. A. If you want to build character, try something else. *Psychology Today*, October 1971, pp. 60-63.

19. Hale, C. J. Physiological maturity of Little League baseball players. *Research Quarterly*, 1956, *27*, 276-282.

20. Seymour, E. W. Comparative study of certain behavior characteristics of participants and non-participants in Little League baseball. *Research Quarterly*, 1956, *27*, 338-346.

21. Coleman, J. *The adolescent society.* Glencoe, Ill.: Free Press, 1961.
22. Opie, I., & Opie, P. *Children's games in street and playground.* Oxford: Clarendon Press, 1969.

It's More Than Just a Game

by **Edward Wynne,** *professor of educational sociology at the Chicago Circle campus of the University of Illinois.*

A colleague of mine has a ten-year-old son who tends to over-eat, and who has been killing a lot of time over the summer. Suppose any of us had the intellectual problem of conceptualizing a social system that would cause the boy to voluntarily become involved in more purposeful activities and to control his diet? What would we propose? Generally, one might assume that any such system would mobilize parent and community support, invite the boy to participate in prestigious and demanding activities, bear a rational relationship to a progression towards more mature roles, and involve traditional symbols of elevated status (e.g., special garments, conspicuous forms of ceremonial praise).

The "solution" was that the boy decided to try and join a community little league football team. In order to meet their weight ceiling he had to cut his weight from 96 to 88 pounds.

Reprinted from the *Socializer*, October, 1977, with permission of the author.

And has, so far, two thirds succeeded (to his parents' joy). He has promised the coach to get all the way down. He regularly shows up on time for practice, which will take three or four hours a day, six days a week, from early August to October.

What were the reinforcers that achieved this dramatic effect? An adult volunteer coach, who treats the game very seriously, and puts in a lot of time. Colorful uniforms for the team (the coach always wears his team jacket). Weekly games, with parents in the audience, referees and trainers in uniforms, cheerleaders and a band, a league with a schedule and a championship game. And an understanding that the team is viewed, by the local high school, as a training ground for its future players.

Some of us may smile—or even grimace—over the "solution" that seems to be working. But perhaps we should withhold our disapproval until we can come up with better operational answers, that attract equal dedication and attain results. And if anyone wants to make fun of the coach, who is presumably in part playing out some role image of his own (he takes movies of the games), he is putting in a great deal of time for nothing, and succeeding in motivating boys where many teachers and group workers are failing. By many objective measures, he is displaying a high level of skill, and producing beneficial results.

Perhaps there are some general lessons to be drawn from this typical incident. If we want to help children to become more mature, we must strive to "de-*trivial*-ize" their lives, make difficult demands on them, provide them with support, and treat their success or failure in meeting those demands as if it were important. But when we treat something as important, it means that there is a sharp difference between success and failure, and that there are conspicuous symbolic differences between these statues. And this is what the team does—there is a dramatic difference between being on the team and off of it. Sustaining that difference takes a lot of adult time and work, in supplying coaching, uniforms, audiences, playing fields and schedules. But that work creates a stage on which boys want to shine. And the stage changes showing up at practice and maintaining a diet, from simple drudgery to part of a potential progression to precious recognition. If more adults give their time to the young in equivalent structures—that establish plausible but significant standards, and conspicuously recognize success—many beneficial socialization effects can occur. But we must realize that "de-*trivial*-ization" means increasing demands and defining failure, as well as providing supports. And that we are dealing with young people who are motivated and reinforced by devices that may seem strange or inappropriate to our overtrained perceptions.

Comments

A few years ago Joan Leite kept her 9-year-old son, Chris, out of a Little League game because he had not been doing as well as he should in school. But she gave him permission to attend practice the next night, whereupon the coach informed Chris's mother that it was not right to use Little League as a means of disciplining Chris. Mrs. Leite complained to league officials, and after some heated arguments and regretful statements the coach was suspended. But the coach then brought suit demanding to be reinstated in his unpaid job. The press had a "ball" with the story—all because a 9-year-old boy apparently didn't do his homework.

Such incidents as these support the position of Devereux and others who urge or demand that kid's sports be given back to the kids. Those in opposition to organized children's sports say, "Let the kids play in the afternoon when parents are too busy to interfere. Let the adults supply the fields and other necessary equipment, but then let the kids play ball by themselves, for the fun of it, the way they used to."

For many adults there is a nostalgia about the good old days of sandlot games. A reminiscing "old timer" contrasted those good old days with the modern day rules of Little League. First he described the rules of today and then how it used to be.

> **Playing Equipment**—*Each team must have at least twelve conventional baseball uniforms. The Official Little League Shoulder Patch must be affixed to the upper left sleeve of the uniform blouse. Games may not be played except in uniforms. These uniforms are the property of the League, and are to be loaned to the players for such period as the League may determine.*

Playing equipment—Each guy came out to the ball field looking like a bum. Shirts were optional. Patches went on pants because they were torn up sliding. Anybody wearing a clean or neat garment was jumped on and rubbed around in the dirt. . . .

Pitchers—*Any player on the team roster may pitch. A player shall not pitch in more than six (6) innings in a calendar week. Delivery of a single pitch shall constitute having pitched in an inning.*

Pitchers—Any player who owned the ball pitched. A player could not pitch on more than seven (7) days in a calendar week, or more than one hundred (100) innings a day, because it got too dark. Delivery of a pitch straight down and the pitcher falling senseless beside the ball constituted exhaustion. . . .

Protests—*Protests shall be considered only when based on the violation or interpretation of a playing rule or the use of an ineligible player. No protest shall be considered on a decision involving an umpire's judgment.*

Protests—A protest was considered only when you were awfully sure you could lick the other guy. There was no umpire, unless some kid was on crutches and couldn't play. Nobody paid any attention to his calls, because he was just another kid.

Field Decorum—*The actions of players, managers, coaches, umpires, and League officials must be above reproach.*

Field Decorum—There were no managaers, or coaches, or any of those big people. Only players who swore and spat. Anyone caught being above reproach got clobbered.[1]

Where do you stand on the issue after reading the views of Devereux and Wynne? Should we return sports to the sandlots of yesteryear? Should we demand that adults step aside and give children their freedom to play? Would the best solution be the total elimination of children's sports programs? Do children benefit more from unstructured play than from organized sports?

Unfortunately, these questions cannot be answered on the basis of extensive research. I believe Devereux has legitimate reason to be concerned about the effects of *some* organized sports programs on the development of children. In some cases sports programs for children do indeed become *over-organized*, usually because there is an over-emphasis on winning. If youngsters had a voice in the planning of their sports participation, I doubt if they would schedule 80 hockey games per season, with thousands of miles of travel, or practices that begin daily at 5 a.m. Left to their own volition, I doubt that youngsters would wrestle 160 bouts a year, stretching from November to the following August. I question whether young swimmers would practice 4 to 6 hours a day for the entire year in the absence of adult coercion. I know that young football players would not spend 2 hours a day executing pro-type drills such as one-on-one, head-to-head tackling. Yet I am completely convinced that children want, enjoy, and benefit from organized sports programs which are well conducted. It is when winning becomes the sole emphasis that organized children's sports are likely to be detrimental, or at least less beneficial than unstructured play. Nothing is more effective than *over-organization* to dampen children's enthusiasm for the game.

I believe the solution to the problem of over-organized sports is not a return to the nostalgic sandlot days of the past. While our memories may recollect the joy and laughter of those leisure summer days, additional thought might also recall some sadness. I vividly remember my own days of sandlot ball. Winning, I assure you, was very important. Sides were chosen to maximize winning, and the kids selected last knew painfully well their evaluated worth! The game was played with as much impassioned fervor as any organized league game, and was often interrupted by endless arguments. We used broken bats precariously taped together; played in fields with sticker patches, mole holes, and broken glass; and put the unprotected catcher dangerously close behind the plate. We wanted to win. At times we fought for our assumed rights. They were fun times, but I cannot say they were more fun than playing organized sports. In fact, it seemed to me that we would not have played sandlot baseball nearly so much had we *not* been playing on Little League teams as well. It was the incentive of Little League that motivated us to practice our skills in sandlot games.

In short, I think that sports programs with poor adult leadership are much more detrimental for youngsters than unstructured play. But organized sports with competent leadership, where winning is kept in perspective, are immensely valuable. Children can benefit from both structured and unstructured play in different ways, and they should have time for both. Society has changed today, and many activities compete for children's attention. I suspect if we suddenly abolished all children's sports programs, we would see much less unstructured play than Devereux would lead us to believe. Children, I am afraid, would let television occupy an even greater proportion of their time than it already does. Just as pot belly stoves, feather beds, and Model A's are things of the past, sandlot play as an *alternative* to organized sports is an anachronistic idea. Today our society thrives on organization. We organize fitness classes, sewing clubs, chess clubs, and hobby groups of all types. We can, of course, do all these activities without an organization, but most people enjoy them more when they are organized. And just maybe, as Edward Wynne contends, organized sports are effective means for "de-*trivial*izing" the lives of our children.

Rather than consider organized and unorganized sports as antagonistic to each other, they should be seen as complementary. Our youngsters should have opportunities to participate in both organized and unorganized sports, allowing them to choose the proportion of time committed to each. And when they choose organized sports, we should give them the best leadership possible—leadership that cultivates an enthusiasm for the sport, where winning is kept in proper perspective, and where fun is the goal which counts the most.

Reference

1. Williamson, D. Tell it like it was. *Saturday Review*, June 21, 1969, pp. 4-5.

SECTION B

Eliminating Kids!

Joe was upset. For weeks he had been out on the football field, practicing every afternoon after class. He had devoted hours to memorizing the plays and struggling through them. Now the afternoon of the big game had come and gone—and Joe had been on the bench the whole time.

Joe's depression deepened. He had counted enormously on playing. He thought of how his parents had made special arrangements to get to the big game. If only the coach had called him onto the field for a minute, he wouldn't have felt so bad.

Joe is not a college student; he is not even a high schooler. He is ten years old and in the fifth grade.[1]

Just how many Joe's are there—kids dedicating themselves to sports, only to be shunned, disappointed, and humiliated? We do not know. Hopefully few, but perhaps many. We do know that the attrition rate is incredibly high. Some youngsters quit because the sport does not appeal to them, their interests change, or they find their talents better rewarded elsewhere. That's fair enough. But how many kids are eliminated by coaches who decide that a youngster cannot help the team win?

Coaches eliminate kids in two ways. They can "cut" kids, telling them in so many words that there is no room for their inadequacies. This often is a cruel blow to youngsters, but perhaps it is even more cruel to permit them to devote enormous amounts of time and energy to practicing the sport only to sit on the bench for the entire season. The second way is indirect. Too often, for those not cut from the team, the sports experience is so miserable that they cut themselves.

In the first reading Hal Lebovitz chastizes coaches for cutting youngsters from sports teams. In the second selection Terry Orlick and Cal Botterill examine why kids are eliminated and suggest how sports can be made less selective.

Reference

1. Sloan, W., & West, D. Don't rush kids into organized sports. *Parent's Magazine*, September 1966, p. 79.

Did You Ever Cut a Boy?*

by **Hal Lebovitz**, *sports editor for the* Cleveland Plain Dealer.

Consider this an open letter to every high-school football coach, principal and superintendent:

Football practice is now under way. The boys have reported; they have been issued uniforms. This is what happened here to one boy not too many years ago:

The boy had just entered high school. All summer he looked forward to the opening of football practice. He enjoyed contact. He had tossed a football around almost from the day he left his crib. His dream was to play on the high-school varsity.

On August 20 he reported for the first day of practice. "You'll have to furnish your own shoes and you'll need $7.50 for insurance," the junior varsity coach told him. The boy rushed out to buy a pair of shoes. Cost $20.

He returned the next day carrying them proudly, paid his $7.50 insurance fee, did calisthenics with the squad and at the

---

Reprinted with permission of *The Cleveland Plain Dealer*, 1964.
*This article was selected as one of the best sports stories of 1964.

end of the session he was cut. So were several other boys—all dropped from the squad after one session of calisthenics.

The boy rushed to a telephone and called his dad's office. Unable to withhold the tears, he sobbed, "I was cut."

"Go back tomorrow," the father suggested gently. "Maybe there was a mistake."

The boy returned, finally summoned sufficient courage to ask the coach for another chance. "Come back in two weeks," said the coach.

Two weeks later the boy carried his new shoes back to practice. "Sorry," said the coach. "We haven't time to look at you now. Come back after school starts."

The boy did. This time the coach apparently had no alternative. He gave the boy a uniform. Within a week he cut the boy once more.

The boy was crushed completely. The father advised, "Try next year, son."

"No," said the boy. "I don't want to be humiliated again."

The boy never did try out again. He never followed the team. His interest in the school was never the same. The cleats on his $20 shoes are slightly worn—from football on the neighborhood lot. They remain the heartbroken memento of his brief high-school football experience.

Later, the father checked with the coach. "We can't handle sixty boys," he offered lamely. "We didn't want your son to get hurt."

If you are such a coach, I strongly urge you to quit. Mr. Principal and Mr. Superintendent, if your school has such a coach get rid of him *fast*. Either that, or drop football, a game in which anybody's son can get hurt.

I speak as a former football coach who never cut a boy. I firmly believe there are lessons to be learned on the football field that have valuable carry-overs in life.

Doyt Perry, head football coach at Bowling Green State University, never cuts a boy. He didn't when he coached in high school.

"I don't care if 100 come out, and we get almost that many," he says. "If they want the football experience, they should have it."

Fortunately most high-school and college coaches have the same philosophy.

Football takes stomach. A boy who doesn't have it will quit of his own accord. The fields are big. They can accommodate large squads. Let the boy hang around. Let him do calisthenics. Let him run, until he's out of breath. Let him scrimmage with the fourth and fifth teams after the regulars are finished.

But don't cut him. If he hasn't got it, he'll cut himself. If he has, he'll stick it out. He'll be a better man for the experience and by the time he's a senior he'll surprise you. He'll help make *you* a winner.

So, Coach, hold that knife. Why plunge it into a boy's heart?

Why Eliminate Kids?

by **Terry Orlick**, *prominent sport psychology professor located at the University of Ottawa (Canada), and* **Cal Botterill**, *instructor at the University of Alberta and a former YMCA director.*

Elimination is a critical problem, perhaps the most critical problem which exists in children's sport.

According to Canadian Amateur Hockey Association statistics, of the 600,000 players registered or affiliated with the C.A.H.A. in 1973, 53 percent were under the age of twelve, 35 percent were from twelve to fifteen, and 11 percent were over fifteen years of age. Hockey statistics over the past five years indicate that only about 10 percent of the players register to continue participating in organized hockey beyond their fifteenth birthday, and similar trends reportedly exist in other organized sports like little league baseball and minor league soccer.[1] This provides clear cut evidence that either kids are being eliminated or they are voluntarily dropping out. Perhaps even more staggering than these statistics is the fact that kids

Abridged from *Every Kid Can Win.* Chicago: Nelson-Hall, 1975. Reprinted with permission of the authors and publisher.

are beginning to drop out of organized sports as early as seven and eight years of age.

In some cases, the elimination of children is calculated and intentional, while in other cases it is completely unintentional. Whether elimination is intentional or unintentional, it has similar effects. Kids come to feel unworthy, unwanted, and unacceptable.

It is absurd that on the one hand we feel that sports are good for kids and on the other hand we set up a system which eliminates poorer performers, girls, late-maturing boys, kids who are not aggressive enough, and so on.

Although the elimination of kids is often unintentional, "cutting" is one form of intentional elimination which can have drastically negative effects on kids. They are "cut" not only physically but also psychologically. Setting limits on the kind and number of kids allowed to be involved is essentially what cutting is all about. This is an all too common occurrence in communities and schools across the nation. An example which comes to mind occurred when two little girls recently went to "try out" for the softball team. Shortly after they left for the field, one of the girls returned home without her girlfriend. Her father asked her what had happened. The little girl replied, "They already had enough people." So it goes. Similarly, we may have 100 boys try out for a basketball team, or 100 girls try out for a gymnastic team—but in each case, only about ten or fifteen *make the team.* Instead of cutting children, we should be personally encouraging them to come out for sport and making it a meaningful place for them.

We should field as many teams as there are interested kids to fill them. It is ridiculous to promote participation on the one hand, and then to cut interested individuals from the team, or to in any way limit their participation. This type of action provides the rejected child with massive negative reinforcement and counters our basic reason for existing (that is, to serve the children). To cut a child because he is not good enough negates our purpose and our responsibility to our children and to society. It is comparable to a doctor refusing to treat his sickest patients to insure that his win-loss record looks good. Those people seeking athletic participation who are cut-off may be the ones who could benefit most from this experience. Just as the least lovable child is the one who needs loving the most, the least athletic child may need athletics the most. The process of cutting is a vicious circle for the one who doesn't make it. He is cut because he is not good enough to make it and is consequently given no opportunity to practice on a regular basis so that he can become good enough to make it—so he is rejected again the following year. We not only are doing an injustice to the individual but also are cutting our own sporting throats. Twenty years later, these cut individuals do not support our programs, and they refuse to pay for new facilities. Through our negative conditioning program we have firmly entrenched in them a negative feeling about sport. The least that this negative feeling will do is to relegate these people to the role of spectators, which is bad enough in itself.

Elimination is a long term process. Although it may occur at an early age, it can last a lifetime. By eight or nine years of age, many children have already turned off sports. In one study, many young children who had opted out of sports indicated that they never wanted to go out again.[2] A seventeen-year-old female cross-country skier of national caliber revealed some possible reasons why many children may not want to go out again as well as why she dropped out herself:

Q. Why do you think you stopped skiing?
A. I liked it when I started but later it wasn't fun anymore.
Q. What didn't you like?
A. There was too much criticism . . . he [the coach] didn't act like he wanted me on the team . . . he never gave any positive suggestions . . . just criticism.
Q. Is there anything else that bothered you?
A. Yes, the coaches ignored the younger skiers . . . in order to get attention you have to be good . . . lots of kids gave it up because nobody took any interest in them.
Q. Is there anything you would like to see changed in the cross-country ski program?
A. Yes, there's no promotion for recreational skiing . . . it's only for the ones who want to compete. The program shouldn't be concerned only with producing racers. Kids may want to compete once they learn how to ski . . . or just ski later on. Now they never hear anything about it.

Her perceptive insights were borne out time and time again in interviews conducted with athletic dropouts (young and old) in skiing as well as in many other sports.

The reward structure which now exists in organized sports does not appear to be consistent with what is in the best interest of the majority of children. There appears to be an overemphasis on winning at the expense of fun involvement. This gives rise to an elitist atmosphere wherein many youngsters eliminate themselves before they start, while others begin to withdraw at seven and eight years of age.

In many cases, organized sport (team or individual) appears to operate as an extremely efficient screening process for the elimination of children.

The findings of a study by Orlick[3] indicate that a major change in emphasis is needed in children's sport in order to operate in the child's best interest with regard to motivation, program, and personnel. Extensive interviews conducted with eight- and nine-year-old organized sports participants, nonparticipants, and drop-outs showed that the children strongly felt that they had to be good either to make the team or to play regularly. Seventy-five percent of the nonparticipant children, *all of whom thought they were not good enough to make the team*, indicated that they would go out for a team if they thought they would surely make it. *Fear of failure*, or the psychological *stress of disapproval, appeared to influence certain children to the extent that they were afraid to participate.* It has become evident that there are many nonparticipants who would like to participate in a variety of sports, and they would participate if they knew they would be acceptable in the sports setting and if they were assured of having a rewarding experience. However, they generally do not feel that this is the case. Rather, they feel that they do not have much to contribute or gain from a sporting system where acceptance is seen as being conditional upon performance.[4]

Children who drop out of sport at an early age appear to be merely reacting to negative situations which are largely due to the structure of the game or the emphasis of the coaches. The majority of the children drop out because they are not given an adequate opportunity to play, or they are not having a positive experience (e.g., it's not any fun). Sitting on the bench, being ignored, or being yelled at for making a mistake, certainly isn't much fun. Generally these kids are not getting positive reinforcement from the coach or from the competitive situation itself. If they are getting any positive feedback, it is outweighed by negative feedback which leads to their decision to drop out. Most negative experiences are related to an overconcern with perfection, particularly at an early age.

The mother of an eight-year-old hockey player summed up the situation well when she said: "How can kids become enthused when they're not allowed to become involved?"

Consequently, children's first sports experiences are vitally important. If their initial exposures are positive and enjoyable they may become "hooked" for life. On the other hand, if these experiences are negative and unenjoyable, they can be "turned off" for a long time. Whether the child does have an early positive exposure to sports and physical activities is largely dependent upon minor league coaches, who collectively come into contact with millions of children, along with the parents and teachers of these same children.

The most important thing you can do to insure that the child gets the right start is to see that the child's participation is fun and enjoyable above everything else. The simple fact is that if children are not receiving some sort of positive rewards from their participation, they will not continue. Having fun, playing, and being a part of the action can be extremely rewarding for kids. In fact, interviews with young kids who played organized sports revealed that "fun" and "action" were the things they liked best about sports. A typical response from an eight-year-old when asked why he wants to play sports is "I like it. It's fun!"

As we begin to move away from this fun orientation, kids indicate that they have progressively more negative and unhappy experiences. For example, kids indicate that what they dislike most about sports include such things as "getting yelled at for doing something wrong, getting hit or kicked, dirty play, sitting on the bench, feeling like a failure." Community leagues and school teams often make reinforcement (e.g., social approval, praise, encouragement) dependent upon successful performance before children have had adequate preparation.

In the beginning, if children are evaluated at all, it should be on an individual basis. If a child has made advancements, he should be rewarded and praised rather than being made to feel like a failure by judging him against some predetermined standard, particularly when the standard is unattainable.

If children feel they are failing, they quickly become discouraged. Failure certainly is not rewarding for anyone, while success is a great reinforcer. However, success and failure are dependent upon the standards which are set for the children. Consequently, the standards or goals should be structured, or restructured, for success.

The most important factor determining whether the child feels he has succeeded or failed is not how high or low the standard is set, but the difference between his actual performance and the standard. In other words, the goals set must be achievable. By setting unrealistically high goals you almost guarantee that the child will feel a sense of failure. If standards approximate the top performances, which they usually do, most children are bound to experience repeated failure because of the continuous gap which exists between where they are now and where they think they are supposed to be; for example, the best. Regardless of how hard they try, most children will never close the gap.[5]

One way to establish realistic and attainable goals for children is to have them compete against their own past performance. In this way, the goals can be set near enough to their actual performance level to insure that any amount of individual improvement will be experienced as success. This will assure frequent success experiences. As the child progresses, goals can be readjusted to meet specific individual needs and still be kept within reach.

Coaches have often minimized or ignored the critical role which failure, or expectancy of failure, plays in shaping a child's behavior in a sports setting. The child operates on his expectations of success or failure. Activities are dropped or accepted with enthusiasm depending upon the degree to which the child expects he can attain the goals.

Children are not going to (and should not) waste their time *failing* when they have the option to become involved in more positive, life-oriented enterprises. For example, both self-improvement and fun are important goals within every child's reach. It is particularly important in the beginning when you are establishing sports attitudes and behavior that these goals be paramount.

If we remove the sense of accomplishment or the fun element we will also remove the majority of the children.

References

1. Orlick, T. D. *Development of children's attitudes toward sport.* Paper presented and workshop conducted at the National Conference on Women in Sport, Toronto, May 1974.
2. Orlick, T. D. Children's sport—A revolution is coming. *Journal of the Canadian Association for Health, Physical Education and Recreation,* January/February 1973, pp. 12-14.
3. Orlick, T. D. *A socio-psychological analysis of early sports participation.* Unpublished doctoral dissertation, University of Alberta, 1972.
4. Orlick, T. D. *An analysis of expectancy as a motivational factor influencing sport participation.* Paper presented at the Third World Congress on Sports Psychology, Madrid, June 1973.
5. Sherif, C. W., & Rattray, G. D. *Psychosocial development and activity in middle childhood (5-12 years).* Paper presented at the first national conference and workshop on the Child in Sport and Physical Activity, Queen's University, Kingston, Ontario, May 1973.

Comments

The problem is clear but the solution is not. It is not easy to provide programs for everyone. There are only so many playing fields, gymnasiums, and pools; there are only so many coaches and officials willing to contribute their time; and there are only so many dollars and equipment. Is it realistic then to talk about providing every child who seeks to play an opportunity to do so? Or, because of limited resources, must we confine sports to the more talented youngsters? The answers depend upon the resources, attitudes, and unique circumstances of each community. But most communities can do much more than they have in the past. They can either marshal more resources or use their existing resources far better than they do.

Many communities will spend well over $100,000 to support a football program for 40 or 50 youngsters, but will not spend $3,000 to begin a soccer program for 500. Too many communities invest their sports dollars in the development of a few top athletes at the expense of the ordinary player. Writing in the *San Francisco Chronicle* some 15 years ago, Charles McCabe observed:

> Sports largely concern themselves with the top dogs: the kids with skills, speed and physical endowment, all nicely balanced. The kids who can win, in short. Excellence has become such a fetish with us that the ordinary, which after all is what the world is composed of, is sometimes cruelly neglected. For we cannot have it two ways. We cannot have a nation of champions, eating the breakfast of champions, and at the same time have a nation of physically fit people with a healthy interest in sports. Being victory-happy results in wild over-emphasis of

sports for the elite who make the squad, and wild under-emphasis . . . for the lads who like sports but aren't red-hots.[1]

The investment in sports programs for superior athletes brings to communities entertainment, esprit de corps, and potential fame. And, of course, it provides gifted athletes with an opportunity to be challenged and to excel. A worthwhile investment perhaps—but is it when the cost is the elimination of less skilled youngsters from sports because there are no playing fields, no equipment, and no coaches for them?

I believe there is value in giving greater recognition to superior athletes, and I believe they deserve the better facilities and equipment. Holding these rewards before youngsters to be obtained for the pursuit and attainment of excellence has considerable value for young children. But I am opposed to providing superior athletes with lavish resources if it is at the expense of less talented youngsters—the youngsters who may benefit most from sport. I am opposed to sport being exclusive, where the only children who have a chance to succeed are those who already are skilled.

Most children do not expect to play on the varsity immediately, but they do wish to have an opportunity to play at some level. Then they can develop their skills with the hope, perhaps, that some day they may be able to play with the varsity. Other children may have no such ambitions; they will be quite satisfied to simply experience the enjoyment of competing in sports. Let us plan to accommodate both groups so that those who wish to strive for excellence have the opportunity to do so and those who wish to play simply for the "fun of it" also have an opportunity to do so.

Some communities have demonstrated that they can offer comprehensive sports programs providing opportunities for the gifted athlete and a rich selection of sports for the less skilled or less ambitious. Many communities have developed feeder teams or minor leagues that provide instruction and competition at graduated levels commensurate with the skill and maturation level of the community's children.

A good example of such a concept is the development of the minor leagues associated with Little League baseball. Yes, Little League has a farm system not unlike the "major" leagues. The minor leagues provide the less skilled youngsters with opportunities to play and learn skills so they eventually can join their more skilled peers. The idea is superb and often it works well, but the old villain—over-emphasized winning—can destroy minor league programs, too. A father of a Union City, Ohio, minor leaguer wrote:

> Perhaps I am most uninformed but I have encouraged my son to participate in minor league in the belief that he would learn baseball, sportsmanship and appreciation for athletics. . . .
>
> My son has been enthusiastic, loyal to practice and games, and understanding when he was not put in the game.
>
> He was totally uninformed as a ball player when he began at eight years of age, and this year is still not proficient enough to make the Little League team. So now he is beginning his fourth year in minor league.
>
> I am amazed that he is still enthusiastic after three years of attending every practice and game and still being on the bench. But now it has come to him that:
>
> 1. In order to play he would have to know how to play better before he began because nobody out there really cares if he learns.
> 2. Winning is more important than the individual, and if he makes a mistake, he is pulled out of the game—if he ever gets in.
> 3. Loyalty and faithfulness to the team are worthless because the new kid who joins the team and is a better catcher is more important than he.
> 4. Since his Dad can't work with the team, his chances of ever playing are extremely limited. . . .
>
> Please tell me why we cannot emphasize helping the boy and de-emphasize helping the winning. . . . If a boy is willing to work, let's not be guilty of slapping him on the bench with a label that he is inadequate.[2]

So far we have considered only the problem of eliminating children by confining sports programs to an elite few. But an equally effective, and unquestionably more insidious, way of eliminating kids is to make the sport experience so miserable that children "cut" themselves. Misguided and thoughtless coaches have found many ways to transform sports into miserable experiences for youngsters. Some place so much emphasis on winning that kids find sports to be too serious, with the fun eliminated through the regimented practice of one boring drill after another. Youngsters turn elsewhere when constantly criticized, badgered, and treated unfairly.

Surely the one thing that is most effective in causing children to quit is simply sitting them on the bench. Some organized sports programs have attempted to legislate that children must play a minimum amount in each game. For example, Little League requires that every player present must play two innings. The intent of the rule is good, but it can be circumvented. Coaches have been known to inform poor players to stay home on the day of a big game. The rule can also be harmful to the youngsters it was designed to protect. Children know when they are being sent into the game because the coach must do so. They know when they are considered inadequate and a threat to victory. They sense the resentment of more skilled teammates and the coach for interrupting "their" game. The value of playing under such conditions is greatly diminished if not lost entirely.

Rather than legislate rules requiring children to play, I believe we need to change the attitudes of many adults—coaches and parents alike—about the values of children's sports. Surely if winning can be relegated to secondary importance (not unimportance, but secondary importance), and the development of the child can be lifted to primary importance, the need for rules requiring limited participation would be unnecessary. The negative practices of adults undoubtedly would diminish if such a change in thinking could be accomplished on a grand scale.

References

1. McCabe, C. Kids who don't make the team. *San Francisco Chronicle*, December 6, 1963.
2. Giannestras, N. J. Pee wee baseball and football—good or evil? *Bulletin of The American College of Surgeons*, 1970, *55*(6), p. 17.

SECTION C

Three Cheers for the Girls

Ten-year-old Jill Wilson had earned a starting position on a local baseball team. She was an outstanding player, which made it all the easier for her coach and boys on the team to accept her—and for the opposing teams to object to her. Although there were no official rules barring girls from playing in the league, no girl had ever attempted to play before. Disturbed about the integration of their league, the other coaches called a secret meeting to seek a solution. They found one.

At the first league game, when Jill came to bat, the opposing team's coach filed a protest with the umpire, claiming that Jill was not officially dressed as prescribed by the league rules.

"But what's wrong," her coach demanded to know. "She has an official uniform, official rubber cleated shoes, an official glove, and batting helmet. She is dressed exactly as the boys."

The opposing coach said he doubted it, wanting to know if she was in compliance with rule 14g: "All players must wear a protective athletic supporter."

After a moment of disbelief, Jill's coach became outraged; the opposing team was demanding that Jill wear a "jock." The coach appealed to the umpire for common sense to prevail, but the umpire, boggled by it all, responded only by saying, "a rule is a rule." The game was delayed for over an hour while coaches, officials, and parents argued whether Jill should or should not be required to wear a jock.

Meanwhile, Jill's father quietly went to a nearby sporting goods store and purchased the item of controversy. Unnoticed by the arguing adults, the father had Jill put the supporter on, but over her uniform. The sight of Jill brought a mixed reaction of laughter and disgust. It was a superb repartee in one respect, but in a much larger sense the entire scene was repugnant. The sight of a young girl wearing an athletic supporter so that she and her team could be permitted to play apparently so shocked the opposing coach that he withdrew the protest and the game continued.

Incredible as this story may seem, it is true. No issue has stirred more emotion and provoked more irrational behavior among adults than the controversy over girls entering the male bastion of sports. Girls of all ages have been challenging officials of school and nonschool sports programs for an equal right to play. As with so many other aspects of sports these days, the issue soon found its way to the courtroom. And once again, Little League baseball entered center stage.

The Young Democrats Little League team of Hoboken, New Jersey had a pitcher named Maria Pepe. When the National Little League headquarters heard that a girl was playing, the Williamsport executives ordered that either Maria be booted off the team, or the team would be booted out of the league. Little League had a strict policy of boys only which, incidentally, had been confirmed by Congress when it granted Little League its charter.

The National Organization for Women (NOW), which happens to be headquartered in New Jersey, took Maria's case to court. Extended argument was heard over 5 days before the presiding officer, Mrs. Sylvia Pressler. On Nov. 7, 1973 Pressler ruled as follows:

> It is my understanding that Little League baseball is a monumentally successful operation . . . as American as the hot dog and apple pie. There is no reason why that part of Americana should be withheld from little girls. The sooner little boys begin to realize that little girls are equal and that there will be many opportunities for a boy to be bested by a girl, the closer they will be to better mental health.

Mrs. Pressler went on to observe, "In essence I am satisfied that children between the ages of eight and twelve perform differently on an individual basis, not on a sexual basis. Just as Little League protects weak boys, they can protect weak girls."[1]

There have been a number of other court cases across the country seeking to permit girls to enter all-male sports programs. Many judgments have been in favor of the girls, but not all. Without doubt though, girls are obtaining greater opportunities to participate in sports than ever before. Certainly the opportunities are not equal to those available to boys, but the inequities are decreasing.

In searching for selections to include in this section, no articles were found that comprehensively examined the issues related to girls' participation in sports. Included, however, is one short piece that says more in fewer words than perhaps any other selection in this book. *The Southpaw* by Judith Viorst will warm the hearts of those who want all children to participate equally in sports and will even bring smiles to male chauvinists. Some of the issues surfacing in court rooms and other problems associated with girls participation in sports are then discussed in the concluding comments.

Reference

1. Dworkin, S. Sexism strikes out. *Ms.* May 1974, p. 20.

The Southpaw

by **Judith Viorst**, *poet, journalist, and author of children's books.*

Reprinted from *Free To Be ... You and Me*, pp. 71-75. McGraw-Hill Book Co., 1974. Reprinted with permission of Free to be Foundation.

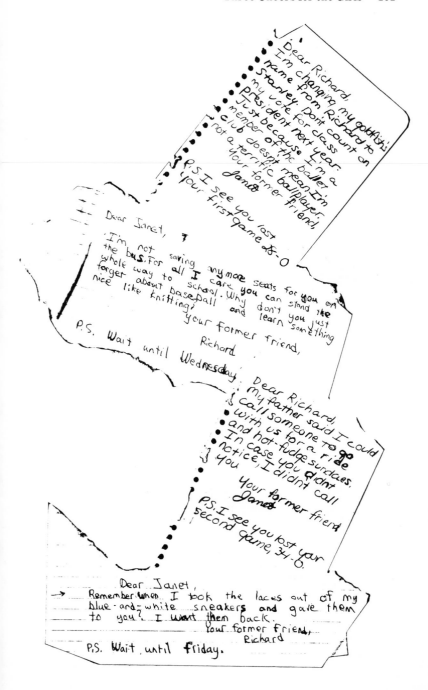

Dear Richard,
I'm changing my goldfish's
name from Richard to
Stanley. Don't count on
my vote for class
President next year.
Just because I'm a
member of the ballet
club doesn't mean I'm
not a terrific ballplayer.
Your former friend,
Janet

P.S. I see you lost
your first game 18-0.

Dear Janet,
I'm not saving any more seats for you on
the bus. For all I care you can stand the
whole way to school. Why don't you just
forget about baseball and learn something
nice like knitting?
Your former friend,
Richard

P.S. Wait until Wednesday.

Dear Richard,
My father said I could
call someone to go
with us for a ride
and hot-fudge sundaes.
In case you didn't
notice, I didn't call
you
Your former friend
Janet

P.S. I see you lost your
second game, 34-0.

Dear Janet,
Remember when I took the laces out of my
blue-and-white sneakers and gave them
to you? I want them back.
Your former friend,
Richard

P.S. Wait until Friday.

Dear Richard,
Congratulations on
your unbroken record.
Eight straight losses,
Wow! I understand
you're the laughingstock
of New Jersey.
Your former friend,
Janet

P.S. Why don't you and
your team forget about
baseball and learn
something nice like
knitting maybe?

Dear Janet,
Here's the silver horseback riding
trophy that you gave me. I don't
want to keep it anymore.
Your former friend,
Richard

P.S. I didn't think you'd be the kind who'd
kick a man when he's down.

Dear Richard,
I wasn't kicking exactly.
I was kicking back.
Your former friend,
Janet

P.S. In case you were
wondering my batting
average is .345.

Dear Janet,
Alfie is having his tonsils out tomorrow.
We might be able to let you catch next week.
Richard

Dear Richard,
I pitch.
Janet

Dear Janet,
     Joel is moving to Kansas and Danny
sprained his wrist. How about a permanent
place in the outfield?
                    Richard

Dear Richard,
I pitch.
        Janet

Dear Janet,
Ronnie caught the chicken pox and Leo broke his toe and Elwood has these stupid violin lessons. I'll give you first base, and that's my final offer.
Richard

Dear Richard,
Susan Reilly plays first base. Marilyn Jackson catches. Ethel Cahn plays center field. I pitch. It's a package deal.
Janet
P.S. Sorry about your 12-game losing streak.

Dear Janet,
Please! Not Marilyn Jackson.
Richard

Dear Richard,
Nobody ever said that I was unreasonable. How about Lizzie Martindale instead?
Janet

Dear Janet,
At least could you call your goldfish Richard again?
your friend
Richard

Comments

Until recently, many segments of our society questioned the propriety of girls playing in sports, but this attitude is changing. I find it difficult to understand why adults are opposed to girls participating in sports per se. Examine for yourself the positions of both the opponents and proponents of girls sports based on testimony in recent court cases.

Opponents: Sports are physically harmful for females.

Proponents: A myth unsubstantiated by medical evidence.

Opponents: Vigorous sports endanger the female's reproductive organs.

Proponents: Also unsubstantiated by medical evidence. Doctors are quick to point out that it is the external male reproductive organs that are more vulnerable.

Opponents: Sports participation delays or impedes menstruation.

Proponents: The reverse appears to be true. Physical exercise improves regularity and lessens cramps.

Opponents: Girls' bones are more fragile and are injured more often.

Proponents: Girls have smaller, but not more fragile bones. Girls do have a slightly higher rate of *minor* injuries, but boys have a much higher rate of *severe* injuries.

Opponents: Heavy blows to the breast will cause breast cancer.

Proponents: Unsubstantiated by medical evidence.

Opponents: Girls suffer severe social consequences from facial injuries frequently incurred in sports.

Proponents: Accurate information on the frequency of permanent facial injuries to boys and girls does not exist. Such an argument implies that girls' faces are more valuable than those of boys!

Opponents: Sports participation for girls develops unfeminine, bulging muscles.

Proponents: Exercise physiologists have found this to be untrue.

Opponents: Girls become masculinized through sports participation and are moved toward lesbianism.

Proponents: Absurd!

Opponents: Girls are not as skilled and the physical inequality would ruin the sense of sport.

Proponents: Girls have comparable reaction time and dexterity to boys. Before puberty they often are stronger and faster, too. Girls, however, have had less opportunity to develop specific sports skills. After puberty boys have a decided advantage in sports demanding speed and strength.

Opponents: Sports place too much psychological stress on girls.

Proponents: And, if true, too much stress on boys as well. Girls respond to stress in essentially the same way as boys do.

Opponents: Male coaches will sexually exploit girls.

Proponents: Possible, but improbable. Equally possible, but improbable, is that male coaches may exploit boys, and that female coaches may exploit boys or girls.

The proponents have convinced me. I see no reason why sports cannot provide the same benefits to girls which we claim for boys—fitness, development of motor and social skills, self-confidence, and feelings of self-worth, to name a few. Actually, I think few people today object to girls playing sports, but they are concerned about (a) girls and boys competing against each other, and (b) whether the development of girls' sports programs will adversely affect existing boys' programs. We briefly examine these two issues now.

Girls Competing Against Boys

No known physiological or medical reasons exist why *prepubescent* boys and girls cannot compete fairly and safely against each other in all sports. Girls have similar cardiovascular and respiratory capacities, they have a slight edge in speed and strength, and they meet the demands of competitive stress as well as boys do. More importantly, girls find sports to be just as much fun, just as great a challenge, and just as beneficial physically, psychologically, and socially as boys do.

But my endorsement of unisexed competition for prepubescent children is not without a warning. Most adults object to unisexed competition because they are concerned for the well-being of girls, but we also need to be concerned about the well-being of boys.

When attending a recent National Regional Kids Wrestling tournament, I saw an attractive, pigtailed 10-year-old girl wrestle an equally attractive bushy-haired boy of the same age. Even though seven other bouts were going on at the same time, the attention of every spectator was riveted on this bout. Young wrestlers who were not competing rushed to matside to watch the spectacle.

The young boy was reluctant to begin the match, needing to be coaxed by his coach. Behind 4-0 at the end of the first period, the boy went crying to his coach. Embarrassed by this unmanly display of emotion, the coach attempted to shield him from the audience. When the referee called for the two wrestlers to begin the second period the boy balked, but the coach pushed him onto the mat and the contest resumed, tears and all. The outcome of the bout was never in doubt; the girl was a superior wrestler, winning 11-2. When the referee declared the girl the winner, with the contestants facing the audience and her hand held overhead, the boy burst into tears again running furiously from the mat to the locker room.

I do not think that children's expressions of intense emotions when disappointed are always something at which to become alarmed. But in this particular case, and I am told that my observation in wrestling is not unique, I sensed that the novelty of a girl wrestling a boy brought so much attention to the match that the stress was enormous, especially for the boy. The young girl seemed well prepared, not only to wrestle, but for the accompanying attention. The boy was not; he had not expected to wrestle a girl.

I'm concerned about the psychological stress in children's sports, although, as we will later see, the evidence indicates that for most youngsters the stress of sports is not too great. But because unisexed competition is still a novelty attracting considerable attention, I wonder whether this added attention may make them too stressful.

Although the stress appeared to be too great for the boy I observed wrestling, in other cases the stress may also be too great for the girls. With today's societal expectations, however, I think the stress is often more likely to be greater for boys. Defeat by the supposed "fairer" sex is potentially more damaging to a boy's feelings of self-worth than when the reverse occurs. Boys are expected to beat girls, not the other way around, even though there is no basis for this expectation. One may argue that young boys should not think this way, but as products of our culture most do.

In spite of my concern for the potential adverse psychological effects of unisexed sports on both male and female participants, I support such integration. I suspect that unisexed sports for prepubescent children will be commonplace in the future. But as they become commonplace, adults will have to be particularly alert, not so much to the physical or skill differences between boys and girls, but to the psychological impact of such competition. Adults can help prepare both boys and girls to understand that victory or defeat is not appropriately attributed to sex differences, but to ability and effort. In time, as the novelty of unisexed competition diminishes, as the physical and emotional equality of prepubescent children becomes obvious, the psychological threat (especially to boys) of competing with the opposite sex will dissipate.

As fervently as I support boys and girls playing together *prior* to puberty, I firmly oppose unisexed sports *after* puberty for sports demanding speed, strength, and endurance. This includes most popular sports—baseball, basketball, volleyball, track and field, swimming, wrestling, hockey, gymnastics, tennis, and golf. *Postpubescent* boys and girls are significantly different physiologically, and these differences establish limits to their performances in sports.

Young boys and girls mature at about the same rate up to the age of 9, but then girls have a growth spurt where they become taller, heavier, and better coordinated. Girls normally terminate their growth between 15 and 16, but the boys' slower but longer growth rate continues until about the age of 20 or 21. The slower growth period of males results in a heavier, larger, more rugged structure with mechanical advantages, particularly in the upper body. Consequently, the male develops a considerable advantage in sports requiring speed and force.

James Michener in *Sports in America* also advocates separate sports programs for postpubescent boys and girls on the basis that defeat to males at the hands of females is psychologically damaging to males. Michener believes that the male's need for dominance over the female is an "immutable genetic inheritance" of the male. He writes that "the separation of boys and girls during the ages of twelve through twenty-two conforms to some permanent psychological need of the human race and that to reverse the custom might produce more harm than good."[1]

Michener's thoughts on this are in left field in my opinion. I know of no evidence—none whatsoever—to suggest that male dominance and separation of the sexes at this age is biologically based. On the contrary, all the evidence indicates that these are learned attitudes—attitudes which incidentally are not found universally.

Although I reject Michener's reason why boys and girls should compete separately, I do think that postpubescent unisexed competition is potentially just as dangerous psychologically as it is with prepubescent children. But if the only basis for separating postpubescent boys and girls is for the *potential* psychological damage to the male or female ego, I would advocate unisexed sports, for I think these attitudes can be changed with time. But this is not the reason. My argument is based on physiological and anatomical differences between postpubescent males and females, and those reasons alone.

I am not sympathetic to the argument that girls who are good enough should also be permitted to play on the boys' teams. Then those boys who are good enough should also be permitted to play on the girls' teams if equality is to be the guiding principle. If such a policy were followed, most girls would play on neither team. But such logic does not always prevail.

Recently the Maryland State Department of Education ruled that girls may compete for places on all-boy teams, but boys cannot compete on all-girl teams, even if a separate boys' team in the sport does not exist. They claim the rule is intended to bring the school athletic programs into line with the Maryland equal rights amendment of 1972. I fail to see the equality in this ruling.

Over the last 5 years numerous legal actions have been initiated to permit girls to play on boys' teams in school and non-school sports programs. These litigations have had the positive effect of publicizing the inequities in sports opportunities for females, but I believe in the long run it will be more profitable for girls to fight for equal but separate programs.

The difficulty with advocating unisexed sports for prepubescent children and separate sports programs for postpubescent children is knowing exactly when to separate them. The variability in maturation is substantial. For example, the onset of puberty varies from as early as 9 years to as late as 17. (The advantage of early maturation in sports will be discussed in the next section.) An accurate means of establishing the physical maturation of children is to measure their skeletal age, which is the measure of the ossification of the wristbones as shown by X-ray. But this system is prohibitively expensive for most children's sports programs. It is my opinion that at present, in the absence of a better proven method, we should use the admittedly crude index of chronological age. I think this age should be set somewhat conservatively in order to diminish the advantage of the early maturer. Thus I recommend that boys and girls should play all sports demanding speed, strength, and endurance separately beginning at the age of 11.

Equal Opportunities

Three things prevent girls from having equal opportunities in sports—organizational rules, customs or social norms, and lack of resources. Many local and national youth sports organizations have willingly or unwillingly changed their rules to permit girls to play. Almost all national youth sports organizations for children under 12 have no restrictions against girls playing or have developed separate girls' programs. Those rules still existing which prevent girls from playing are almost entirely at the local level. For children over 12 some national organizations, like Babe Ruth baseball, have refused to admit girls. I think they are correct to do so because Babe Ruth baseball is for youngsters 13 to 15 years of age. But I also think that separate baseball programs ought to be provided for girls of that age who wish to play.

When discussing rules preventing girls from participating in sports, we cannot ignore the highly controversial legislation known as Title IX of the Education Amendments Act of 1972. Even though in this book we are not primarily concerned with school sports programs the significance of this piece of legislation for helping to irradicate the inequities in girls' opportunities cannot be ignored. The Act simply says "No person in the United States shall, on the basis of sex, be excluded from participation in, be denied the benefits of, or be subjected to discrimination under any educational program or activity receiving federal financial assistance."

In the past 2 years junior high schools, high schools, and colleges have been frantically attempting to comply with this new law. It has been tremendously helpful in stimulating the development of interschool sports teams for girls, yet it also has led to some undesirable practices. Girls' programs are modeling boys' sports programs more and more and thus acquiring the problems associated with recruiting, scholarships, and gate receipts.

A less overt but more potent means of preventing girls from playing are the cultural attitudes which have erected social barriers against female participation in sports. In the past, boys have been socialized into sports through the family, school, community, and the media. Girls were socialized to become the caddies of sports—the jumping, screaming, dancing sideline cheerleaders. Although it is acceptable to be a "tomboy" until the age of 9 or 10, girls thereafter encounter pressure to put away their boyish behaviors and assume their proper feminine role in society—which, when translated, means "get off the playing fields, and go back to the sidelines and cheer."

While these societal attitudes still prevail, they are changing. It is more acceptable today than ever before for girls to participate in sports, and more girls are seeking to do so. Adult women who have been deprived of sports during their youth resent their missed opportunities and enthusiastically support the movement to permit their daughters to play sports. Today many people—males and females alike—find nothing unfeminine about girls who participate in sports, who are intensely competitive, and who achieve. Instead, they admire and respect girls for their accomplishments, just as much as they do for boys. But there still are some who hold the antiquated view that sport is macho.

The third factor hindering girls from having an equal opportunity in sports is the lack of available resources. Money for new programs is difficulty to obtain; and leaders of boys' sports programs resist and resent girls' sports leaders asking and sometimes demanding to share available resources. They believe that any diminution of boys' sports reduces the local program's chances for fame and fortune. Boys' sports are perceived as more important both to the boys' and the community's development. Girls' sports are seen as less important because they are less developed, fail to attract huge audiences, and are not played seriously enough. These are perhaps accurate charactertistics of girls' sports today, but that does not make girls' sport less important. If anything, these characteristics may make girls' sports more attractive to the participants.

For some time to come it will be a difficult task for girls' sports programs to coequal boys' programs. The girls' programs at presnt tend to get poorer facilities, less monetary support, and inconvenient practice and game schedules. Communities have only so much money and so many facilities to use for sports. As both boys and girls seek increasing opportunities in sports, greater scrutiny will be made of the present resources of all-male sports programs. The pressure to provide girls' sports programs may indeed mean a reduction of lavish expenditure and the abolition of male dominance of playing facilities.

Reference

1. Michener, J. A. *Sports in America.* New York: Random House, 1976, p. 130.

SECTION D

The Maturation Game:
Midgets Vs Giants

When observing and talking with youngsters today I often marvel at their knowledge and skills. Not only do they seem brighter and more adept than my generation at the same age, they also seem more mature. When I interviewed a young boy recently I asked him the simple question, "What is your age?" His response was, "Well, that depends, sir. If you're asking about my anatomical age, it's 7. If you're asking about my intellectual age, it's 11. If you're asking about my social-emotional age, it's 9. But I suppose you're asking about my chronological age which is 8!"

Although I was astonished to hear his answer, this bright lad was quite correct—each of us has many ages. But usually we use chronological age as the sole index of children's development. This is certainly true in children's sports. Chronological age and sex are the usual means for classifying or grouping youngsters for competition, although in some sports like wrestling, weight is also used. And in other sports chronological age and skill level are sometimes used jointly to classify competitors. We know though that chronological age is not always closely related to children's physical, intellectual, or emotional maturity levels.

Individual differences in youngsters' physical maturation present substantial problems in making competition in many sports safe and equitable. From about 10 to 16 years, the range of individual differences in physical structure at any given chronological age is greater than at any other time in the human life span. Boys of the same chronological age may differ by as much as 60 months in their anatomical or skeletal age. Skeletal age, the best indicator of a person's physical maturation, is a measure of bone ossification revealed by X-raying the hand and wrist bones. The degree of ossification is compared with norms for children of different chronological ages. For two boys, both 13 years of age, one could have a skeletal age typical for boys aged 10 and the other for boys aged 15. These same boys may vary as much as 15 inches in height and 90 pounds in weight. Thus in sports where speed, strength, and power are likely to determine the outcome, matching children by skeletal age should make competition safer and more equitable.

The child who matures early obviously has a substantial advantage in sports—the same advantage postpubescent boys have over postpubescent girls. Some sports-avid parents are quick to recognize this advantage, delaying their children's entrance into school for the express purpose of giving them an additional year to mature for sports participation.

The advantage of the early maturer in sports is described in a delightful article, titled *Healthy Hormones*, written by Catherine and Loren Broadus. Then in the second selection Morty Morris argues that in the long term, the success of children in sports is not at all related to how early they begin intensive training in a sport. Instead, it is determined by the child's biological clock. This does not speak well of the common practice of having children specialize in one sport at an increasingly earlier age. In the concluding comments, I discuss how the early maturer's advantage may become a disadvantage and the problems associated with "maturation matching" of children for safe and equitable competition.

Healthy Hormones

by **Catherine** and **Loren Broadus,** *former coaches and fans for their three Little League sons. The authors are now at the Lexington Theological Seminary.*

"THAT BOY HAS A MUSTACHE!" the lady shouted in a state of shock. "The pitcher has a mustache," she repeatedly told the person sitting to her right, to her left, in front of her, and behind her. "Don't tell me he isn't over 12 years old." The stands were buzzing with the big news of the boy with a mustache.

This was a small town of about fourteen thousand Protestants and two hundred Roman Catholics. Everyone knew everyone else or knew someone who knew those people they didn't know. However, it took these local people 15 minutes to discover the identity of this boy, which must be some kind of record. He was from the "Catholic community," which was a few miles out of town.

"Where is he from?" the excited lady asked. No one answered. She stood up, looked around and then leaned over

Reprinted with permission of the authors from *Laughing and Crying with Little League*, pp. 13-15. New York: Harper and Row, 1972.

three people and asked, "Do any of you know where that boy is from?"

"He's a Catholic," a friend replied. I still do not know what that has to do with his mustache. I have known Protestants who grew mustaches.

The game began and what some people feared occurred. He threw his first pitch and the fans had trouble seeing it, it was so fast.

"Oh Lord! He'll kill somebody."

"He can't be 12!"

"I've never seen anything like him."

"Somebody had better check his birth certificate."

While all of this conversation is taking place, the boy's farmer father sat silently, grinning as if he had studded Man o'War.

Eleven pitches and the side was retired. The boy stepped up to bat and knocked the ball out of sight. "Oh God, now I know someone will get killed. If he ever hits one to our boys it will break their hand or head."

"He shouldn't be permitted to play!"

All of this conversation was taking place between the parents of the opposing team. While they complained, we good guys clapped our hands, winked at the father, and thanked God for Catholics or whatever it was that enabled this boy to grow his Samsonlike mustache.

"So they say he's from the Catholic community," another lady mused, "I don't understand it."

Catherine [first author] solved the problem of the boy's early development. She turned to the disturbed people and informed them that the nuns were spiking the boy's milk with hormones.

The conversation eased a little and the winners told jokes while the losers wept.

Needless to say we had a winning season and the conversation was the same for every game. To this day there are people who still do not believe that the 12-year-old man was a 12-year-old boy.

If your son has a mustache, or even heavy fuzz on his upper lip, you may have to carry his birth certificate to every game to prove his age to opposing parents. The women will talk to other people about your forging the birth certificate, but they will leave you alone.

Incidentlly, a birth certificate has to be presented at the beginning of the season. If your son is chosen on the All-Star team, prepare to present it again! No one seems to trust anyone in this game.

Don't Rush Your Kids

by **Morty Morris,** *former director of recreation for the Village of Croton-on-Hudson, New York.*

The trend among coaches during recent years has been to start the boys young, to keep them coming. The only unhappy part is that some have begun to start them too young. Though it is a pernicious practice, it has undoubtedly produced results. However, even better results would be obtained if these coaches who have proved both their knowledge of the sport and the ability to put it across, would only consider maturation and saturation, with the emphasis on the former. In their zeal they often ask too much of boys and girls and give them tasks far beyond strength and abilities.

Success Depends on Maturation

Every coach has had boys return to school after the summer recess with the ability to perform well and easily the very

Abridged from the *Journal of Health, Physical Education and Recreation,* October 1952, pp. 18-19; 56. Reprinted with permission of the publisher.

assignment that was unsuccessfully hammered at during the preceding season. Questioning usually discloses that little or no practice was had during the vacation. The explanation lies in maturation and saturation.

The mind and body seem to absorb so much and then, like a wad of cotton under the faucet, can absorb no more. However, a layoff, even a short one, will reopen the boy's learning of new and advanced skills.

Maturation cannot be overemphasized. A coach would definitely not expect to teach a third grader to hook shot accurately with both hands for he finds it impossible to teach his high school varisty to be equally adept at this same skill. While he would recognize the absurdity of such a program for the third grade, he is undoubtedly trying to teach his ten-year-olds to do things that would be more suited to a boy of 12 or 13.

Another valid reason to consider carefully maturation among our youngsters is the trite maxim "Nothing succeeds like success." Most boys will give up and lose interest after several failing attempts to develop a skill, but victory after a fair amount of struggle and difficulty will definitely build enthusiasm. Walk into any gym and watch the boys shooting baskets. It is the unusual lad who is practicing to master a new shot. Most of the boys will be shooting pet shots, for we all tend to perform actions we do well or know well. This eventually settles the player into deep ruts.

Rushing boys and girls along can also ruin promising athletic careers. Many a vaunted high school star proves a dud in collegiate circles because he was "burned out" before ever reaching his peak. The toughest job a high school coach has is to keep his pitching staff from throwing hooks and screwballs and a wide variety of "stuff." Coaches who develop their athletes according to maturation will protect these lads from their own folly.

Wide Experience Best

The sad part is that the coach is not being as efficient in his coaching methods as he imagines. Maturation can do with greater, more evident efficacy much of the task that is now so laborious. The eight-year-old can be worked upon for countless hours and will become quite adept at catching a baseball or football. However, when compared to a boy of like ability who has been permitted to progress with skills better suited to his ability, you will find no difference at the age of 11.

If anything, the latter boy will hold the edge. He will show more enthusiasm and receptivity. In addition, his background and range of experience from activities such as tumbling and apparatus, group games, dancing, and swimming will give him a broader base on which to build further development. It is common sense that, with all other things being equal, the boy with the widest experience from which to draw knowledge and technique will prove the player of superior value to the team.

What Coaches Must Do

Rather than hide our heads ostrichlike in the sand, we must face the situation and understand our position. Until education assumes the lead and patterns thinking in proper channels, rather than following opinion formulated by a misinformed and often misdirected public, we coaches must consider our own survival and our own welfare. I am not against competition for I feel it has many virtues but I am against any system where a coach must sacrifice all else to save his job through winning teams.

It is impossible to set down definite lines or to name certain ages and grades as the spot for certain activities. Location and the climate, plus the background of the students and any number of items could cause a change in readiness and you will find that even in your own classes there will often be a wide divergency of ability and growth. However, an alert, interested educator will be able to adjust his program for the common good.

Premature Training Useless

Let us return to our original statement of the uselessness of premature training. As has been proved by experiments on birds and animals, the fundamental motor skill development comes largely through maturation. Arnold Gesell and Helen Thompson proved this also by using twin babies in an experiment in stair climbing.

It is therefore apparent that we are wasting valuable time and effort by trying to force the development of our athletes. What we can and should do is to try to perfect co-ordination of reactions that the boys already have as a result of normal growth.

Emotionally too, in our zeal to develop teams, we can do irreparable harm to youngsters. Boys maturing slowly may not be able to participate on a satisfactory basis with their mates. A social problem can easily develop and these boys will forever be lost to varsity competition. Often if they do develop into varsity material they can upset the entire spirit and well-being of the club.

Like Pyramid Building

In summary I would like to compare my theory of developing young athletes to pyramid building. The higher, sturdier pyramid must always be the one with the wider base. In analogy, your superior athlete is the one with the most experiences and background. His growth has been unforced and natural. His enthusiasm has not been killed by any overemphasis nor by impossible heights to scale. Success has always been within reach through an honest effort. He has not been "burned out" nor made a psychological problem. Best of all, I think I will have developed a good citizen.

Comments

The Early and Late Maturer

We have all seen the Catholic boy with the mustache in one sport or another. But how many boys and girls in sports have an advanced biological clock, and how much faster do their clocks run? Creighton Hale,[1] the present director of Little League baseball, studied the physical maturity of boys participating in the 1955 Little League World Series. He assessed physical maturation using the Crampton pubic hair scale, a less precise means of determining maturation than skeletal age. Hale reported that 46% of the boys were postpubescent, indicating they were mature for their chronological age of 12 or under. In fact, these postpubescent players equaled the norms for height and weight of the average 14-year-old boy. Hale also reported that most of the starting pitchers, first basemen, and left fielders were postpubescent; and every boy who batted fourth or cleanup, the key position in the batting lineup, was postpubescent.

Krogman[2] replicated Hale's study with the participants of the 1957 Little League World Series, but used skeletal age as the measure of physical maturity. He found that 71% of the boys were advanced in skeletal age, with 45% being over one year advanced. In an extensive study by Clarke[3] of young athletes in Medford, Oregon, boys who made the interscholastic teams at elementary and junior high school were 11 to 13 months advanced in skeletal age, body size, strength, endurance, and power in comparison with their nonathlete peers. Other scientists[4,5] found that the best predictor of success in football and track was not a measure of motor skill or physical size, as might be expected, but skeletal age.

Both observation and scientific evidence lead us to the irrefutable conclusion that physically maturer children are more likely to succeed in sports. Yet there is some doubt as to whether these children gravitate to sports or whether participation in sports hastens the maturation process. It is a proverbial chicken-egg question. Do sports select out the physically mature youngsters, or do sports cause youngsters to mature faster? After substantial investigation, researchers have found no evidence indicating that competitive sports hasten physical maturation, but they have found considerable evidence that the rate of maturation is genetically predetermined under normal conditions. Hence, all factors considered, it is highly probable that sports tend to select out physically mature youngsters.

This selection process often eliminates late maturing children from sports. And, more significantly, even after they physically catch up, many will never re-enter sports. By then late maturing children have missed the advantage of early training and they have lost interest because of early failure.

But differences in physical maturation may also hurt the early maturer. There is an old cliche which says, "The earliest light burns out first." Its meaning in sports is that the star of the midget league is the first to lose his position of stardom. For those youngsters whose light goes out so that they no longer enjoy the prestige and status of being a star athelte, the psychological adjustment may be a difficult one. The problem may be accentuated when coaches mistakenly attribute a youngster's fall from stardom not to the improvement of the other youngsters, but to the erroneous belief that the early maturer is no longer putting forth the needed effort. Because both the coach and the youngster fail to understand the biological basis for his initial advantage in sports and his subsequent loss of it, some youngsters become frustrated and quit.

But just how often do early maturing children get passed by as the slower maturing children move through puberty and into postpubescent adolescence? The Medford growth study,[3] an impressive 12 year longitudinal investigation, helps answer this question. Of the athletes studied, 45% were stars in elementary but not junior high school, 30% were stars in junior high school but not in elementary school, and only 25% were stars in both elementary and junior high school. In other words, only one out of four star athletes in elementary school maintained such a rating 3 to 4 years later in junior high school.

I think every young athlete and certainly every coach of children's sports should be cognizant of this fact. This information should serve to encourage slow maturing children to persist, for more than likely their day is coming. It should warn fast maturing youngsters that some day success may not be obtained so easily. And it should tell every coach that the practice of eliminating youngsters who may be slow maturing is foolish. How many kids have been turned off sports by coaches who cut them from the team? How many have been humiliated by their awkwardness because their biological clock ran slower? How many youngsters have had their self-esteem shattered in sports, their attitudes toward sports soured by a coach or parent who failed to understand that **kids mature at different rates and the single most important factor determining their success is their physical maturity**?

Maturation Matching

Maturation matching simply refers to arranging competitive sports groups according to maturity rather than chronological age. Skeletal age is the most reliable method for matching children on physical maturity, but the use of skeletal age is not an entirely satisfactory solution either. First, the cost of X-raying and scoring children is high, about $30 per child. Second, the additional exposure to radiation is a potential health hazard. And third, children of the same chronological age not only differ widely in physical maturity, but also in mental and emotional maturity. If one criterion is used for grouping, such as physical maturity, then the differences in mental and emotional development are likely to be substantial.

Hence the most difficult problem in maturation matching for young sports participants is determining the criteria to be used. This question is related to three others:

1. What are acceptable ranges in maturity for grouping young people to safely engage in different sports?
2. What are the practical constraints of the situation when grouping—for example, the number of children per category, available facilities, coaches, equipment, etc.?

3. What should be the degree of self-selection into groups
   by young people?

We have no satisfactory answers to these questions. We do
not even have adequate means to measure mental and emotional maturity. Yet I believe we can do better than hap-
hazardly grouping children according to age or grade as we so
often do.

Two types of maturation matching may be done. One is to
match children *to* sports suited to their maturity level. And
the second is to match children *within* a sport to make competition safe and equitable.

One elaborate classification system that counsels youngsters into different sports is called the Selection Classification
Age Maturity Program (SCAM), which is being used experi-
mentally in the New York State public school sports program.
It classifies students on the basis of physical fitness, skills, and
physical maturity. The physical maturity of boys is measured
by an examination of their hair rather than chronological age
or skeletal age. Boys' facial, underarm, and pubic hair are
examined and compared with normative charts. "Boys with a
good five o'clock shadow . . . should not be throwing vicious
body blocks into boys with only peach fuzz on their cheeks"[6]
writes Sophie Gerber about the system. Girls, on the other
hand, do not have their hair scrutinized, but are asked at what
age they experienced menarche, their first menstruation.

This simple method of measuring physical maturity com-
pares quite well with skeletal age for youngsters who are
pubescent or postpubescent (but not with younger children).
The relationship between genitalia development and muscle
and bone development is well documented.

Student athletes are also tested for agility, strength, speed,
endurance, and skill specific to the sport of their interest. All
this information is converted to an achievement score based on
norms for each grade, ranking each student on a scale from 1 to
10 (underdeveloped to superior). Then using tables which
specify the demands of each sport on the basis of strenuousness and physical contact, the student is matched to a sport
suitable for his or her present level of development.

The system has enthusiastic supporters because the injury
rate in its first year of use was reduced from 32 per 100 to 3 per
100. SCAM also is relatively simple, inexpensive, and not

overly time consuming to use. It works best for large school systems or recreation and park districts which offer a wide range of sports.

But the system has limitations. First, it does not match children *within* sports. This need for matching within a sport is reduced, however, by better matching of students to suitable sports. Second, the use of hair and menarche as indices of physical maturation are useful for pubescent and postpubescent youngsters, but not for prepubescent children. Third, late maturing children will always be counseled away from contact and collision sports, but once they catch up it may be difficult to shift into these sports. And fourth, the system disregards mental and emotional maturity as criteria for classification. Despite its limitations, I believe SCAM is better than permitting children to enter sports without any counseling regarding their readiness.

Maturation matching within a sport is even more difficult than matching children *to* a sport because precise measurement is needed over the full range of development to achieve effective matching. The appearance of secondary sex characteristics as used in SCAM permits only crude classification and is limited to pubescent and postpubescent children. Skeletal age is the only measure of physical maturation capable of measuring the full range of physical development, but, as previously explained, it is impractical. So it is understandable that sports officials continue to rely on chronological age or grade as the only functional means of matching children for competition.

Yet there are some things league officials, coaches, and parents can do to diminish the probability of mismatching children in sports:

1. Weight should always be used in conjunction with chronological age in all collision sports. The more homogeneous the grouping on these two criteria the better.
2. Skill tests specific to the sport should be used so that children can be matched for equitable competition. In contact and collision sports, closer matching on skills also reduces the risk of injury among the less skilled players.
3. More limited age ranges within each grouping will decrease the extreme differences among players. For example, rather than an 8-team league of 9- to 12-year-olds,

two 4-team leagues, one of 9- to 10-year-olds and one of 11- to 12-year-olds is better.

4. A governing council of league officials should have the authority to move players up or down in classification when they are obviously biologically advanced or delayed, regardless of chronological age. Such flexibility should be available to league officials when in their judgment it is in the best interests of all players. Such decisions, of course, could easily be the source of much controversy in programs where winning is foremost in the minds of the adults involved. But if the development and the safety of all children are to be foremost, then such decisions will have to be made.

5. By providing a wider range of sports programs and varying the skill level and intensity of competition, children will have greater opportunity to self-select a level of competition appropriate for their maturation level. All-too-often, children have but one choice—to compete at a very intense level or not to play the sport at all. If at least two, three, or four different levels of competition were available based on skill and the degree of competitive intensity, children would probably match themselves quite well to the competition best suited to their development. This may be one of the best ways for children to match themselves on mental and emotional maturity as well.

6. Parents should use their good judgment to help counsel their children into appropriate competition—perhaps in consultation with a physician, physical educator, or coach. Parents who believe their children are substantially behind in physical maturation may want to have their skeletal age measured. But parents know better than anyone the mental and emotional maturity of their children and should consider these factors in conjunction with physical maturation when helping to counsel them into sports.

Early Training

Adults who push youngsters into intensive sports programs at seemingly earlier and earlier ages appear unaware or doubtful of the importance of children's biological clocks in determining their capacity to learn sports skills and thus to benefit from early training. Or perhaps they believe that early intense competition in sports will hasten the maturation process, even though there is no evidence to support such a view.

Over the years a number of outstanding college and professional coaches, as well as knowledgeable sport scientists, have professed that superior high school and college athletes are more likely to come from elementary schools which do *not* include interscholastic sports.[7] Instead, a program that teaches a broad base of skills, one which does not exclude youngsters whose potential may not yet be demonstrated, and where facilities and instruction are available not to a few but to all children, is much more likely to produce successful teenage and adult athletes.

Intensive training to acquire specialized sports skills at too early an age has a number of disadvantages:

1. The chances are great that the late maturer is likely to fail.
2. Early specialization usually is achieved at the expense of developing a broader base of fundamental movement skills such as balance, agility, and coordination.
3. Early specialization usually occurs at the expense of learning other sports, especially lifetime sports skills.
4. Early specialization may channel children into sports not best suited to their talents.
5. Frequently youngsters feel considerable adult-imposed pressure, especially after experiencing some initial success. This drives them to excel at one sport even though they find it work and devoid of fun, and would rather participate in a variety of other sports. Yet, fearing failure, they are hesitant to risk competing in other sports in which they are less experienced.
6. Specialization all-too-often means a heavy emphasis on winning and a de-emphasis on having fun.

A few youngsters may benefit from these specialized sports programs, and these few may indeed become our heroes of the Olympics and professional sports. Some of our highly specialized, intensely competitive children's sports programs are efficient sorting machines. They identify and train the few youngsters whom we hope to hoist onto the Olympic pedestal and revere as idols, thereby justifying the huge expense for elite sports. But at what price? How many youngsters are lost along the way? How many are told they are not good enough? How many are either physically or psychologically burned out from too intensive training and competition? No one really knows. But every sports administrator, coach, and parent of young athletes must consider the possibility and reach a conclusion in accordance with his or her observations.

I do not disapprove of intensely competitive programs per se, but I am opposed to programs that become *too* intense and require *too* much specialization *too* early. It is a judgment of degree of intensity, a judgment which must be made specific to each sport program. To me, it is too intense when 6-year-old youngsters train in the swimming pool 4 hours a day, 50 weeks a year. It is too much specialization when an 8-year-old boy is designated a left tackle and plays that position the rest of his football career. It is too early when 4-year-old youngsters play 30 games of competitive ice hockey per season.

And this leads us to the question which parents most frequently ask coaches and sports administrators: What is the appropriate age for my child to begin competing? Unfortunately, at this time we do not have scientific evidence that tells us precisely the optimal age for children to begin competing in sports programs. Surely, though, it varies from sport to sport. We do have some helpful knowledge, however, about the physical and psychological development of children. We know, for example, the optimal ages for children to learn different basic motor skills. We know that sports skills are learned hierarchically, that is, simple movement skills must be acquired before complex skills can be learned. We know that teaching complex sports skills before children are physically ready is of little benefit, and any initial advantage gained is lost when other children reach appropriate maturation levels. We also know that children do not develop the motive to compare their skills with other children until about the age of 6.

In judging when children should enter competition, we also can benefit from the opinions of knowledgeable educators, physicians, coaches, and parents. The opinions of these people vary widely: some believe that children can begin competing as early as age 3, others argue that children should not compete until age 12, and still others oppose sports competition at any age! But most experts who have given serious thought to the question recommend that competition may begin between the ages of 6 and 10 years. Based on these opinions, and on pertinent information from the child development and sports research literature, age recommendations are given in the table below for three types of sports.

Age Recommendations for Beginning Sport Competition for Normal Developing Children

TYPE OF SPORT	CHRONOLOGICAL AGE
Collision	10 years
Contact	8 years
Noncontact	6 years

Examples of collision sports are football and ice hockey. Contact sports include baseball, basketball, soccer, and wrestling —any sport where physical contact is an integral part of the game but collision-type contact is not. Examples of noncontact sports are swimming, tennis, and golf.

Knowing that chronological age is not the best index of physical maturation, these recommendations require careful interpretation. Parents must judge whether their children are maturing at a slow, normal, or accelerated rate in relation to chronological age. Children should be delayed from entering sports when they are deemed to be substantially slower in physical maturity. And, if at all possible, they should be permitted to enter sports earlier when they are biologically advanced. It is easier to delay slow maturing children's entrance into sport, but usually it is impossible to place an accelerated child in a higher age classification because league rules do not permit such flexibility.

When children are ready to compete, they normally will express interest and enthusiasm for becoming involved. Parents should support their children's desire to compete when they are physically ready, but they should be careful to distinguish between support and pressure. Some parents can effectively communicate their subtle expectations that their children must participate successfully in sports as soon as they are old enough. Sports are unlikely to be enjoyed by children who feel such pressure.

References

1. Hale, C. Physiological maturity of Little League baseball players. *Research Quarterly,* 1956, *27,* 276-284.
2. Krogman, W. M. Maturation age of 55 boys in the Little League World Series, 1957. *Research Quarterly,* 1959, *30,* 54-56.
3. Clarke, H. H. Characteristics of young athletes. *Kinesiology Review,* 1968, 33-42.
4. Rochelle, R. H., Kelliher, M. S., & Thornton, R. Relationship of maturation age to incidence of injury in tackle football. *Research Quarterly,* 1961, *32,* 78-82.
5. Cuming, G. R., Garand, T., & Borysyk, L. Correlation of performance in track and field events with bone age. *Journal of Pediatrics,* 1972, *80,* 970-973.
6. Gerber, S. Are kids too young to avoid sports injuries? *Science Digest,* 1975, *78*(4), p. 44.
7. Knapp, C., & Combes, H. A. Elementary interscholastic basketball—Does this produce superior high-school players? *Journal of Health, Physical Education and Recreation,* November 1953, pp. 12-13; 37.

SECTION E

Sticks and Stones May Break My Bones...But Will Sports?

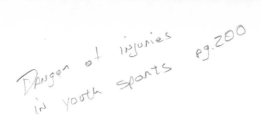

Danger of injuries in youth sports pg. 200

How many of our children die because of heatstroke, de-hydration, broken necks, and concussions resulting from gladi-ator warfare under the guise of sports? How many young-sters are maimed by bean balls, spear tackles, and body checks? Are dislocated knees, little league elbows, and cauli-flower ears the accepted price to pay for the possible thrill of victory? Critics of children's sports frequently pose these questions and then answer by relating horror stories of young-sters being maimed or killed, and citing statistics such as the following:

- —38 young people die playing football each year.
- —17 million sports injuries requiring a doctor's attention are estimated to occur among all ages in this country each year.
- —Approximately 40,000 crippled knees result from sports each year.
- —For youngsters under 15 years, there is one sports injury each year for every three players.
- —Among 1 million football players of all ages, 250,000 are injured, with 80,000 being serious—for example, frac-tures, concussions, internal injuries, or death.
- —Among 100 Little League and Middle League baseball par-ticipants in California 69 sprains, 5 broken bones, and 146 bruises and cuts were reported for one season of play.
- —Based on 771,810 Little League participants, 15,444 or 2% sustained injuries sufficiently severe to require medical attention.
- —5–8% of high school wrestlers are injured each year, resulting in their missing an average of 3 days of school.
- —For 16,500 junior high school football players in New York, 11.2% were reported to be injured each season.

Just how risky are sports to a child's health? These statistics, the best available, actually help very little in answering this question. Some of the statistics do not differentiate between children of varied ages or adults; some fail to consider the obvious differences in risk associated with different sports; and some do not distinguish between minor and major injuries. To know that 86 out of 100 high school football players are injured during their playing years tells us little. Perhaps 70 of those injuries are merely strained or pulled muscles. To know that 38 youngsters died playing football last year is a frightening figure, but less so to the father of a 10-year-old when he learns that most of these deaths occurred among 15- to 18-year-old boys and that Pop Warner football has never had a fatality in all the years of its existence.

In the absence of accurate statistics, how do we evaluate the risk to which children are exposed in certain sports? One way is to examine the frequency of injury in other activities in which children engage, especially those injuries occurring during unorganized play. For example, the Consumer Product Safety Commission tells us that 375,000 young people were injured in skateboard accidents in 1977, compared to some 370,000 in all the nonprofessional football games in the country. Over 400,000 bicycle injuries were suffered by children between the ages of 5 and 16 in 1976. And for the same year, nearly 6,600 youngsters between the ages of 5 and 14 were injured from fireworks. Some sports such as swimming are obviously safer when organized by adults. In 1973, 1,580 children drowned during recreational swimming whereas none drowned during organized swimming.

Are children's sports safe or hazardous? The answer depends on your point of reference—safe or hazardous in comparison to what? Obviously some sports are safer than others; basketball compared with football, tennis compared with ice hockey. It cannot be denied that a certain percentage of children are hurt in sports, some seriously—a few so severely that they die. Should sports in which the injury risk is higher than in other sports, such as football and ice hockey be banned for children? Should all collision and contact sports be banned? Shall we at the same time ban children from bicycles, skateboards, and swimming holes?

The answers are not simple. Parents, of course, want to protect their children. It is their responsibility. Yet the decision to permit children to participate in sports—particularly sports in which injury risk is higher—is difficult when accurate information about the frequency, severity, and causes of injury is lacking. It is difficult when youngsters pressure parents to let them join their friends who are playing sports. And it is difficult when physicians, educators, and coaches themselves are unable to help parents weigh the potential benefits against the potential risks.

I am of the opinion that most sports *can* be made sufficiently safe so that the benefits far outweigh the risks. What we must do is concentrate our efforts on making children's sports as safe as possible. The three articles in this section focus primarily on how to reduce the injury risk in children's sports. Fred Allman reviews some of the opinions of physicians about sports injuries and suggests some steps to help reduce unnecessary risk. In the next article, the disqualifying conditions for sports participation are summarized in tabular form by the American Medical Association. Merritt Low then provides valuable information to assist not only medical personnel, but also coaches and parents, to determine intelligently the disqualifying conditions for sports participation. Although Low's article is somewhat technical and verbose, every adult working with youngsters should study this article carefully. Definitions of technical terms have been inserted in brackets throughout the article.

Competitive Sports for Boys Under Fifteen: Beneficial or Harmful?

by **Fred L. Allman, Jr.**, *physician with special interest in sports medicine.*

Few subjects incite more controversy among physicians than the question of competitive and body contact sports for boys under the age of 15. A recent national poll of physicians by *Medical Tribune* indicated that 43.5% of physicians polled expressed unqualified opposition to body contact sports, while 40.5% felt that such activities were not too hazardous if properly supervised.[1]

The physicians that oppose contact sports seem to be mainly in agreement with Dr. Carl V. Lendgren who has stated, "These are the tender years when muscles lack the fibrous toughness needed for protection. Ribs and skull bones are too fragile and even the skin is tender and easily torn. Judgement, as well as body, is immature. Broken wrists, legs, torn ears, lacerated faces in these children represent too high a price for the fun or training they may receive."[2]

Abridged article from the *Journal of the Medical Association of Georgia*, November 1966, Vol. 55, pp. 464-468. Reprinted with permission of the publisher.

Proponents for contact sports generally agree that the benefits of competition outweigh the hazard of injury if the program is properly supervised.[2]

In order to fully evaluate the benefits of competitive sports, a better understanding of the hazards involved in such activities must be undertaken.

Acute Injuries to the Musculoskeletal System

Much has been written and even more said about the potential danger of permanent impairment to growth because of epiphyseal injuries. Many physicians agree with Dr. Lendgren and feel that these are truly "the tender years." Certainly there can be no question that our youngsters who compete in contact sports do on occasion sustain injuries, and these are sometimes serious or even fatal. In spite of the strong feelings that many physicians have regarding the potential harm of epiphyseal injuries, very few statistical studies have been reported regarding these injuries. As a result of this information void, an attempt has been made over the past few years to obtain data from areas where contact sports are allowed during this age span.

Drs. Larson and McMahan recently reported on a review of 1,338 consecutive athletic injuries.[3] In their survey 20% of the injuries occurred in the age group below 15. Only 6% of those injuries were epiphyseal injuries. The youngsters in that age group comprised 60% of the school population. Also of importance, their report indicated that 40% of the injuries occurred in the 15–18 year age group which comprised only 15% of the total school population. (Therefore the high school students appeared to be the most vulnerable to athletic injury.) The conclusions reached by these authors was that although epiphyseal injuries did occasionally occur, they did not necessarily mean deformity, and that the benefits derived by children participating in athletics outweighed such an indefinite potential.

The late Frank Barnes, surgeon in Smithfield, North Carolina, gathered data from several communities where midget football was played. A review of injury records revealed that injuries of any type were unusual and fractures were extremely rare (see table).

Midget Tackle Football

Kingston, N.C.
  400 players, 1 fractured wrist
Morehead City, N.C.
  260 players, 59 games, 7 injuries (3 fractures)
Smithfield, N.C.
  110 players, 3 seasons, 0 fractures
Raleigh, N.C.
  224 players, 1 dislocated shoulder
Elizabeth City, N.C.
  100 players, 12 seasons, 9 fractures
Durham, N.C.
  350 players, 1 fractured toe

Gallagher reported on records of 650 students at Phillips Academy over a seven-year period, ages 13–18 and stated that there were "few epiphyseal injuries."[4]

Seventeen Dallas, Texas, junior high schools representing 1,253 football participants reported only a small percentage representing epiphyseal injuries.[5]

The injury incidence of 16,500 Junior High Football players in New York was 11.2% with no mention being made of epiphyseal injuries representing a problem.[6] In 1957 junior high schools in New York representing approximately 2,000 participants in tackle football reported two or less injuries in 21 schools and five or less injuries in 38 schools.[7]

Yearly records have been kept on participants in the YMCA Tackle Football Program in Atlanta.[8] These represent the Y-Guys who are in the second and third grade, and the Gray-Y representing grades four through seven. There are 1,450 participants, and prerequisites for competition are minimal, being only tooth protectors, suspension helmet and soft shoes with rubber cleats. Yet, total injuries in 1965 were 31—there being only six fractures (four forearm, one metacarpal and one finger), hardly enough to classify the program as a health hazard. Certainly, during this same ten-week period at least six youngsters out of nearly 1,500 non-participants would have fallen from a tree, or a bicycle, or been struck by an automobile, producing a much more serious injury. Some might even have had time to engage in a mischievous act or embarked upon a career in crime.

Although rare, fatalities do occur as the result of contact sports. However, one of the largest tackle football programs for youngsters, The Pop Warner Program, has had over one million participants in the past 34 years without a fatality, a record that speaks well for the leadership and organization within the program. "What constitutes undue risk from participation in sports remains intuitive. Understanding what goes into a yardstick of risk plus a respect for the limited utility of fatality-risk figures are a sound combine for rebuttal of intemperate conclusions."[9]

Late Effects of Microtrauma

Too often history records the disaster which in earlier years had been considered prudent. Little did the luminous watch dial painters realize that in 30 years most of them would be dead of bone cancer because of the effects of radium. Nor even now do many fully realize the harmful effects accumulated over the years by the habitual use of cigarettes.

Although sports activities have been present since the beginning of man, they have not had the organization and the altered techniques of today. The "wear and tear" on joints, especially the neck and knee of football players, and the elbow and shoulder of baseball pitchers may produce changes which do not become apparent for many years. It becomes necessary therefore to be on the lookout for techniques that may be especially harmful and to make certain that these are eliminated from the athletic program. Probably the greatest offender of this generation of football players is the procedure known as "spearing." This is blocking or tackling with the head —the main purpose being to inflict pain or discomfort to the opponent by using the front or top of the helmet to strike the player in the sternum or back. This not only may produce serious acute injury, but is most certain to produce degenerative changes in the cervical spine if continued over a sufficiently long period. Coaches in the professional and college ranks argue that their boys are prepared for this activity by special exercise programs that help to strengthen the cervical spine. Serious doubt must be given that any spine could be prepared for such activity when continued over a period of years. More important, however, is the fact that the high schools and midget programs frequently mimic the colleges and the pros—and therefore they also teach spearing. Most youngsters cannot possibly have adequate musculature to protect them properly during this type of activity. Even if acute injury is avoided, chronic changes are sure to occur if the practice is continued throughout the years of football competition.

Organized leagues in baseball are now available for youngsters beginning at age six. If a boy is good he will usually go from one league to another, play for his school in the spring and the league in the summer. Many young pitchers throw curve balls, sliders and fast balls, but few are taught the importance of warming up slowly and cooling off slowly. Prolonged pitching over many years without adequate conditioning, and pre and post performance care of the arm, will surely result in degenerative changes about the elbow and shoulder. Adams,[10] Bennett,[11] Middleman,[12] Meyer and Dively[13] have noted these shoulder and elbow changes, and called attention to the importance of proper recognition and care.

Specialization Too Early

Although there are certain skills that are specific for each sport there are other factors which are basic for the hard core of sports fitness and there are generally speaking the same for nearly all sports. Basic fitness work should always include the practice of skills of many sports, even though they seem unrelated to one's special event. This is especially important during the early years of training. Other sports are basic training in skill learning.[14]

"A candidate for football should be a year-round athlete. This does not mean that an aspiring young halfback should devote his attention to football per se during the off season. Nor does it mean that he must participate in competitive sports all year long. Rather, it means that every athletic minded boy should be enjoying a high level of physical readiness for sports regardless of the season. The payoff is more injury free time to spend on refinement of skills when competitive practices begin—especially for a contact sport like football."[15] (A comment by the National Federation of State High School Athletic Associations and The Committee On The Medical Aspects of Sports of The American Medical Association.)

The recent success of the Soviet athletes in the Olympics has been attributed in part to the fact that they have learned that specialized athletic performance rises highest when founded upon a broad base of multisports training. Youngsters in Russia are encouraged to engage in many sports.

The development of motor skills depends partially upon maturation. It therefore becomes necessary to utilize the potentiality which is associated with changes in the function ability of the individual. If this potentiality is neglected then the same high level of performance that might have been attained will never be reached.

Skill training concentrates on teaching the correct technique for the individual based on his or her own natural movement. Studies at the Laboratory of Applied Physiology at Southern Illinois University have demonstrated that there may be at least three distinct patterns of throwing. Each pattern can be highly successful within itself; however, the methods of teaching throwing attempt to have a boy throw in a standard pattern which means changing his basic pattern.[16]

Much has been learned in recent years by observing champions during top performance competition. While a study of these champion athletes has helped others to improve performance, these techniques have for the most part evolved over a number of years. It therefore may be very incorrect to try and teach this same technique, which has been acquired by one athlete over a number of years, to the beginning athlete who has not yet reached the same level of maturity.

References

1. Sports report. *Medical Tribune*, June 5, 1963.
2. Boys in contact sports. *Medical Tribune*, November 7, 1964.
3. Larson, R. L., & McMahan, R. O. The epiphyses and the childhood athlete. *The Journal of The American Medical Association*, 1966, *196*, 607-612.
4. Gallagher, J. R. Athletic injuries among adolescents: Their incidence and type in various sports. *Research Quarterly*, 1948, *19*, 198-214.
5. Dallas Independent School District, Dallas, Texas. Participation and injury report, Junior High School Football, 1961. Personal communication.

6. Emerson, R. S. Sports report. *Medical Tribune*, January 6, 1964.

7. Lane, R. G. Midget tackle football. *Proceedings of the Athletic Workshop*. Georgia Recreation Commission, February 2-3, 1966.

8. Young, B. Northside Branch YMCA, Atlanta, Ga. Personal communication.

9. Clarke, K. S. Calculated risk of sports fatalities. *The Journal of The American Medical Association*, 1966, *197*, 894-896.

10. Adams, J. L. Injury to the throwing arm. *California Medicine*, 1965, *102*, 127-132.

11. Bennett, G. E. Elbow and shoulder lesions of baseball players. *American Journal of Surgery*, 1959, *98*, 484-492.

12. Middleman, I. C. Shoulder and elbow lesions of baseball players. *American Journal of Surgery*, 1961, *102*, 627-632.

13. Diveley, R. L., & Meyer, P. W. Baseball shoulder. *Journal of The American Medical Association*, 1959, *171*, 1659-1661.

14. Doherty, J. K. *Modern track and field*. Englewood Cliffs, N.J.: Prentice-Hall, Inc., 1963.

15. Physical readiness for football. Comment by The National Federation of State High School Athletic Associations and the Committee on The Medical Aspects of Sports of the American Medical Association, July 1966.

16. Bender, J. A. Personal communication.

Disqualifying Conditions
for Sports Participation

American Medical Association

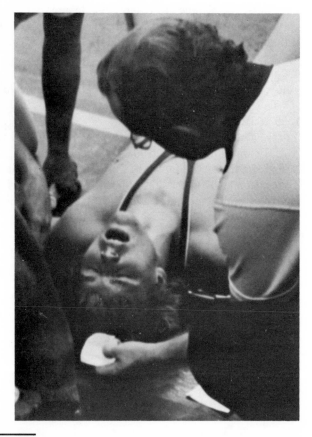

Conditions	Collision[1]	Contact[2]	Noncontact[3]	Other[4]
GENERAL				
Acute infections:				
Respiratory, genitourinary, infectious mononucleosis, hepatitis, active rheumatic fever, active tuberculosis	X	X	X	X
Obvious physical immaturity in comparison with other competitors	X	X		
Hemorrhagic disease:				
Hemophilia, purpura, and other serious bleeding tendencies	X	X	X	
Diabetes, inadequately controlled	X	X	X	X
Diabetes, controlled				
Jaundice	X	X	X	X
EYES				
Absence or loss of function of one eye	X	X		
RESPIRATORY				
Tuberculosis (active or symptomatic)	X	X	X	X
Severe pulmonary insufficiency	X	X	X	X
CARDIOVASCULAR				
Mitral stenosis, aortic stenosis, aortic insufficiency, coarctation of aorta, cyanotic heart disease, recent carditis of any etiology	X	X	X	X
Hypertension on organic basis	X	X	X	X
Previous heart surgery for congenital or acquired heart disease*				
LIVER				
Enlarged liver	X	X		
SKIN				
Boils, impetigo, and herpes simplex gladiatorum	X	X		

[1]Football, rugby, hockey, lacrosse, etc.
[2]Baseball, soccer, basketball, wrestling, etc.
[3]Cross country, track, tennis, crew, swimming, etc.
[4]Bowling, golf, archery, field events, etc.
*Each patient should be judged on an individual basis in conjunction with his cardiologist and operating surgeon.

Conditions	Collision	Contact	Noncontact	Other
SPLEEN				
Enlarged spleen	X	X		
HERNIA				
Inguinal or femoral hernia	X	X	X	
MUSCULOSKELETAL				
Symptomatic abnormalities or inflammations	X	X	X	X
Functional inadequacy of the musculoskeletal system, congenital or acquired, incompatible with the contact or skill demands of the sport	X	X	X	
NEUROLOGICAL				
History or symptoms of previous serious head trauma, or repeated concussions	X			
Controlled convulsive disorder**				
Convulsive disorder not completely controlled by medication	X	X	X	
Previous surgery on head	X	X		
RENAL				
Absence of one kidney	X	X		
Renal disease	X	X	X	X
GENITALIA*				
Absence of one testicle				
Undescended testicle				

**Each patient should be judged on an individual basis. All things being equal, it is probably better to encourage a young boy or girl to participate in a non-contact sport rather than a contact sport. However, if a particular patient has a great desire to play a contact sport, and this is deemed a major ameliorating factor in his/her adjustment to school, associates and the seizure disorder, serious consideration should be given to letting him/her participate if the seizures are controlled.

***The Committee approves the concept of contact sports participation for youths with only one testicle or with an undescended testicle(s), except in specific cases such as an inguinal canal undescended testicle(s), following appropriate medical evaluation to rule out unusual injury risk. However, the athlete, parents and school authorities should be fully informed that participation in contact sports for such youths with only one testicle does carry a slight injury risk to the remaining healthy testicle. Following such an injury, fertility may be adversely affected. But the chances of an injury to a descended testicle are rare, and the injury risk can be further substantially minimized with an athletic supporter and protective device.

Sports and the Young Athlete

by **Merritt B. Low**, *retired school physician.*

The young athlete, for the purposes of this discussion, is defined as the child thirteen years of age and younger. Disqualifying conditions can be permanent and absolute as well as temporary or partial, the child himself as well as the sport or game involved being of relevance. Boxing has no place in programs for children of this age because its goal is injury and because the educational benefits attributed by some to it can be realized through other sports.[1] It is convenient to divide sports into contact or collision-type, noncontact endurance type, and others.[2] By "others" I mean sports that are primarily recreational and noncompetitive. Endurance sports and "others" merge, of course, at times. Examples of the first of the three categories are football (including tackle and touch), ice hockey, basketball, baseball, softball, wrestling, lacrosse, and soccer;

Reprinted with permission of the author and publisher from *The Journal of School Health*, October 1969, *39*(8), pp. 514-522. Copyright, 1969, American School Health Association, Kent, Ohio 44440.

of the second category, cross country and track, tennis, rowing, canoeing, swimming, skiing, skating, bicycling, and squash; of the third category, golf, bowling, archery, hiking, climbing, horseback riding, field events. Collision sports at the preadolescent level should be undertaken by a school or community only when there is exemplary medical and educational supervision. Probably the incidence of serious injury or accident is no higher (and may indeed be lower) under these conditions than in situations where there is unsupervised free play. So far as I know there are no good statistics available on this point, and they would indeed be hard to come by. Subjective evaluations often enter and color the picture. Whereas "football" (or any sport) may be superficially and categorically indicted at times for an accident, accurate investigation may in truth reveal that the situation was one of the grossest kinds of unsupervised general "fooling around," with the football itself merely an innocent "prop" for mismatched horseplay.

Children of this age are not miniature adults or "little pros" and must not be treated as such, for sports benefits are not automatic. These boys and girls are in the process of rapid growth and maturation, physical, psychologic, and social—in their rapid approach toward adulthood. There are numerous special problems when we consider the overall picture of the young athlete and his possible opportunities and all the disqualification features. In the first place, it is extremely important to obtain an adequate, accurate, individualized health and sports history, in order to help the sport fit the child and the child the sport. This should be in association with a physical and psychological appraisal too, with periodic reviews of all these features. One of the biggest problems, of course, is mismatching, from incorrectly equating chronologic and physiologic age and ability. Other pitfalls are ill-fitting, hand-medown or imitation equipment, incomplete recovery and/or inadequate evaluation of apparently minor injuries, [and] cumulative physical or emotional fatigue.

The situation is often an ambivalent one, between persons who say, "any kid can and should play football to become a man" and others who state "all contact sports should be outlawed for children this age"—both unrealistic ends. The children themselves have ambivalent feelings and unmolded ideas too, polarized and tending often to be either complainers or

noncomplainers, unable or unwilling to be maturely self-evalu-
ating, and being very sensitive to the feelings if not the words
of the important adults around them.

In these areas of flexibility and motion and change we indeed have to develop a reasonable, realistic approach to disqualifying conditions. Permanent or temporary disqualification must be based on special physical and psychological con-
siderations, with a positive, knowledgeable, conservative
approach, avoiding maximizing or minimizing the problems.
Pain, swelling, and *disability* are still the three major symptoms and signs on which to base temporary disqualification
and no child should be allowed in sports if any of these are
present. In fact, symptomatic abnormalities at this age always
merit analysis from physical and psychological aspects. "No
Sports" should also be the rule in the presence of acute infection. The absence of fever for at least 48 hours following a
respiratory infection is often a good criterion for the resumption of ordinary sports and games—though the particular individual's past history, the sport involved, the weather, and the
residual signs and symptoms are factors which have to be individualized. Other acute infections require individual yard-
sticks—[e.g.] rheumatic fever and hepatitis (cessation of all
symptoms and signs of process-activity, including the evidence
of laboratory tests); mononucleosis (a month's time or more
after the acute process); boils and other staphylococcal infections (individualized, depending on clinical cure and potential
hazard to others). Size, growth, obvious immaturity, blood
dyscrasias [poison], diabetes, asthma require combined judgment in individual cases with the physician in the leading role
but able to picture the whole child as a developing person and
willing to stay flexible and commit himself beyond hidebound
easy conservatism.

Ultraconservatism is in fact an abdication of responsibility
on the physician's part. The physician has to be the final
arbiter, and nowhere in pediatrics does he have more responsibility and opportunity as the family advisor. Tables are available[2,3] to help, but the tables do not always fit the child, and vice
versa, in the overall consideration of the individual. The total
consideration is especially necessary in the doubtful situation.

The "paired organ" concept—no collision sports for the individual with absence or serious impairment of function of one of

a pair of body parts—has to be examined. The easiest thing to say is "No Collision Sports," yet I am not sure we have incontrovertible factual evidence here to back up this dictum universally, and we certainly need a data base which would include the accidents that happen outside the supervised play areas with children excluded from supervised sports. To play may be to risk accident, but not to play is not to be a child-person. Situations are more apt to be hazardous than individuals [are] accident prone. The child's past history [of] serious illnesses and accidents has to be considered; and more importantly in both diagnosis of the injury itself, and clearance to return to sports and games, an exact history of the individual accident in particular and how it happened, and illnesses likewise must be considered in the individual case.

I shall now take up individual conditions, organ systems, and special features of importance for this particular age group. First the central nervous system and sense organs [are discussed]. A child with a history of fractured skull requires individual consideration regarding qualification for contact sports. Epilepsy may be a cause for exclusion from certain sports and games. The signs and symptoms and relative control of seizures are extremely variable and specific guidelines hard to promulgate. Time of occurrence, type of seizures, severity and frequency of attacks, and adequacy of control measures (great advances in the past few decades) all affect the judgment involved, and the facts must be faced and not glossed over. It is true, however, that mental and physical activities tend to be seizure deterrent.[4] Hyperventilation (stressful less so than voluntary) on the other hand may precipitate attacks. The danger of exacerbation of pre-existing organic pathology should be a deterrent if such pathology is known to be present. There is little evidence that closed head injuries resulting from collision sports aggravate a pre-existing epileptic disorder, so by and large every effort should be made to minimize restrictions. General agreement would obviously exist about sports (gymnastics, certain kinds of swimming) where direct injury or death would likely follow a seizure of the moment. An experienced and informed adult or "buddy" should always be present and have knowledge about the individual epileptic child.

Acute cerebral concussion must be clearly defined, graded

and classified,[5] if we are to know what each of us is talking about. No child with even a mild concussion should return to a game until cleared by a physician. Those with moderate or severe concussions should not return at least for several days, and until cleared medically. A second concussion should be cause for barring for the sports season; three concussions should be cause for barring from the sport involved.

Absence or loss of function of one eye (amblyopia), and even severe myopia, should be causes for barring or steering away from collision sports unless extreme measures for protection are conscientiously and completely followed. (I can still remember the boy barred from hockey who injured his good eye fooling around unsupervised while the team was playing.) Certainly some positive approach must be outlined in the non-collision area for these active, often otherwise well-coordinated children. The same formula should be used for those with significant hearing impairment.

A word about teeth, nose, and facial injuries, which may assume additional significance for girls. The physician in consultation with the orthodontist must at times advise in regard to protection of the child's mouth and face during the period of intense orthodontia so often an important feature of this time of life. Usually such bracework is not incompatible with continuing sports (except for the time consumed) but sometimes special mouth guards must be added for protection of teeth damaged or under special treatment. In fact, the general use of face and teeth guards in football should be prescribed for youngsters, with other sports with special risks included. A very conservative approach too is indicated in the convalescent period following relatively minor nasal and facial contusions, lacerations, abrasions, [and] repeated epistaxes [nosebleed]. It is not important at this period of life to get back into the game at all costs.

Any structural weakness of head (previous operation) or spine should preclude most contact sports and any back symptoms of significant duration, even with no history of injury or only a vague one, should have a thorough medical investigation, including X-rays, to be certain about structural and developmental weaknesses causing or contributing to the problem. One word of caution regarding X-rays must be inserted. Sometimes we find "X-ray evidence" which does not quite jibe with the clinical situation or which is an incidental finding of doubtful significance. Correlation with the clinical findings and symptoms is a must. "Repeat" films may at times be helpful. Furthermore, just as disc patients should not do toe-touching, so should spondylolisthesis [spinal column deformity] patients be warned against back-arching, or be prevented from doing it by bracing. Thus a boy with spondylolisthesis may have more trouble serving a tennis ball than being a football lineman, and a "disc" patient do better in soccer than diving or basketball. Asymptomatic spondylolisthesis or osteochondritis [bone inflammation] or chondrosis [formation of cartilaginous tissue] found in the course of other examinations need not be of too much concern unless there is discomfort or sciatica.

The cardiorespiratory systems require specialized consideration in this age group. "Colds" and their complications plague child athletes. Antibiotics give the physician something to fall back on in case of bacterial complications, and perhaps permit a little less cautious approach than in the pre-antibiotic era. Criteria for resumption after temporary disqualification are: return of well-being and uninterrupted sleep patterns, normal temperature for two or three days, and the absence of signs and symptoms (especially coughing) associated with increased activity. Objective advice is necessary—some children want to go back to sports too soon, others "never." The child must be helped to pay neither too little nor too much attention to his health. Asthma and bronchitis are individual problems in each case. Certain sports can be psychotherapeutic in the asthma area, and there are no allergens on the ski slopes. The stresses of competition on the other hand must at times be toned down if there is significant pulmonary insufficiency.

The heart is an area in pediatrics constantly undergoing new liberal concepts, and the days of a murmur as a cause for physical inactivity are gone. It was, and still is, very easy to make a pronouncement, and that is that. Now we must sort out the problems and take a balanced view of the development of the child as a whole. We still lack good data bases for objective analyses and recommendations and the area is still a nondefinitive one characterized by widely divergent personal opinions, medical and other.

Some general observations can be made. Insignificant mur-

murs should be recognized, with consultation if necessary, and ignored. They are common in this age group ($\pm$ 33 percent) especially with activity and stress and anxiety. Fortunately, pre-adolescent children (and Mother Nature) tend to have built-in subconscious judgment in the area of functional capacity, which should be respected. This furthermore can fairly quickly, easily, and obviously be improved with fitness programs. Sinus tachycardia [excessive rapidity of the heart beat] especially before games is very common and not important. Sinus arrhythmia [irregularity of the heart beat] likewise is common and usually unimportant, as are premature beats (extrasystoles) especially in pre-stress situations where there is anxiety. Vasomotor instability and medically non-significant syncope (fainting) require little attention; hypotension is rarely seen (systolic pressure below 75 mm.) and is not important. At least 15 percent of boys of this age have transitory hypertension (systolic pressure above 135 mm. of mercury), though it is rare to find diastolic pressures above 85 mm. This hypertension, which may not be of a true type, tends to disappear, though as a matter of medical interest it would indeed be worthwhile to have some long-term adult follow-ups of the group. Always one must be on the watch for coarctation [narrowing] of the aorta or the rare pheochromocytoma [vascular tumor] or other systemic conditions. "Heart pain" is apt to be pre-exercise anticipatory, or of the stitch-in-the-side type, but post-exercise pain should be investigated. Cardiomegaly [enlargement of the heart] should always be a cause for concern, and usually limitation, and a thorough cardiac evaluation should be undertaken. Cardiac surgery is not necessarily a cause for permanent disqualification, each child being considered on the basis of his own status.

Conditions requiring special bewareness in children are congenital or acquired aortic stenosis [narrowing of the opening of the heart], isolated pulmonic stenosis [narrowing of the opening between the pulmonary artery and the right ventricle] to a lesser degree (because symptomatic shortness of breath tends to limit physical activity before there is great cardiac—right ventricular—strain), and aortic regurgitation and mitral stenosis [narrowing of the opening of the mitral valve]. Serious pulmonic stenosis usually is associated with electrocardiographic changes also, though this instrument is far from infallible with many conditions in children. The aortic lesions impose unacceptable and sometimes untolerated strains on the left ventricle, and of added concern is the fact that children with aortic stenosis do tend to be of the mesomorphic athletic type. These children should be disqualified from competitive sports. Shunt lesions (atrial and ventricular septal defects) need not as a rule be of great concern or cause for children's disqualification from regular sports, unless there is associated cardiac enlargement or electrocardiographic change. Cyanotic [lack of sufficient oxygen in the blood] heart disease usually carries with it its own self-imposed limitations. Radiologic cardiac enlargement with or without electrocardiographic changes should preclude collision and endurance type sports except on a non-competitive (time, self, or other persons) basis. Regular exercise is another matter—a cardiac patient even in childhood can be more physiologically fit through proper care, attention, and exercise than a non-cardiac who neglects these things. Further studies with the use of cardio-pulmonary functional indices may be helpful with children. In doubtful situations a cardiologist can be of great help, though the final decision rests on the personal physician and family. As mentioned heretofore, active rheumatic fever is cause for disqualification temporarily from all sports.

Inguinal hernia [hernia of the intestine in the groin area] is a cause for disqualification from sports categories one and two, until three weeks after surgical repair. The same goes for abdominal surgery. An enlarged liver, spleen, or kidney has to be studied, obviously, before sports clearance.

Orthopedically minded persons are on both sides of the fence in regard to children's sports, and some sit on top. Basic problems are inaccurate early diagnosis and ineffective treatment, with failure to recognize underlying pathology. X-rays should not be thought to be infallible; and clinical judgment, a good history of the mechanics involved, and special views or repeat films should be obtained when the physician's index of suspicion is high, as it should always be. Improved knowledge and techniques have characterized the past two decades. The bugbear of epiphyseal injuries [injuries to cartilage in area where bone growth takes place] is apparently not so great as has been supposed by some.[6] The real hazard is not the injury, but failure to recognize it and provide proper treatment. About 6 per cent of athletic injuries in nine to fifteen-year-olds are said to be epiphyseal.

Sleeplessness (a good question always to find out about in this age bracket), pain, tenderness, swelling, and disability cannot be dismissed lightly and should be cause for disqualification until thoroughly investigated. Incomplete recovery is another hazard, which can make for further injury or injury elsewhere. In addition, there are of course congenital or acquired anatomic and/or physiologic inadequacies of the musculoskeletal system which should obviously be associated with disqualification for certain individuals in individual sports. The lanky, long-necked, loose-jointed child presents specific hazards in collision sports and the heavy, poorly coordinated [does] also.

One must be wary of all hip and upper leg limps and complaints in the adolescent, for fear of not diagnosing an early slipping femoral epiphysis, which requires immediate withdrawal from sports and instant treatment. In this connection it should never be forgotten that radiating knee pain is a classical symptom of slipping femoral epiphysis. One should always X-ray the right place! Groin pain can be confusing too, but the hip limp is often characteristic though slight. In younger children (under 9 years) similar signs or symptoms may indicate Legg-Perthe osteochondrosis [a disease in children of the growth center at the head of the femur] or coxa plana [inflammation of the capitular epiphysis]. Epiphysitis of the elbow and heel (apophysitis) and other areas should limit sports. Aponyms and acronyms are available for those interested. Cysts, tumors, and osteochondritis dissecans [inflammation from the splitting of pieces of cartilage into the joint] require disqualification from sports if not exercise.

A good history will often pick up a dislocating patella (more common with knock-knees, more common in girls) which requires protection, prevention of recurrence in so far as possible, disqualification from sports conducive to its re-occurrence, and disqualification during orthopedic or surgical treatment. In doubtful or mild dislocations of the patella an elastic pull-on type of knee brace with a "doughnut" hole for the kneecap and a high build-up of sponge rubber laterally may "hold" this situation for ordinary physical activities. Osgood-Schlätter [inflammation of the protuberance of the tibia] condition or tibial tubercle epiphysitis is a common problem, of varying severity and unpleasant duration, and one where there are varying opinions on disqualification. I have seen over 150 of these cases in the past 25 years and have yet to see permanent disability. Often these children are physiologically precocious and sports minded. Rest at times of exacerbation of pain and tenderness, and protection for collision sports have been my only rules, and the boy himself has been given a voice in the planning for the months of intermittent attention required. A basketball knee-pad seems to offer more bump protection than an Ace bandage. With other conditions (osteochondritis dissecans) the patient should have no voice. Knee injuries must always be diagnosed early and accurately, must always mean disqualification until complete anatomic and physiologic recovery (or stability) is present, and return to sports should also be delayed until the quadriceps muscle on the affected side is up to or greater than the normal one. Children are always willing to participate in such visible rehabilitation, but will usually neglect it if not supervised. Fractures and sprains should be completely treated, with no rush to return to sports permitted. After a week or ten days of disqualification, an ankle sprained should have extra protection (taping) for the rest of the season. During periods of enforced restriction due to injuries, some positive approach to exercise, conditioning, and time consumption should be associated with the temporary disqualification. Partial disqualification is hard to effect and enforce.

Genitourinary conditions deserve special attention. Active renal disease until the condition is quiescent, or hematuria following injury till the urine is free of blood and a normal intravenous pyelogram [an X-ray of the kidney and ureter] has been obtained, mean disqualification from all sports. So-called postural albuminuria [presence of albumin in the urine] must be distinguished from true renal disease, is common enough especially after increased activity, and is not a condition requiring restrictions. Absence of one kidney or serious disease or anomaly of a kidney should be a cause for disbarring from collision sports (and sledding, competitive skiing, and similar pursuits). The questions of the lone testis and the undescended testis remain controversial; here is an area where authorities disagree. Without doubt, the testis overlying the pubic ramus is in some jeopardy, the testis in the scrotum much less so. In thirty years experience with over 4,000 pre-adolescent boys in a boys' boarding school, the only testicular injuries I have seen have never been associated with supervised collision sports. Proper equipment and supporters are mandatory, however, and if any steering is feasible it is probably best to help direct the athlete with only one normal testis into non-collision sports. Left-sided varicoceles [varicose enlargement of the veins in the scrotum area] are fairly common in this age group and need no special attention. As far as the pediatrician is concerned it behooves him to look earnestly for associated urinary tract anomalies where there are other congenital anomalies (ears, heart especially); also in association with lower tract anomalies. Possibly disqualifying conditions, even conditions of general life import, may be revealed from such studies.

Endocrine, chronic and metabolic disorders require special individualized appraisals, but team participation for the diabetic or other handicapped child should not be barred (or unduly encouraged) on the basis of the condition per se. Objective consideration and advice, depending on the whole situation and the child as a maturing person should have thoughtful attention and decision-making.

The problems regarding girls' participation in sports in this age group revolve around preconceived non-medical social attitudes and myths and the medical truth that in fact a pre-adolescent girl (by school grade and age) can be an adolescent one physiologically speaking. Variations in maturity are well known. Yet there is ample evidence that girls in endurance sports such as competitive swimming can approach their peaks at 12–13 years of age. Girls for a variety of reasons have less accidents and causes for disqualification, as long as we accept the fact that menstruation is a condition rather than a disease, and that whereas it may or may not affect performance it should not affect qualification.

Matching for competition is difficult, with regard to size, weight, and age. The developmental level of physical maturation is the best criterion. There appear to be emotional as well as potential physical stresses during the pre-menarchal growth spurt of girls and these have to be taken into account in the area of cumulative fatigue as a cause for temporary disqualification. Problems of early menstrual irregularity (normal) and excessive bleeding may become factors for consideration in individual cases, though there can be beneficial psychophysiologic effects on dysmenorrhea in healthy sports attitudes and situations. Participation in most sports need not be curtailed during menstruation.

Most agree that sports for girls are beneficial both physically and psychologically, with some reservations (usually emotional) on social advantages. For what sports then are girls qualified? For those under 9–10 years the same concepts apply as for boys, with perhaps the reservation that it is best in the long run to encourage the life-time, endurance type of activity. Physical causes for disqualification are similar to those for boys. After menarche collision sports (except softball, soccer, field hockey, basketball) are generally not pushed; and the same disqualification rules apply for non-collision sports as for boys.

Lastly, there are so many cooks in the soup of children's athletics that even in this area of qualification for sports the areas of responsibility have to be well delineated, lest the child become lost betwixt the adults, with the evils of fragmentation and divided-irresponsibility taking over. The people involved are the athlete himself, the physician, the parent, the coach, the school, and at times a sponsor. Furthermore, in this age period of strong peer loyalties the captain or team mate must exert as positive a responsibility as he can in relation to truthful evaluation of the other fellow's injury or attempted "cover-up." Legal threats must not result in buck-passing and abdication of responsibility. Sympathetic courts, mushrooming of insurance programs, the increasing role of government in medicine, definitions of the school's, the doctor's, and the parents' responsibilities all can present paralysis producing milieus or situations giving rise to imprudent headlong impatience. A good program of sports for children and a sound science and philosophy of qualification and disqualification involve good communication and cooperation between these various individuals and groups. The doctor must have the prime authority because he has the prime responsibility; the parent next. There are no magic tables or formulas for decisions. To live and grow is to move and play.

References

1. *Competitive athletics for children of elementary school age, joint statement.* Chicago: American Academy of Pediatrics, Committee on the Medical Aspects of Sports (American Medical Association), American Association for Health, Physical Education and Recreation, and the Society of State Directors of Health, Physical Education and Recreation, 1968.
2. *A guide for medical evaluation of candidates for school sports.* Chicago: American Medical Association, 1968.
3. Rocky Mountain Pediatric Society (Ed.). *Disqualifying conditions for contact and non-contact sports.* Denver, 1966.
4. Committee on Children with Handicaps (Ed.). *The epileptic child and competitive school athletics.* Chicago: American Academy of Pediatrics, 1968.
5. Subcommittee on Classification of Sports Injuries (Ed.). *Standard nomenclature of athletic injuries.* Chicago: American Medical Association, 1966.
6. Larson, R. L., & McMahan, R. O. The epiphyses and the childhood athlete. *The Journal of the American Medical Association*, 1966, *196*, 607-612.

Comments

Sport Injury Data

We have only limited evidence regarding the incidence and severity of injury in collision, contact, and noncontact sports. But from the more reliable information available, I believe the frequency of serious injury in collision and contact sports is often greatly exaggerated. By serious injury I mean broken bones, dislocations, cuts requiring sutures, or other injuries incapacitating players for more than a day or two.

Creighton Hale's[1] study of injuries in Little League baseball is one of the few comprehensive surveys which has been conducted. Hale found that only 2% of 771,810 boys sustained injuries sufficiently severe to necessitate medical attention. The distribution of types of injury for the 15,444 injuries reported were as follows:

41% contusions (bruises)	5% dental
19% fractures (mostly fingers)	3% abrasions
18% sprains	2% concussions
10% lacerations	2% miscellaneous

When it is considered that these children were exposed to approximately 148 million pitched balls, plus the many other potential sources of injury in baseball, the number of severe injuries was remarkably low.

Godshall[2] compiled an injury report for 1,700 boys in a Pop Warner league in Souderton, Pennsylvania over a period of 12 years. Although there were a number of minor injuries (bumps and bruises), there were only two major injuries, both leg fractures. Several experts estimate that 90% of all injuries in children's sports are minor, consisting mostly of bruises and muscle pulls.

Both Hale and Godshall, as well as several other research- ers, report that as children grow older *both* the frequency and severity of injuries increase. Prepubescent children are much less likely to be injured than postpubescent youngsters, with boys between 15 and 18 years of age sustaining the highest injury rate. For example, Larson and McMahan[3] reported that of 1,338 sports injuries reported to 4 orthopedists in Eugene, Oregon, only 20% involved children 14 and younger, whereas 40% occurred in the 15 to 18 age group, and the other 40% were for adults 18 and older.

Two factors appear to cause the rising injury rate with in- creasing age. First, older children have greater body mass and speed which result in the generation of greater force (whether it be in the form of two youngsters colliding or one throwing or striking an object toward another). The second factor is an associated increase in the intensity of play as skill improves with age.

A much publicized injury in children's sports is "little league elbow," so named because its etiology often is pitching in little league baseball. Medically termed epiphyseal damage, little league elbow refers to injury of the growth centers of the bones or the epiphyses.

The anatomy of a growing bone consists of a central shaft called the diaphysis and two end portions called the epiphyses. Each epiphysis is separated from the diaphysis by cartilage, and this area of separation is the main zone of bone growth. When this zone ossifies, growth is no longer possible.

Epiphyseal damage may occur not just to the bones forming the elbow, but to any bone which is placed under constant physical stress. This physical stress (which some medical re- searchers believe causes the epiphyses to ossify prematurely) is known to result from tremendous impact on the epiphyses due to the violent action of repeatedly throwing or striking objects in certain sports.

Although critics would have us believe that nearly every youngster who pitches in organized baseball will be disabled for life with little league elbow, the frequency and severity of this injury constitute a highly controversial topic among sports medicine researchers. For example, Adams[4] reported that 76 of 80 9- to 12-year-old baseball pitchers had some degree of epiphyseal injury, but only 7 of 47 nonpitchers had similar injuries. These results led Adams to conclude that little league pitchers should be limited to two innings of pitching per game and that curve balls should be prohibited until the age of 14. But Larson and McMahan[3] reported that for boys under the age of 15, only 1.7% of all injuries reported were epiphyseal. They concluded that most of these injuries could be corrected with prompt attention resulting in little chance of permanent damage.

Two extensive studies of little league elbow among 9- to 12-year-old boys were conducted in 1974—one in Eugene, Oregon, and the other in Houston, Texas. The Houston study[5] found that 17% of 595 pitchers had a history of elbow symptoms, but only 1% had symptoms which kept them from pitching at some time. The Eugene study found that 33% of 120 pitchers had some degree of epiphyseal damage although in the majority of cases this damage was slight.

Certainly the research is not decisive, but while awaiting more definitive evidence, several tentative conclusions may be made. First, although epiphyseal injuries occur less frequently than some have claimed, there is no doubt that they do occur at least in a small percentage of boys who pitch regularly. Second, it appears that symptoms do not always arise during the little league playing years; instead they sometimes do not require medical attention for the first time until the child is 13 or 14 years of age. Thus, perhaps the low reported incidence of epiphyseal injury for youngsters 12 and under represents underestimates of an injury that is not detected for several years. In some cases pitchers admit having pain when in little league, but hesitate to mention it for fear of not being allowed to play. A third conclusion is that limitations on the frequency of pitching and the elimination of curve balls until bone ossification is complete are recommendations well worth heeding, even if they only reduce the incidence of epiphyseal injuries from 2% to 1%.

One of the questions which critics of youth sports have often raised concerns the long-term physical effects of intense competition on children. Some claim that damage to the epiphyses and to the knee, elbow, and shoulder joints is one of the causes of arthritis. Others say that the extreme pressure on vertebrae and back muscles is a major cause for back problems in the advancing years. Others have suggested that the enlargement of the heart through intensive training makes an athlete who has quit training more susceptible to heart problems. Examination of all the evidence presently available indicates that these claims are entirely unsubstantiated. In fact, what limited research has been completed on the long-term effects of intensive training on humans suggests that the effects are positive rather than negative.

One other question which has been raised is whether or not intensive sport training influences the growth of a young athlete. Two studies[7,8] found that high school wrestlers did not grow as much as the average high school boy. They suggested that the reported 2 cm less growth in height was a result of either the strenuous activity or the reduction in normal caloric intake characteristic of wrestlers. After reviewing the evidence on this question, it was concluded by those involved in the State of Michigan Joint Legislative Study on Youth Sports Programs that

> Physical training beginning as early as 10 years of age for girls and boys may enhance static dimensions and function capacities. However, it should be pointed out that occasional negative results have been reported from high-stress programs. Cardiovascular function has been enhanced consistently. Mild to moderate physical training during childhood has not been found to produce detrimental structural or functional effects during adulthood.[9]

Boxing

Before considering how to make sports safer, a comment is needed about the "sport" of boxing. It should be banned, forbidden, and eliminated forever as a sport for children. Hats off to our elders who eliminated boxing from the public schools and as an intercollegiate sport in the 1950's. They did so for good reason: it is the *only* sport where a major objective is to inflict harm on the opponent. No other sport awards victory to the contestant or team who *intentionally* injures the opponent.

I am unsympathetic to the argument that boxing as prescribed by Olympic rules eliminates the intent to harm. Baloney! If that were true, why not penalize the boxer who knocks out an opponent and award victory to the athlete who most often lightly taps his opponent in the head and stomach without being lightly tapped himself? Or better yet, why not tap the opponent only in the shoulders and stomach and eliminate hitting the head? Certainly amateur boxing contains a great deal of skill and is exciting to watch; but in spite of the current emphasis on the skill and the supposed de-emphasis on the big punch, the knockout is still a major goal and a certain means of victory.

Boxing is not a sport for children, nor is it a sport for adults. The recent growth of boxing after a sharp decline in the 1960's is disturbing. Golden Gloves, the major amateur boxing organization for youth under 16, has 40,000 members today, having doubled its membership since 1972. And an estimated 250,000 youngsters are boxing in local clubs not affiliated with Golden Gloves.

Much of boxing's recent rejuvenation can be attributed to television—its extensive coverage of boxing at the Olympic Games and recent efforts to promote amateur and professional boxing in the Unites States. Although generally I am not critical of the television industry, and I enjoy most of the sports shown, I am opposed to its promotion of boxing. Thus, I was delighted to hear Howard Cosell report that the recent series of fights shown on television, with the exception of the magnetic Muhammad Ali, obtained low viewer ratings.

Professional organizations such as the American Medical Association, the American Academy of Pediatrics, and the American Alliance for Health, Physical Education, and Recreation have unanimously opposed boxing for children. They do so with justification. The potential for serious injury, particularly to the brain, is greater than in any other sport. Parents are neglecting their responsibility to protect their offspring when they permit them to participate in boxing. Any benefit that boxing can offer is equally available in numerous sports which are much safer. Enough said!

Reducing the Risk

These professional organizations have also made useful recommendations intended to reduce the injury risk among youngsters competing in all sports. They include:

1. *Proper physical conditioning in preparation for competition as well as adequate warm-up immediately before competing.*

2. *Good protective equipment that is correctly fitted and facilities that are well maintained.*

3. *Modification of rules, game equipment, and facilities to suit the maturity level of the participants.*

For example, midget football has eliminated the kick-off, because this aspect of the game resulted in numerous injuries. Steel spikes have been eliminated and batting helmets required in little league baseball, both contributing to the reduction of injury. The hard shell football helmet and face mask have reduced certain types of injuries, but unfortunately appear to be the cause of others. Current research is attempting to develop a helmet that provides the same protection against impact, but has a soft outer shell so that it does not injure those who are hit with it. Shorter spikes have reduced knee injuries to a limited extent, and ensolite mats have increased the resiliency of wrestling surfaces so that they are much safer. Synthetic equipment of all types—poles, pads, pits, floor surfaces, eye glasses, etc.—have all helped make sports safer.

4. *Better maturation matching.*

5. *Available medical care.*

A child should be examined by a physician at least once a year. The doctor should thoroughly examine the child's health history and evaluate his or her capability to participate in accordance with the American Medical Association's guidelines for disqualifying conditions.

Many recommendations state that a physician should be present or readily available at practices and games. If "readily available" means the nearest hospital, I concur. If it means that a physician needs to be present at every practice and game, I do not. It simply is not feasible. Just to be present at games, it is estimated that the 350,000 practicing physicians in this country would have to leave hospitals and medical offices to spend 8 hours every week of the year on the sidelines of athletic fields and gymnasiums. Although it would be a good precaution to have doctors on the sidelines, I think we would all prefer doctors to spend those 8 hours per week attending to those who are sick or injured.

6. *Competent coaching.*

Undoubtedly the most effective preventive measure is the presence of a competent coach. Ultimately it is the coach who must ensure that the above criteria are met and that youngsters do not engage in activities that are overly hazardous. It is the coach who must make certain that kids are not only physically prepared to compete, but have sufficient skill to safely control their bodies in collision and contact sports. It is the coach who must know the hazards of spear tackling and the danger of heat prostration when youngsters are deprived of water on hot, humid days. It is when incompetent coaching results in needless injury that the critics' cries of outrage are justified.

But coaches are not the only adults responsible for the safety of young athletes. Officials play an important role in making certain that competitors play safely. Parents, too, must assume responsibility for their children's well-being—not pushing when their children are injured, communicating openly with the coach, and informing he or she when their children are injured or ill.

A dangerous over-reaction to the potential risk of sports injuries is to place children in a protective cocoon. Over-protective parents who do not permit their children to experience the common activities of childhood, who constantly guard them from the physical and social maladies of our society, are failing to vaccinate their children against the perils of adulthood. Thus they expose them to psychological risks of adjustment equalling or exceeding the physical dangers of sports.

As inevitable as stepping in bubble gum at a ball game, kids will get hurt when they play. Whether it be sandlot or organized sports, when children scurry about—running, jumping, falling, colliding—injuries will occur. It is an immutable fact of life. But we can make sports safer for our children; we can eliminate unnecessary risk while obtaining the full benefits of sport participation. That must be our goal.

References

1. Hale, C. J. Injuries among 771,810 Little League baseball players. *Journal of Sports Medicine and Physical Fitness*, 1961, *1*, 80-83.
2. Godshall, R. W. Junior League football. *Journal of Sports Medicine*, 1975, *3*, 139-144.

3. Larson, R. L., & McMahan, R. D. The epiphyses and the childhood athlete. *The Journal of the American Medical Association,* 1966, *196,* 607-612.
4. Adams, J. E. Injury to the throwing arm: A study of traumatic changes in the elbow joints of boy baseball players. *California Medicine,* 1965, *102,* 127-132.
5. Gugenheim, J. J., Jr., Stanley, R. F., Woods, G. W., & Tullos, H. S. Little League survey: The Houston study. *The American Journal of Sports Medicine,* 1976, *4,* 189-200.
6. Larson, R. L., Singer, K. M., Bergstrom, R., & Thomas, S. Little League survey: The Eugene study. *The American Journal of Sports Medicine,* 1976, *4,* 201-209.
7. Clarke, K. C. Predicting certified weight of young wrestlers: A field study of the Tcheng-Tipton method. *Medicine and Science in Sports,* 1974, *6,* 52-57.
8. Tipton, C. M., & Tcheng, T-K. Iowa wrestling study. *Journal of the American Medical Association,* 1970, *214,* 1269-1274.
9. *Joint legislative study on youth sports: Agency sponsored sports - Phase I.* State of Michigan, November 1976, p. 22.

SECTION F

If Only My Knees Wouldn't Shake!

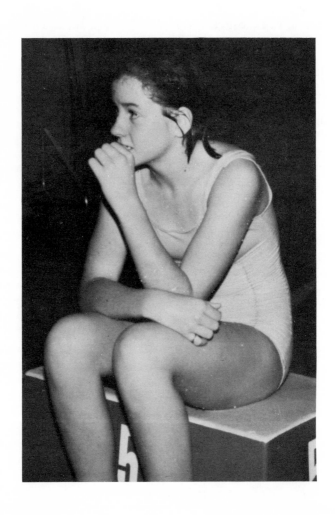

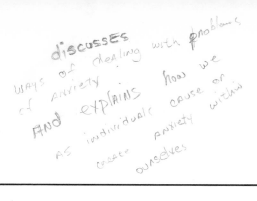

discusses ways of dealing with problems of anxiety and explains how we as individuals cause or create anxiety within ourselves

"I'd get so nervous before a big game that I wouldn't be able to play until I vomited," recalled a college football star about his former playing days in midget league. Other athletes have said that as youngsters they became so figety and irritable the day before a big event that they could not get along with their family or friends. A hockey coach told of a young lad who became so nervous when he was sent into the game for the first time that he lost control of his bladder. Some critics claim that the stress in kids' sports is comparable to the stress experienced by soldiers in combat. Others have likened it to the stress associated with surgery, dental repair, or giving a speech.

Rather than sports contributing to the emotional health of the nation's young, could it be that they are actually contributing to the rising incidence of mental illness? Critics have been quick to say yes. They cite horror stories of youngsters being emotionally scarred and burned out by coaches who place too much pressure on them to perform like adults. But how many youngsters are really emotionally damaged or burned out by the stress of sport? Does this happen in all sports, or is it limited to certain sports or to certain conditions within sports? What types of children are prone to high anxiety states in sport, and what can we do to help these youngsters?

There are many psychological topics that are pertinent to children's sports, but none is more prominent than the continuing debate about whether or not sports are too stressful for youngsters. In this section we will look at how stressful sports are for children, the causes of stress, and how stress may be controlled or reduced.

In *Thoughts of a Star* by Marty Novak, we get a glimpse of a young boy's feelings in a pressure-packed baseball game. Bill

Meyer and Dan Zadra follow with some useful advice on *How to Beat the Jitters* when participating in sports. In the concluding comments we look at what sport psychologists have learned about the causes of stress in sports and whether the stress is too great.

Thoughts of a Star

by **Marty Novak,** *freelance writer and children's novelist.*

Wow! This is the most important Little League game I've ever played. If we can win, we'll go to the state tournament.

Golly, I'm batting third today rather than sixth. Coach said he moved me up because I've been hitting pretty good lately. He'll expect me to hit today.

Oops! Got to get my bat and helmet. I'm on deck.

Oh boy, is my heart ever thumping. Why do I get so nervous? Sure hope I get a hit.

"Come on, John. Get a hit."

If John gets on and I can knock him in . . . sure would be nice to get a lead early.

That kid on the mound looks really tough. Wow, he's fast. I sure hope he isn't wild.

I wish I'd gone to the bathroom before the game. I wonder if baseball players ever call time out so they can go?

Crack!

Reprinted with permission of the author.

"Way to go, John."

John got a single. Now I've got to come through. The coach expects it of me.

Yes, I hear you yelling, Mr. Krebiehl. I'll watch the ball. I won't swing at any bad pitches. And I'll try not to hit into a double play—thanks alot!

"Strike one!" yells the umpire.

Oh darn, I wasn't ready. I was listening to old Krebiehl. Better step out and get myself together like they do in the major leagues.

I've got "cotton mouth" so bad my tongue is stuck to the roof of my mouth. Oh, no. The ump and the catcher are laughing at me. I tried to spit, but just slobbered on my chin. I bet they couldn't spit with cotton mouth either.

O.K. pitch, now I'm ready. Throw me one right down the middle—and not too fast, please!

It looks low, better not swing.

"B-a-a-l-l one!" says the ump.

Now throw me a good one. Here it comes.

Crack!

Oh, that felt good.

Nuts! A line drive right to the third baseman. The lucky bum.

Well, this is it. Bottom of the sixth. We're behind 2 to 1. If we don't score at least one run this inning we won't go to State.

Let's see, I'm the fifth batter this inning.

I better go to the bathroom—just can't wait anymore.

Hurry, you don't want to miss the action.

Um-m-m, I thought I needed to go. Oh, well. Whoops, my zipper is stuck. Oh, no. Come on, hurry! Get it fixed. Oh, nuts! No more time.

"Hey Mom, my zipper is stuck. Have you got a pin?"

"Oh good, but hurry."

"Thanks, Mom!"

Splash.

Oh, you jerk, you stepped right in the mudhole by the water fountain. Now you have one white shoe and one black one.

Wow, look! Gerry and Mike are on first and second and John is up to bat. There's only one out. I'm on deck.

"Where's my bat? Who's got my bat? Give me that!"

The dumb batboy is sitting over there playing with my bat.

"Come on, John. Get a hit."

Boy, have I got the butterflies.

I think I'll kneel down. No, I better take some practice swings. Maybe I'll swing two bats. No, one is better.

Oh, there's the pitch to hit, John.

"Oh, no!"

John hit the ball to the pitcher. It'll be a double play; we'll lose the game. But look, the pitcher's not going for a double play. He threw it to first. John's out—that's two outs—but Gerry and Mike are now on second and third.

Oh, boy! Now it's all up to me. If I get a hit, we go to State. If I make an out, the season is over.

O.K., here goes. Boy, my knees are shaking. I hope it doesn't show.

Here comes the pitch.

It's bad—don't swing.

"Ball one, outside," says the umpire.

Oh, now what does Mr. Krebiehl want? He wants to talk to me.

"Yes, coach, I know Doug is the next batter and the best hitter on the team."

"O.K., coach, I'll look for a walk."

Boy, has he got confidence in me!

Look at Mom and Dad. They look as nervous as I feel. My heart must be going a mile a minute. Even swallowing is hard.

O.K., here comes the next pitch.

"Strike one!"

Boy, it was a good pitch. I should've swung. But maybe I'll get a walk.

Here comes the next pitch. It looks outside.

"Strike two!"

Nuts! I didn't think that was a strike. Now I'm in the hole.

O.K., no looking for walks now. Step out a second and get ready. You don't want to lose this game. Everybody is counting on you. The umpire says let's go, so let's go.

Here it comes. It looks high . . . I think.

Whew, ball two, said the umpire.

Two and two is the count. My hands are so sweaty I can hardly hold the bat.

"Time out. I need the rosin."

O.K., my hands are dry. That helps. I think I'll spit. No, I don't think I will!

Here comes the ball. It looks good.

Thunk!

Foul ball. Geepers, that was the one to hit.

O.K., I'm ready. Now the pitcher is pawing around the rubber. Come on, throw it in here.

He's ready now. Here it comes. It's right down the pipe.

Crack!

It's a fly ball to left field.

Oh no, the left field is going to catch it. No, he can't reach it. WE WIN!

———————

"That was a great hit, son."

"Thanks, Dad."

"You must have been really nervous that last time at bat?"

"Oh, a little. But I knew I could do it."

How To Beat the Jitters

by **Bill Meyer,** *sportswriter for* Young Athlete *and* **Dan Zadra,** *also a sportswriter and editor of* Young Athlete.

The bases are loaded. It's two outs in the bottom of the ninth, and the whole team is watching as you step into the batter's box. There's a powerful pitcher out on the mound, and he's really sizing you up.

Suddenly, your knees get wobbly, your heart starts pounding, and there's a funny feeling in the pit of your stomach. It's the jitters!

Every athlete in the world knows about the jitters. It's that terrible, nervous feeling that always seems to come just at the moment of our greatest opportunity.

In basketball, it might be just when we're about to shoot that winning free throw. In golf, it's that five-foot pressure putt. In football, it's running that go-for-broke fourth-down play, or preparing to kick that important field goal.

Have you ever had an experience like this one: you study all week long for an important English exam, but when you finally

Reprinted with permission from *Young Athlete*, September 1975, pp. 42-43.

sit down in class to take the test, you can't seem to remember any of the answers? When the test is over, you walk out of the room shaking your head in bewilderment, and then BINGO! Suddenly, you can remember every answer, clear as a bell.

The same thing often happens in sports. We never seem to have trouble remembering our plays or moves, either before or after the competition. But *during* the competition, that's when the jitters try to take over.

The bad thing about the jitters is that they often make it difficult for us to do our best. A nervous boxer loses strength and coordination. A nervous diver is often too stiff to leave the board properly. And a nervous quarterback will often throw a simple pass into the dirt.

The *good* thing about the jitters is that they're actually very easy to overcome. Here are three simple tips that great athletes use to keep "cool as a cucumber" under pressure:

Tip #1—How To Stop Worrying

One of the biggest causes of the jitters is worry. Worry is nothing more than thinking about what we *don't* want to happen. Sometimes we spend so much time thinking about how we might lose, that we forget to think about how we might win. Instead of thinking about how well we're going to do, we spend all our practice time thinking up imaginary disasters for ourselves.

For example, two weeks before a big event we say to ourselves: "What if I blow it? What if I slip and fall? What if I get sick? What if we lose? What if I forget the answers? What will everybody say?"

By the time the big day rolls around, we've got ourselves so worried that we can't even imagine ourselves doing well. The result is called "the jitters."

How do you stop worrying? It's actually very simple. Every time you catch yourself thinking about imaginary disasters, just stop and turn your thoughts around. Take a moment and think about how good and wonderful it's going to be to succeed. Don't waste your time imagining that you're going to strike out; instead, think about how good it might feel to hit a home run.

Remember, we can only concentrate on one thing at a time. If we concentrate on what we want (and forget about what we don't want), we'll be much more relaxed and effective when the day of competition actually arrives.

(P.S. When you're about to shoot that important free throw, don't stand at the line and worry about missing. Before you shoot, take a deep breath of air and imagine the ball leaving your hands in a perfect path to the basket. After you've seen a beautiful "swish" in your mind, *then* shoot the actual shot. It works!)

Tip #2—How To Prepare For New Situations

Whenever we attempt to do anything for the first time, we tend to be nervous, awkward or uncertain.

Playing against a new team on a foreign field or court; facing that visiting wrestling opponent for the first time; playing our first varsity game under the lights; or moving from local competition into the state finals. In these and similar situations many athletes find themselves tight and jittery. And by the time we relax and loosen up, the game may already be over.

Again, the solution can be simple. Many athletes find that they can turn new, scary situations into familiar, friendly situations simply by using good mental preparation.

For example, Dick Hannula, a Wilson High School senior from Tacoma, Washington, recently shattered two swimming records held by Mark Spitz and Mike Bruner. Asked if he was nervous during the races, Hannula replied, "No, because I had swum those races a thousand times in my mind before I ever swam them in the pool. All I had to do was remember how I won in my mind, then do it in the pool."

Last year, 13-year-old Brad Shuman of Seattle, Washington captured first place in the J-Stock Speedboat competition in Dayton, Ohio. Later the same day, his younger brother, Scot, did the same thing in the J-Stock Hydro class. Both boys were very relaxed and confident, even though this was their first national competition. The secret, said Brad, was this:

"Before the race, we ran every turn on the course over and over in our minds. We imagined ourselves pulling ahead, and always crossing the finish line first. That made the real race a lot easier."

Fifteen-year-old Russian gymnast Olga Korbut won the hearts of millions of people with her poised and graceful performance at the Olympic Games. How did Olga stay so relaxed? She told reporters that she had been studying pictures of the crowded pavilion for months, and imagining herself performing with complete confidence in front of thousands of people.

Olga did the same thing that many football coaches have been doing for years: she gave herself a scouting report. A good football coach will show his team movies of the opponent. He will help his players anticipate the strategy, the playing field, the uniform colors, and locker rooms ... even the expected size of the crowd. That way, there are very few surprises on game day.

Professional football player Rick Redman says that game day is the easiest day of the week. "After all," he says, "by game day I'm just repeating a game that I've already played (and won) several times in my imagination. Each time I win in my mind, I get less and less nervous, and more and more anxious to play."

Try it yourself. Gather as much detailed information as you can about your opponent and the expected playing conditions. Then you can repeatedly imagine yourself playing and winning the competition in vivid detail. By game day, you'll have nothing on your mind but an instant replay of an old, familiar situation.

Tip #3—How To Handle Mistakes

Fear of making a mistake is another big cause of the jitters. How many times do we step into the batter's box hoping and praying for a walk? Sure, taking a swing at the ball could mean that we'll strike out; but it could also mean that we'll hit a home run.

Everyone knows that Babe Ruth held the world record for most home runs in a single season. But few people remember that he held the world strike out record at the same time!

Babe Ruth was a great athlete who gave himself the right to make mistakes. The Babe used to say that, "Every time I miss the ball, I get excited. It means that I'm just one swing closer to my next home run."

Thomas Edison made more than 3,000 "mistakes" on his way to inventing the electric light bulb. Edison looked at his mistakes the same way a great athlete looks at an error. He never got discouraged, and with each mistake he learned an important lesson that took him closer and closer to eventual success. When we turn on an electric light today, we remember Thomas Edison not for his 3,000 mistakes, but for his final, perfect win.

Every athlete strives for improvement. But we can only improve if we allow ourselves the right to make new mistakes. These mistakes give us the information we need to get better. The "wrong way" often tells us more about the "right way."

An athlete should never be afraid of looking foolish. Many people laughed at Roger Bannister's strange running style; but the laughter stopped when Bannister became the first person to run a mile in less than four minutes. No athlete looks foolish if he or she is truly giving a 100 percent effort. And no matter what the final outcome, the crowd always loves and appreciates the athlete who gives it a try.

Remember: Our mistakes are really beautiful pieces of information. Let yourself relax and make a few. Learn from every one, and then forget them.

The next thing you know, the terrible jitters will be gone.

Comments

Causes of Competitive Anxiety

There are many specific causes of anxiety in sports, but after investigating these causes for some time I believe they reduce to two general factors that work together to produce high levels of competitive anxiety. These two factors are the *uncertainty* children have about the outcomes of competing and the *importance* they attach to these outcomes. The more uncertain children are that they will be able to meet the demands of the competitive situation in order to obtain a favorable outcome, and the more important these outcomes are, the greater the anxiety will be.

There are many sources of uncertainty in sports for children, and some coaches appear to be more skilled at making kids feel uncertain than they are in teaching the techniques of the sport. For example, coaches keep children uncertain about whether or not they will make the team or the starting lineup. They keep them uncertain as to whether they will get to play in the game. Some coaches constantly remind their players about the uncertainty of winning and especially make them feel uncertain about their own individual capabilities. The coach, along with parents and teammates, may also make children feel quite uncertain about their social status or importance on the team. Adults often create these feelings of uncertainty—not with the intention of making children anxious, but with the intention of motivating them.

Many factors also make the outcome of sports more or less important to children. Sports provide a means by which children can evaluate themselves by comparing their abilities with those of their peers. Obtaining a favorable evaluation is important not only to children's self-concept, but also to their standing with peers. They know that success in sports is rewarded with social status and social mobility.

The presence of adults, especially those whose evaluation children value, also increases the importance of sports. Children seek the praise of adults, and they dread their displeasure. Indeed, unfavorable evaluation may not only mean disesteem, it may mean losing the opportunity to play.

Sports can be made more important in other ways. The game can be given publicity through the media—letting all know how a young child has played. Pagentry can be added, such as homecoming queens, cheerleaders, and award banquets. And, of course, children can be offered trophies, ribbons, medals, and trips to far away places for victory and other accomplishments. These are but some of the ways both uncertainty and importance of outcomes may be increased, thereby intensifying the anxiety in children's sports.

Some adults seem particularly callous to the factors that increase uncertainty and importance. Consequently they are insensitive to the emotional states of young athletes. For example, regardless of whether youngsters appear to be anxious or not, some coaches feel impelled to motivate the team with the traditional pregame pep talk. This pep talk typically will remind youngsters that the game is one of the most important they will ever play, that their opponent is very good, and that the outcome of the game is dependent upon their very best effort. For the already anxious youngster, this pep talk is as helpful as bloodletting for curing pneumonia.

Sensitive coaches, on the other hand, are aware of the many factors which increase or decrease uncertainty and importance, and they find ways to diminish these two causes of anxiety when children appear to be over-anxious. Coaches can discover means for accomplishing this by putting themselves in the place of the child. Such empathetic understanding will guide coaches in helping children find optimal emotional states for enjoyable and successful sports participation.

Individual Differences

To help children in managing their anxiety, it is important for coaches to be able to identify those youngsters who are likely to experience high levels of anxiety. This is not as easy

as it may seem. Children differ widely in both what they perceive to be threatening in sports and how they respond to the
threat.

It is easy, of course, to observe the youngster who displays
all the overt signs of anxiety—nail chewing, jitteriness, stac-
cato speech, and tense facial expressions. But some youngsters
are much more covert with their emotional states. They may
feel that the display of nervousness is a weakness which should
be concealed.

How well can coaches predict the competitive anxiety of
their athletes? In one study with female coaches, Julie Simon
and I[1] found that many were poor judges. The coaches accurately predicted their athletes' anxiety less than 10% of the
time. And these were not volunteer coaches—they were professional coaches in high school and colleges.

A seldom recognized aptitude of successful coaches is the
ability to distinguish the different emotional states of each
athlete and to respond on an individual basis. How coaches
acquire such an ability is not clear, but an obvious prerequisite
for developing this competency is realizing its significance.

Anxiety and Sports Performance

For most coaches, the major interest in anxiety is knowing
how it affects performance. Sport psychologists have been
equally interested in this question, conducting more research
on it than any other topic. In spite of all this research, we know
little.

In brief, sport psychologists have discovered what most
coaches already know—there is an optimal arousal* state for
performing sports skills. If youngsters are not aroused
enough, or if they are aroused too much, they will not perform
as well as they might; but if their arousal level is just right,
their performance will be the best of which they are capable
(see Figure below). This optimal arousal level varies, however,
with different sports skills. Some sports skills, like putting in
golf or shooting in archery, are best performed under lower
levels of arousal; sports such as basketball and baseball are

---

*Arousal is the term commonly used when referring to the entire
continuum of a person's psychological activation. *Anxiety* is restricted to high arousal states which produce feelings of discomfort.

better played at slightly higher levels of arousal; and skills like weightlifting or tackling and blocking in football are accomplished better under even higher levels of arousal. In other words, the research suggests that there is an inverse relationship between the precision of motor control required and the arousal state that is optimal for performance; that is, the optimal arousal level increases as the precision of motor control decreases.

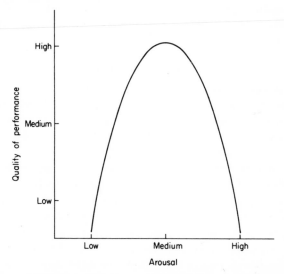

Proposed Relationship Between Performance and Arousal

The optimal arousal level also varies among individual athletes. Some athletes best perform certain motor skills with considerably less arousal than other athletes. Although researchers are able to measure arousal and anxiety, so far they have not been able to measure them with sufficient precision to be able to accurately determine these optimal states. Apparently the distinction among not being sufficiently aroused, being optimally aroused, and being over-aroused or anxious is very, very fine. Moreover, sport psychologists have insufficient knowledge about how to help persons make minute adjustments in their arousal level in order to achieve an optimal state. At the present time, coaches are best advised to use their judgment, based on careful observations, in helping each athlete find an optimal arousal level.

Today many techniques for managing anxiety have been popularized, and some coaches in children's sports are beginning to experiment with these techniques. I do not think it is desirable to use techniques for managing anxiety with young children. If sports are so stressful that children must engage in relaxation training, autogenetic training, transcendental meditation, or even hypnosis, then something is wrong with the sport environment. Rather than treating the disease, coaches should prevent it. The prevention is to reduce the uncertainty and importance placed upon the outcomes of competing in sports.

Are Sports Too Stressful for Children?

With all this concern about the psychological stress in children's sports, we need to stop and assess just how stressful children's sports really are. Two studies are reviewed which are representative of the available evidence and of the difficulty in answering this question.

The first study was conducted by Dale Hanson[2] with Little League baseball players. By attaching small electrodes to the players' chests and a small transmitter to their belts, Hanson continuously monitored each players' heart rate on a receiver located behind the dugout. Increased heart rate, of course, is a common indicator of heightened anxiety or stress. When sitting on the bench before the game, the boys' heart rate averaged about 95 beats per minute, when they played in the field the average rose to 127 beats per minute, and when they batted it increased to 167 beats per minute. After the game, when sitting on the bench again, their heart rate dropped to 100 beats per minute.

In the second study, Julie Simon[3] compared the anxiety states of boys participating in seven different sports (baseball, football, hockey, basketball, swimming, gymnastics, and wrestling). She also compared the anxiety experienced in these seven sports with the anxiety youngsters experienced when taking an academic test in school, when participating in physical education activities, and when competing in musical contests, either as members of a band or as soloists. To measure anxiety Simon used a psychological scale constructed specifically to measure children's emotional states at a specific moment in time. Children completed this scale minutes before they began engaging in the activity. They could score from 10 (low anxiety) to 30 (high anxiety) on this scale.

The results are shown in the Figure on page 246. It was the soloists in music rather than the athletes who scored highest in anxiety. The two most anxiety-provoking sports were wrestling and gymnastics, both individual sports. In fact, when all the individual sports were compared with all the team sports, the children in the individual sports were significantly more anxious. As can be seen in the figure, physical education classes and academic test situations elicited little anxiety. It is noteworthy that the average anxiety scores for each sport did not reach even the midpoint on the anxiety scale.

So what do the studies of Hanson and Simon tell us about the stress in children's sports? Does a heart rate of 167 indicate too much stress? Is an anxiety score of 19.5 too high on a paper-and-pencil test where scores range from 10 to 30? Hanson suggests that it is; Simon concludes it is not.

Remember these are average heart rates and average anxiety scores. Some children scored higher and some lower. Hanson found great variation in heart rate to the different situations in baseball; one batter's heart rate climbed to 204 beats per minute while another's never rose above 145. Simon reported similar variation in anxiety scores. How high must a child's heart rate rise to indicate stress? How high must an anxiety score be to suggest that a youngster is *too* stressed? What percentage of children are so stressed in sports that they are psychologically injured?

We have no absolute answers to these questions. It depends on the child and the sport, or more precisely, the specific situations within sports. Some children in certain sports situations may be highly stressed, other kids in the same situations may not be. Based on the research to date and on my observations of children's sports programs, I believe that the critics have made too much of competitive stress. It does not appear to be as great a problem as they would have us believe. This is not to say, however, that competitive anxiety is not a problem for *some* youngsters in *some* sport situations. It is only to say that it is an extremely small percentage of children who find the stress of sports to be too great. In fact, it may be that children's sports are often more stressful for adults—the coaches and parents—than they are for children.

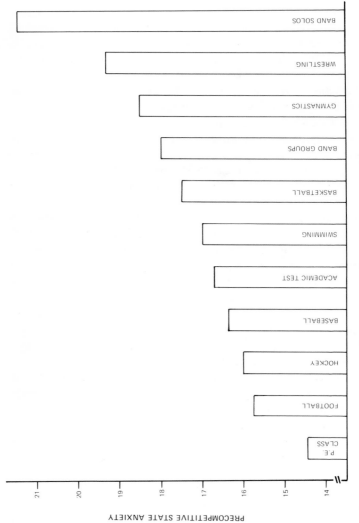

State Anxiety in Sport and Nonsport Evaluative Activities

It also may be that some stress is beneficial for children. For years, child psychologists have contended that youngsters who often have the most difficult time adjusting to adulthood are those whose parents constantly protect them from stressful experiences during childhood. Proponents of children's sports often have argued that the stress in sports helps children to prepare for the stresses in life. But if some stress is beneficial, the questions arise just how much stress is beneficial, and how much is *too* much?

We know that all competition contains some uncertainty about the outcome, and thus is potentially stressful. Yet it is this same uncertainty in competition which makes sports challenging, and motivates youngsters to seek out competitive sports experiences. However, too much uncertainty, and uncertainty about some things can be very stressful. The perplexity of competitive stress is that there is a fine line between uncertainty being a challenge and uncertainty being overly stressful. And this fine line is unique to the psychological makeup of each youngster. Consequently, **one kid's challenge is another kid's stress.**

Competitive stress may be likened to a virus. A heavy dose all at once can make a child ill. A small dose carefully regulated permits the psyche to build antibodies and to successfully resist subsequent stress. The key to whether children's sports are opportunities for learning to cope, or jungles where a high degree of coping is essential to survive, is dependent on the objectives emphasized by parents, coaches, and league administrators. When the predominant emphasis is toward children's physical and psychological development, toward having fun, and not just toward winning, the chances increase that children will not be overly stressed.

The key to how much stress children can handle, and indeed benefit from, depends greatly on their feelings of self-worth and their concept of themselves—how secure, how confident, how well they know who they are. Youngsters can have a great deal demanded of them without being *overly* stressed if they are secure in knowing who they are. Children can grow from the stress in sports if they know that their family, peer group, and coach consider them worthy persons regardless of the outcome of their performance in the game.

Adults can help children develop healthy attitudes about

competition by demonstrating that success or failure does not change their respect and affection for them as individuals. Children who feel their success in sports is associated with the affection and value they have as individuals obviously are risking a great deal each time they compete. But when children know that their worth as a person to their family, coach, and peers is not dependent on their performance in sports, then they feel confident to risk failure in pursuit of the benefits of sports participation.

References

1. Martens, R., & Simon, J. A. Comparison of three predictors of state anxiety in competitive situations. *Research Quarterly*, 1976, *47*, 381-387.
2. Hanson, D. L. Cardiac response to participation in Little League baseball competition as determined by telemetry. *Research Quarterly*, 1967, *38*, 384-388.
3. Simon, J. A. *Children's anxiety in sport and nonsport evaluative activities*. Unpublished doctoral dissertation, University of Illinois, 1977.

SECTION G

Is Sportsmanship Dead?

In the previous pages many incidents were described which represented poor sportsmanship in children's sports. But more often than not, these incidents involved unsportsmanlike behavior on the part of adults, not children. Yet we must be cautious in reaching the conclusion that the behavior of most adults in children's sports is unsportsmanlike. The reporting of sports news is like any other news; the negative incidents make the headlines. "Pee Wee Hockey Coaches Display Good Sportsmanship" is not nearly as sensational as "Coach Kicks Referee—Charged With Assault." The negative, the extreme, the bizarre attract our attention.

Seldom do we hear or see the reporting of good news, such as the incident in Utah several years ago when Scott Bennett of Murray High School and Brad Howes of Cottonwood High School were running neck and neck in a cross country meet. As they approached the finish line Howes suddenly stumbled and fell. Bennett stopped, helped Howes to his feet and crossed the finish line with him. The race was called a tie. Bennett was quoted as saying afterward, "I just couldn't think of anything else to do."

With two out and the tying run at third in a pee wee baseball game in Lincoln, Nebraska, a ground ball was hit to the second baseman who threw it to the first baseman. Umpire Jim Reynolds called the runner out and whirled away to return to his position. He failed to see first baseman Billy Summers drop the ball on the low throw. A terrible argument followed between Reynolds and the opposing coach. But the argument stopped when Billy, standing directly between the two adults, announced that he had dropped the ball. At first Reynolds was flabbergasted. He did not know what to do with such straightforward honesty. In the end, though, Jim Reynolds declared the runner safe and the tying run scored. Billy's team lost the game, but Billy and all who witnessed his honesty perhaps won something more significant than a game.

Each of us probably can recall several incidents like these when admirable sportsmanship was displayed, when playing fairly overrode the motive to win. Perhaps to our own dismay we can, with at least equal clarity, remember incidents of extreme unsportsmanlike behavior. In this section, cheating and violence—two of the most frequent forms of extreme unsportsmanlike behavior—are examined in two true stories. Both stories received considerable national publicity. *Watergate on Wheels* is the unhappy story of the cheating scandal that marred the 1973 Soap Box Derby. Ross Thomas Runfola's *A Model of Legalized Violence* tells the story of a young black Canadian hockey player who resorted to violence after extreme goading. Runfola's account was awarded the Best News-Feature Story in Sports by the *New York Times* in 1973.

Watergate on Wheels

by **Gwen Gibson,** *freelance writer.*

During the last year, America's attention has centered on moral crises. There was, of course, the burgeoning Watergate scandal in Washington, D.C. And, in microcosm, there was the teen-age "Watergate on Wheels"—the 1973 All-American Soap Box Derby, whose 14-year-old winner had to be disqualified for "cheating" and "professionalism."

The Derby has seemingly survived its stain of illegality; it will be run again this year in Akron, Ohio, on August 17. The 1974 race, according to Ron Baker, general manager of the newly formed committee that will supervise the competition, will be a "clean event" for boys and girls between the ages of 11 and 15.

The Derby has survived, but what about blond, blue-eyed Jimmy Gronen, the youngster who was stripped of his 1973 championship because his racer had been rigged to gain an illegal lead at the starting gate? How has Jimmy survived?

Jimmy Gronen lives in Boulder, Colo., with his aunt Viola Burden Lange and her husband, Robert B. Lange. The Langes are a prominent, prosperous family. Robert Lange, Sr., trim, handsome, vibrant, is a sporting goods manufacturer. His wife, Viola, a willowy blonde, is a talented artist. The Langes have three children—two daughters and a son, Bob Lange, Jr., who won the 1972 Soap Box Derby.

The fact that shy, polite Jimmy Gronen and the influential Langes were involved in the 1973 Derby scandal stunned Boulder. Most residents reacted protectively toward Jimmy. But there was some bitterness and resentment toward Lange, Sr.

It was Lange who admittedly advised Jimmy to install the electromagnetic nose in his fiber-glass racer. Such a device can pull a car ahead by as much as eight inches at the beginning of a race—if the starting blocks are made of steel. And until this year, the blocks used in the race *were* made of steel.

In a race where the winner is rarely more than a fraction of a second ahead of the runner-up at the finish line, such a jack-rabbit head start can be decisive—determining the outcome of the race almost as soon as it has begun.

Officials said later that the complicated mechanism found in Jimmy's racer was something no 14-year-old could have masterminded. A magnet had been hidden in the nose of the car. It was connected, through a network of wires, to a three-cell battery in the tail of the vehicle. The whole system was concealed beneath the fiber-glass body under several layers of paint. The magnet was activated when Jimmy leaned back and pressed his protective helmet against two secret switches embedded in the headrest of the car.

In this rigged racer, Jimmy won the 1973 national Soap Box Derby, a trophy, a champion's jacket—and a $7,500 college scholarship.

The day after the race, however, Noel Michell, the chairman of the 1973 Derby, dug into the headrest of Jimmy's car and discovered the secret switches. Michell and others had become suspicious because Jimmy's car consistently seemed to pull ahead of the other racers in the first minutes of each heat, when the cars gather momentum. Official photographs had deepened their suspicions.

Once the switches were discovered, the car was X-rayed and the full dimensions of the scandal came to light.

Jimmy's disqualification—the first in the Derby's 40-year history—was announced at a press conference on Monday, August 20. His title and his $7,500 scholarship were transferred to the runner-up, 11-year-old Brett Yarborough of Elk Grove, Calif. By this time, Jimmy and the Langes had left Akron for a late summer vacation; Jimmy had his gold satin champion's jacket and his unengraved trophy with him.

Inevitably, editorial writers suggested that the Soap Box Derby scandal was an outgrowth of the Watergate syndrome and the obsession with winning at any cost.

Amid all the furor, it was Jimmy who found himself caught in the national spotlight—in the most negative way possible for a sensitive teen-ager. The headlines read, "Gronen Accused of Foul Play" and "Soap Box Derby Racing Tarnished by Boulder Boy."

The feedback must have been particularly painful for Jimmy, since his life had already been touched by tragedy.

Jimmy moved in with the Langes in 1972 after his own family had been torn apart. His father, John Gronen, died of a stroke in 1967, when Jimmy was eight. His mother, Mrs. Winifred Burden Gronen, kept her three children together for five years until she became ill. She was eventually hospitalized at the Methodist Hospital in Rochester, Minn. Jimmy's younger brother and sister went to live with their mother's other sister, Mrs. Betsy Burden MacLeod of Gardiner, N.Y.

Jimmy's mother and her sisters are from Dubuque, Iowa— as is Bob Lange. Lange started a plastics company in Dubuque soon after graduating from Harvard. Eventually he developed a revolutionary line of plastic skis, ski boots and ice skates that are now—according to company spokesmen—widely used in the winter Olympics and the National Hockey League.

In 1968, Lange opened a plant in Broomfield, Colo., near Boulder, and made it the home office of the Lange Ski Boot Corp. His two brothers came along as company vice-presidents and all three Lange families moved to Boulder.

The Lange firm sponsored several prestigious local sports events, including a Denver tennis tournament and a ski competition. For several years it also sponsored cars in the Soap Box

Derby elimination races held each June in Boulder by the city's Junior Chamber of Commerce.

So it was a big, active and influential Lange clan that Jimmy Gronen joined in 1972 at the age of 13.

He must have been impressed and perhaps a bit intimidated. Friends say he regarded his cousin Bob Lange, Jr., a bright, self-assured lad one year older than Jimmy, as a big brother. And he looked up to his Uncle Bob as mentor, guardian and father figure.

Jimmy took to Soap Box Derby racing naturally because his cousin and uncle were Derby buffs. Indeed, Alex Hunter, the Boulder District Attorney, says that Lange, Sr., had become a "Soap Box Derby addict."

The elder Lange had been a Soap Box Derby racer himself as a boy. Then, in 1969, he saw his son, Bobby, become interested in the competition—first as a fan. Then, in 1970, Bobby built a racer, entered the Boulder competition and lost. In 1971, he built another racer. This time he won the Boulder competition, but was disqualified because of mechanical failure in his brakes. The Langes vigorously protested the disqualification, but it stood. Bobby thereupon made himself a corded bracelet, which he called the "disqualification band," and vowed not to remove it until he became Boulder's Soap Box Derby champion.

After that, Bobby Lange began building his 1972 car. He drove it to victory in the Boulder race as well as in the national finals in Akron. Like Jimmy, he won a $7,500 college scholarship.

This was the backdrop for the big Soap Box Derby scandal of 1973.

"An Engineer's Dream"

Jimmy Gronen, according to Lange, built his own racer. On June 24, 1973, he entered the Boulder Derby in a precision-made racer which, in the words of one father, "was light-years ahead of anything else in that race—it was an engineer's dream." Jimmy defeated a field of 39 contestants. His prize was a $100 scholarship, a trophy and a spot in the national race.

After the Boulder race, Jimmy's winning car was kept by the local Jaycees until one week prior to the Akron race. Then it was turned back over to Jimmy so he could repaint it for the national competition.

The Soap Box Derby was started in 1934 by the Chevrolet Division of General Motors as an activity for youngsters 11 to 15—to foster youthful backyard ingenuity and fair play. It has been held annually, except for four years during World War II. When Chevrolet dropped out as sponsor in 1972, the Akron Chamber of Commerce took over.

Under the original rules, contestants were to design and build their own racers, which were to be propelled by nothing but gravity.

Jimmy Gronen may not have fully realized how much he was flaunting these original rules when he streaked to victory inches ahead of young Yarborough. He was too excited. At the on-track ceremony that followed, Jimmy slipped into his champion's jacket and, smiling broadly through the braces on his teeth, posed for pictures. His cousin, Bob Lange, Jr., who was with him, quipped: "It's sort of like winning two years in a row for me."

One of the first things Jimmy did after the ceremony was to call his sick mother and give her the happy news. Later, propped up on his motel room bed, he munched on potato chips and held an impromptu press conference. He said his victory was "kind of unbelievable. I'm really surprised."

Two days later, Jimmy's world crumbled when his disqualification was announced.

In Akron, Summit County prosecutor Stephen Gabalac launched an inquiry to see if criminal charges could be filed. In Boulder, D.A. Alex Hunter began an investigation and turned up some allegations—not so much about Jimmy, but about the car in which Bobby Lange, Jr., had won in 1972.

For one thing, Hunter said, the 1972 car had been shipped to the California Institute of Technology to be tested in a wind tunnel. "And we think an engineer from the Lange plant went along with the car," the D.A. said later. "We *know* that high-salaried engineers from the [Lange] plant advised Bobby and that a great deal of sophisticated equipment was used to bore and test the linings and axles—things like that, things an average youngster wouldn't have access to. High-powered lathes were used on this car, as well as instruments that can measure in minute details. So all told we had to estimate that $10,000 to

$20,000 worth of professional expertise had gone into it."

Hunter said he knew that similar expertise had gone into the design and construction of Jimmy Gronen's 1973 car, but the prosecutor didn't put a dollar value on the 1973 racer.

Even Hunter conceded that the Derby rules in effect in 1973 were ambiguous. They allowed youngsters to accept adult "counseling" but not adult "assistance." They specified that only $40 could be spent on materials for any one racer, but this excluded wheels, axles, steering assembly, paint and—again—counseling.

According to 1973 Derby President George W. Brittain, this meant that there *was* no limit to what could be spent on a car.

Lange's Defense

Lange, silent until this point, finally presented his side of the case in a letter dated August 27, 1973, and addressed to Jack Tracy, the Boulder Junior Chamber of Commerce official who ran Boulder's 1973 Derby.

In the letter, which Lange authorized Tracy to make public, Lange said that the electromagnet had been built for the 1973 race "by Jimmy, but entirely at my suggestion . . . and I accept whatever responsibility may arise from this decision."

He denied charges that professionals had worked on his family's 1972 and 1973 racers. "Neither of these cars were professionally constructed in the sense that anyone other than the respective boys themselves built the cars on their own," Lange wrote, "and it is foolish to suggest that any substantial expence went into them, except in the area of advice and counsel . . . which is permitted under the Derby rules."

Lange also stated that for years Derby rules had been "consistently and notoriously" violated by some participants without censure or disqualification. The rule most persistently broken, he said, was the one requiring a youngster to build his own racer. As Lange put it:

"It is common knowledge that it is next to impossible for any 11-year-old boy or girl to build a racer that can win at Akron. It is all that a mechanically inclined and dextrous 14- or 15-year-old boy can do to carry out the superfine mechanical, construction and machine work required.

"As a result of this and other factors, there has grown a

body of interested adults who are professional car builders and professional participants in the Derby."

Commonplace Violations

One of these pros once offered to build a car for his son for $2,500, Lange said, adding, "I promptly refused." He said he knew of other cases in which professionals had hired kids as "chauffeurs" in order to enter as many as four cars in a local race. "I determined that Jimmy should build and install a magnetic nose so as to be competitive with the professional cars he would be racing against," Lange stated.

Then, in a note of humility, he added: "I knew that this was a serious violation of Derby rules, and consider it now to be a serious mistake in judgment. . . . It would have been far better for him not to participate or to take the disappointment of losing rather than to expose him to the shock of his disqualification and the unfair criticism that followed."

In the following weeks, a number of knowledgeable persons supported Lange's contention that violations of Derby rules had long since become commonplace. Tom Jenkins, a veteran of the pit crew at Akron, told the Associated Press that at least 68 major violations occurred in the 1973 race. He said about 50 cars had illegal welding on bodies, brakes and axle assemblies, and that many others had been fashioned of fiberglass from molds costing several thousand dollars.

None of this exonerated Lange, but prosecutor Gabalac in Akron and D.A. Hunter in Boulder both seemed to soften their attitude toward him. Gabalac dropped his "criminal" investigation and the charges against Lange were limited to two misdemeanor counts of encouraging a child to violate a state law.

The case was settled on October 23, 1973, through a "nonjudicial adjustment" in the courtroom of Boulder Juvenile Judge Horace B. Holmes. Lange paid $2,000 to the Boys Club of Boulder and agreed to refrain from participating in Soap Box Derby racing for two years. There was no plea and no finding of guilt or innocence. Judge Holmes noted that the purpose of a "non-judicial settlement" is to provide disposition of a case without putting the minor involved through the ordeal of a trial.

In handing down his decree, Judge Holmes deplored what he termed the "inconceivable lack of morality" in the Soap Box

Derby scandal. But later, talking in his chambers, he indicated some sympathy with Lange.

"He got caught up in what I call the 'Little League syndrome,'" said Holmes. "So many times in the Little League and in other sports, parents have become so involved that they compete with each other, and what you have is no longer a kid's sport."

The settlement protected Jimmy from more public exposure, and most agreed that it should have. But many Boulderites felt it left a number of questions unanswered.

Were the 1972 and 1973 racers built in part at the Lange plant? The technique used to build fiber-glass vehicles like those Bob and Jimmy raced is strikingly similar to the fiber-glass-and-resin technique used by the Lange Company in fashioning its quality laminated skis.

And what happened to Bobby Lange's 1972 car?

In the past, national championship cars became the property of the All-American Soap Box Derby in Akron, where they went on museum exhibit. But the Derby was in a state of flux in 1973—having lost its sponsor, Chevrolet. So when the Boulder Junior Chamber of Commerce asked permission to exhibit the Bobby Lange car back in the world champ's home town, the request was granted. The car was sent to Boulder and it was, indeed, exhibited.

Where is Winning Car?

Then the Jaycees turned it over to the Lange family. And sometime after that, in the words of Mrs. Lange, "It just disappeared. We don't know where it is. We were away at the time, and when we came back, it had just disappeared." (No theft report was filed with Boulder police.) D.A. Hunter eventually abandoned his efforts to examine the 1972 car. He said he had to endorse Judge Holmes' decision that what happened in 1972 wasn't material to the 1973 case.

As this article went to press, Jimmy Gronen—according to Akron officials—had not returned his unengraved national trophy, nor the uncashed check for $100 he received for winning the Boulder elimination race in June, 1973—this despite the fact that the Boulder Jaycees wrote to the Langes in January, 1974, requesting the return of these awards.

Gerald Sloat, an attorney representing the Boulder Jaycees,

said: "We can't prove that Jimmy had the electromagnetic system in his car when he raced in Boulder. But in view of Judge Holmes' decision, we've asked [Jimmy] to return the $100 check and trophy voluntarily, as an act of generosity, so we can close the books on this matter. So far we've had no response, but the check has not been cashed."

Lange has said that Jimmy did not use the magnet in Boulder—and that "even if he did, it wouldn't have worked because the starting blocks were made of wood."

Fritz Gassman of Denver, who built the starting blocks used in Boulder in 1973, disagrees. The blocks were made of iron and covered with carpeting that was not thick enough to stymie a magnet, Gassman said.

Lange still seemed to feel that he and Jimmy had been singled out for criticism—that a double standard had been applied because others who cheated had not been taken to task. He told acquaintances that he had accepted Judge Holmes' decision "because a trial was the last thing Jimmy needed." He implied he could have won a trial by jury, however.

He threatened a number of times to bring suit against the Soap Box Derby, although prosecutor Gabalac said, "Trying to imagine what he would pray for is beyond comprehension."

Lange also demanded that the other nine winning cars in the 1973 Derby be inspected. They were examined and found to be "clean."

The adverse worldwide publicity that resulted from the Gronen incident was too much for the Akron Chamber of Commerce. On December 28, 1973, the Chamber announced that it was dropping the All-American Soap Box Derby "because it has become the victim of cheating, fraud and hoax."

In January, 1974, the Akron Jaycees formed a "Save the All-American Committee." This evolved into the new independent committee, headed by Ron Baker and composed of Akron Jaycees and other Ohio entrepreneurs. Baker was confident that a new and better Derby would rise eventually from the ashes of the old one.

New starting blocks will render any magnet ineffective, Baker said, and new "realistic and enforceable rules" are in effect.

None of Baker's dreams of a "clean, new Derby" meant much

to Robert Hale of Boulder, who had seen his son Rodger lose to Jimmy Gronen in the 1973 Boulder race.

"What really bothers me is that Lange can afford to send his kids to college a lot better than I can. That scholarship money would have meant a lot to Rodger," said Hale.

Sympathy for Jimmy

Reaction toward Jimmy Gronen was gentler. Almost everyone in Boulder—the Jaycees, the district attorney, Judge Holmes, Jimmy's friends, teachers and classmates, even Rodger Hale's father—seemed to want to shield the boy from undue criticism.

A teacher at Centennial Junior High School said that despite all anyone could do for him, "Jim was definitely hurt at first. Kids can be cruel at that age, and he had to pay for his mistake. But Jimmy has a lot of resilience and I think that where *he* is concerned, the matter has been dropped."

An adult who knows Jimmy said that he had become a little more subdued and a little more guarded in making friends. "But I don't think he has suffered any emotional damage," she said.

In California, the mother of Brett Yarborough, who became 1973 national champ when Jimmy was disqualified, had some particularly sympathetic observations.

"We felt awfully bad about Jim Gronen," she said. "My little boy played with him at the camp they have for the participants at Akron and he was really a nice kid. The whole thing must have been very hard on him. Fourteen is a tender age to have the whole world come down on you. I just hope the whole experience wasn't ruined for him."

It's a safe assumption that everyone concerned shares her sentiments.

A Model of Legalized Violence

by **Ross Thomas Runfola,** *former newspaperman, now a professor of social sciences at Medaille College.*

As a mirror reflection of American life, the most popular sport in America is professional football: brutal, precise, competitive, and highly standardized. In football, as in much of American society, the competitor is The Enemy, and the all-consuming passion is to win, often at any cost.

In Canada, sport is also a reflection of the culture; significantly, then, the most popular sport in Canada is professional hockey. Like the American brand of football, hockey also serves as a model of legalized violence—only on a simpler and grander scale befitting a society that still contains a frontier.

Hockey, of course, allows for the most aggressive type of behavior with a formalized rule structure. In hockey, one is free to use whatever personal resources one might have to defeat the opposition as efficiently as possible, including public humiliation through verbal baiting as well as pure physical power. No other team sport in recorded history accepts fighting as such a crucial aspect of the game.

No one has yet been able to chart acceptable parameters for hockey violence. The inability of the hockey establishment to give definition as to what constitutes "civilized violence" was personified recently when the Ontario Hockey Association suspended Gerry Henderson, president of the Bramalea Junior B hockey team, for two years when he withdrew Bramalea from the playoffs after such a violent and brawl-filled first game with the Hamilton Red Wings that he feared for the lives of his players.

A tragic footnote to the suspension of the Bramalea official is the manslaughter conviction of Paul Smithers for the death of Barrie Cobby on February 18, 1973, in a post-game brawl following a midget league hockey game.

Henderson, a concerned official, is considered a threat to the good order of organized hockey; Smithers, a young hockey player, is considered a threat to Canadian society. Both stand guilty of an inability to distinguish the hazy ethical line that separates acceptable and unacceptable levels of hockey violence.

The case of Paul Smithers is the greater tragedy because he stands broken and disillusioned at 17 years old. It is all the more tragic because in some ways—with one notable exception —he is a typical young Canadian. The exception is that he is black. A product of a developing middle-class suburb of Toronto, he lived quietly in a modest townhouse with his parents and 8-year-old brother. There was nothing very important to clutter his young life. Who to ask to the next dance? What record album to buy? And, of course, the next hockey game.

Hockey was a large part of his life. The numerous medals and trophies that filled the bookshelves in his bedroom bore visual proof both of his hockey proficiency and his youthful priorities.

By most standards, then, Paul Smithers was like many youngsters growing up in Canada who skate at 5 and dream of playing in the NHL. If he was somehow different from his peers, it was because he was an extraordinary hockey player, the best player in the Mississauga Midget League. Paul Smithers was also the only black player in the league.

Black hockey players are virtually nonexistent for numerous reasons, including the very small number of blacks living in

Canada. Few blacks live in Mississauga—only a couple of hundred out of a population of more than 200,000. Despite this, the Smithers family experienced few problems. Paul's mother, Joyce, who is white, explains why: "We never bother other people and they don't bother us. We are a quiet family that sticks close together."

The quiet, everyday life of the Smithers family ended forever the night of February 18. Paul Smithers had a game that night against Applewood, but his parents did not attend because they were celebrating their wedding anniversary.

Unknown to them, a few miles away at Cawthra Park Arena, a nightmare was unfolding. *The Toronto Sun* coldly captured the tragedy for them in bold print: MURDER AFTER HOCKEY: BOY CHARGED. As Don and Joyce Smithers stared tearfully at the banner headline the next day, it appeared to them that *The Sun* had already convicted their son.

When their son played for Cooksville in the Toronto Metro Hockey League, he was keyed up for every game. After his parents moved from Toronto and he was forced to play in the Mississauga Hockey League, the poor quality of the coaching and officiating caused him to quit playing for part of the previous season.

A member of the opposing Applewood team, Barrie Ross Cobby, also would have been happier playing in another league. After he was dropped from the Dixie Beehives, Cobby had no choice but to play in the Mississauga Midget League. In the lesser league, he was as much a star for his team as Smithers was for Cooksville.

Only a few weeks before the game of February 18, Cobby wrote an essay in school on the lesson he learned from reading *The Adventures of Huckleberry Finn.* The book showed young Cobby that "Negroes are human. I often wondered if they were any different, although I don't think I was prejudiced. . . . But most important of all I learned about friendship between two races and I hope that some day we'll be able to get along together."

The essay by young Cobby arguing racial harmony obviously did not include Paul Smithers. A member of the Cooksville Midgets recalls that Cobby always directed racial barbs at Smithers whenever the teams met. While tough talk and baiting are as much a part of hockey as fighting, Smithers remains convinced that his blackness and not his ability made him the target for verbal abuse.

And so young Smithers laced up for the Applewood game with mounting anxiety. The game met Smithers' worst fears. It was not hockey they were playing at Cawthra Arena on February 18; they were waging a war, a war orchestrated by a crowd that at times appeared to be emotionally deranged.

Never before had Smithers been conscious of the crowd. But against Applewood, his ears rang whenever play stopped or he skated into the corner to dig out the puck. As the game progressed, the crowd reaction assumed an increasingly ugly character almost in perfect cadence to the illicit violence and racist baiting on the ice.

At the trial, several witnesses, including John Barme, coach of the Applewood Midgets, testified that his team subjected Smithers to numerous racial slurs. Early in the game, Barrie Cobby told Smithers, "I'm going to get you, you black bastard." As the verbal assault escalated, Cobby called Smithers a "stupid nigger" and a "coon" and his mother a "nigger lover" and a "white pig."

At one point, the game threatened to get completely out of hand when the entire Applewood team and parents in the arena started to taunt Smithers and yell, "Get the nigger." As Smithers describes it, the referees ignored his plea to take action to halt the tripping, slashing, and verbal abuse. Soon afterward, Cobby speared Smithers. Just before he entered the penalty box, Cobby challenged Smithers, "Let's fight, you stupid nigger." Smithers scored a goal while Cobby was serving the penalty. The goal only served to further incense Cobby and the crowd. Eventually, Cobby and Smithers were ejected from the game for their continuing battle.

Just four months past his 16th birthday, Smithers reacted to Cobby's challenge to fight by waiting for him outside the Applewood dressing room. Almost a year and half later, Smithers' father attempts to capture his son's mental state after the Applewood game:

"Paul was just a young boy. Who can say he should have controlled his emotions when players and fans were calling him 'nigger' every game? He was bound to explode."

The inevitable explosion came when young Smithers followed Cobby outside the arena to the parking lot, determined to get an apology or a fight. Smithers punched Cobby once and was then grabbed by four Applewood players. With his arms and neck pinned, he kicked out instinctively as Cobby lunged toward him. Cobby crumpled to the group, cluthing his groin. Minutes later he was dead, choked on his own vomit.

A tragic accident by any standard. At the trial, not one doctor could say with any medical certainty that there was a direct connection between the kick to the groin and the death of Cobby. A pathologist attributed Cobby's death to the inhaling of his vomit, but found no evidence of bodily harm. Dr. William Butt, the Mississauga coroner, testified that even extreme tension could have caused the vomiting.

If Smithers' attack on Cobby had occurred during the game, Smithers would have been liable for a five-minute major penalty. Off the ice, he was liable for a term in prison.

In view of the extenuating circumstances, Judge B. B. Shapiro of Peel County Court informed the all-white jury that it could find Smithers guilty of common assault rather than manslaughter under the same criminal code section. In a surprising move, the jury found Smithers guilty of the harsher manslaughter conviction. Judge Shapiro had little choice but to sentence Smithers on June 4 to six months in the Brampton Adult Training Center. Outside the courtroom, Len Cobby, father of the dead boy, was visibly upset by the sentence. "I think it's a pretty poor effort," he told a crowd of reporters, "when Smithers gets six months for taking 50 years from my boy."

Early the next afternoon, Smithers was released on bail pending appeal. Minutes after his release, I haltingly asked him why Cobby's mother sent him a Christmas card in which she refers to her son as being in "profound sleep." As tears well in his eyes, I quickly shifted the subject to why he thought he was convicted of manslaughter. Without pause, he blurted out, "Because I'm black." But then he quickly offered an opinion designed to be more acceptable to his father, who is standing nearby.

"No. The fact that I'm black is not the point. Any 12 decent people would have found me not guilty. I think I got a bad deal from the jury, especially in view of the medical testimony."

As Paul Smithers waits for his appearance, expected some-time in the fall, Don and Joyce Smithers are attempting to pre-pare their family for an uncertain future. They recently pur-chased a 25-acre farm in Orangeville, Ontario, to rebuild their shattered lives.

It will not be easy. Although their son Paul had never been in trouble before the hockey incident, the week after he was found guilty the Mississauga police went to the Smithers home to question him about the robbery of a corner gas station.

"Luckily, I was in the hospital for typhoid fever, so they couldn't get me for that," said Smithers.

Who, then, is to blame for a tragedy that has taken one young life and threatens to destroy another? Barrie Cobby, who grew up with a Manichean "Good vs Evil" view that is so much a part of the contemporary sports scene? Paul Smith-ers, who finally resorted to physical violence after a season of particularly cruel verbal violence? Or societies that increas-ingly tend both to glorify violence and desensitize young people to the growing spectacle of human brutality by teaching them techniques of controlled violence to crush opposition on rival teams?

Perhaps the most important question is also the one that is the most difficult for Canadians to contemplate. The popular heroes in Canada are men who express themselves in the most aggressive and assertive ways. Dare anyone confront the thought that perhaps fans at Cawthra Arena were screaming insults at a black, 16-year-old youngster because he symbolized the assertiveness and unbridled aggression that they them-selves demand in "the future custodians of the Republic"?

It is, after all, the widespread belief of fans that outcomes in the sporting arena are inextricably intertwined with outcomes in the real world that gives the Paul Smithers case a social significance that transcends the sports world. In a word, how far removed is Mississauga from Mississippi?

Comments

Sportsmanship

When asked what they thought sportsmanship meant, American children responded with such answers as:

Playing by the rules.
Being a good loser.
Being a good winner.
Respecting the decisions, requests, and opinions of others.
Being even-tempered.
Respecting the efforts and abilities of others.
Taking turns and letting others play.

Some youngsters felt that sportsmanship meant being a good player, while others felt it meant playing for fun rather than playing to win. Some saw sportsmanship as helping others, and others thought it meant minding their own business.

Sportsmanship is one of those words for which we think we know the meaning but find it difficult to define precisely. Sportsmanship conjures up thoughts about fairness, honesty, respect for authority, self-sacrifice, and sound character. In short, sportsmanship is moral behavior in sport, and moral behavior refers to behavioral patterns approved by society or some segment of society. Moral behavior, and more specifically sportsmanship, may therefore vary from place to place and time to time, depending on the reference group used to determine normative behavior. What is good sportsmanship in England may be frowned upon in Japan, and what is socially sanctioned in baseball may be unacceptable in tennis. There is no such thing as a general quality of sportsmanship; approved behavioral patterns are specific to the norms of particular reference groups.

But some behavioral patterns have far wider acceptance than others. Behaviors that give an opponent an equal opportunity to compete are widely approved, while behaviors that endanger the life of a fellow athlete are widely disapproved. Even in violent sports such as football and hockey, actions that threaten an opponent with serious injury are severely censured by fellow players.

Not being able to clearly establish what is and is not sportsmanlike behavior has plagued the few sport scientists who have attempted to study the sportsmanship of young children. These researchers have constructed questionnaires which ask children to indicate their approval or disapproval of certain behaviors. Two studies[1,2] using these procedures concluded that the more children participate in sports, the poorer their sportsmanship attitudes become. These findings, if correct, would be a severe condemnation of children's sports—the very activities which we claim foster moral development! Yet when examining the questionnaires, it becomes obvious that these researchers were imposing their standards upon those whom they were studying. Who is to say that these researchers' judgment of what is and is not sportsmanlike behavior is correct?

Consider the following situations selected from sportsmanship questionnaires:

1. Each time a member of the visiting team is given a free throw in basketball the home crowd sets up a continual din of noise until the shot has been taken.
2. A tennis player frequently calls out, throws up his arms, or otherwise tries to indicate that his opponent's serve is out of bounds when it is questionable.
3. During a golf match Player A makes quick noises and movements when Player B is getting ready to make a shot.
4. A basketball team uses one player to draw the opponent's high scorer into fouling situations.
5. By using fake injuries a team is able to stop the clock long enough to get off the play that results in the winning touchdown.

Are all these acts unsportsmanlike? Do you define sportsmanship by adherence to the letter of the law or the spirit of the rules? Do you consider it unsportsmanlike when you or others boo players? Is it acceptable to boo the pros but unacceptable to boo kids? Is it a player's moral obligation to inform an official of an incorrect call against his opponent? Is it poor sportsmanship to foul deliberately in basketball to gain a tactical advantage? What antics, if any, are acceptable methods for attempting to "psych out" or upset opponents to keep them from performing at their best? Is stalling toward the end of a game to keep the opponents from having an opportunity to score unsportsmanlike or just good strategy? Do you consider it unsportsmanlike for spectators to leave the game early when their team is losing?

The skulduggery that went on in the 1973 Soap Box Derby and the tragedy in Mississauga are clear examples of unsportsmanlike behavior. But for those situations just described there is little consensus. You may personally feel strongly about these situations in sports, but be assured that there are numerous people who disagree with whatever position you take. It is this difference of opinion about approved behavioral patterns in sports that results in ambiguous norms.

Because there are no precise norms for sportsmanship, it makes it difficult for youngsters to learn what is and is not sportsmanlike behavior. Children sometimes find it impossible to distinguish between being aggressive and committing an act of aggression in sport. They seek to learn when it is considered good strategy to stretch the rules and when it is considered cheating. Children wonder whether they are supposed to do as they are told or as they see their coaches and parents do.

Religious and educational leaders for years have proclaimed that America is having a moral crisis, and this crisis begins with our children. We must scrutinize children's sports and ask: Are these sports programs contributing to the moral development of children or are they helping to create a moral crisis?

Children learn moral behavior by observing and listening to other children and adults. Through the media young children are exposed to many adult athletes. They see remarkably skilled athletes dedicating themselves to achieving excellence. They see these athletes praised and rewarded for their feats. They identify with their heroes; they idolize them. But they also see these athletes commit acts of violence; they hear of cheating in recruiting, tampering with equipment, and the use of illegal electronic surveillance equipment. They frequently hear of team bickering and athletes who play with concern for only themselves and total disregard for their teammates and supporters. They see spectators disrupting games by throwing smoke bombs on playing fields or pennies on gymnasium floors. Youngsters seemingly delight in recounting to their friends the details of a drunken brawl they saw in the stands, players fighting with each other, coaches swearing at officials, and fans spitting at players.

I have little doubt that the impact of observing such behaviors is negative. Research has demonstrated repeatedly that children learn much of their social behavior by observing others, especially those whom they hold in high regard. And certainly this is a nation whose children idolize sports stars. Therefore, there is little question in my mind that adult athletes are powerful models influencing the thoughts and actions of young athletes.

But there is a last line of defense against the negative modeling of some adult athletes. **It is the behavior of those adults who work closely with the kids—primarily the coaches and parents.** If these adults demonstrate and reinforce sportsman-like behavior and help children *understand* what is appropriate behavior in sports, they can counteract the effects of negative sports models.

Those adults who coach young athletes must not only demonstrate sportsmanlike behavior, they must consistently reward and punish good and poor sportsmanship. Children who respect their coach and love their parents seek the approval and affection of these adults. Yet in the absence of clear rules of behavior children test out their actions to discover what is and is not approved. Through selective reinforcement coaches and parents can do much to direct the development of sportsmanship. Through reasoning, they can help children understand *why* it is inappropriate to model the negative behavior of some adult athletes.

It is when the coach and parents fail to exert this leadership that we have cause to worry. It is when children's coaches themselves model the negative aspects of adult sports that we have little reason to expect youngsters to develop good sportsmanship. It is when parents behave like children because their children do not play like adults that poor sportsmanship is learned. It is when adults tell youngsters to display good sportsmanship but then demonstrate unsportsmanlike behavior that sportsmanship is unlikely to develop.

Sportsmanship also is unlikely to develop when adults choose to overlook youngsters engaging in inappropriate behavior. Adults who lack self-confidence, who wish to be "pals" rather than leaders of young athletes, may tolerate cheating, abusive language, and fighting. Some adults are inconsistent in how and whom they reward and punish. Such incongruity is particularly troublesome and painful for children to understand. All-too-often they discover that it is related to the skill of the athlete; the youngster with greater skill is permitted to deviate more from appropriate standards of behavior than the less skilled youngster.

Children find these inconsistencies extremely difficult to reconcile when attempting to form rules about moral behavior in sports. For example, children see that fighting among adult athletes is tolerated, yet they are not permitted to do so. Do they conclude that fighting is inappropriate except for professional athletes, or that fighting is inappropriate until they become adults? Special treatment, hypocrisy, and conflicting models of behavior all decrease the likelihood that children will mature morally through sports participation.

Aggression

The more I observe children's sports, the more I am convinced that children seldom are violent in sports. Most violence occurs in adult sports, and the little aggression that occurs in children's sports is usually instigated by adults—particularly for youngsters under the age of 13. Two exceptions come to mind, but they apply mostly to older children. One is the disturbing report that the widely publicized violence in professional hockey is occurring increasingly among younger and younger hockey players. The second is the many reports of violence at high school football and basketball games. But these reports usually indicate that the violence does not involve the players or coaches, but rather spectators and hoodlums who congregate at the playing sites.

For the most part, I think that the violence among young athletes has been well-controlled. Children's sports are well-policed by officials who can use expulsion from the game as a deterrent to severe unsportsmanlike behavior. In fact, adults would do well to model their sports after children's sports with respect to the enforcement of rules against unsportsmanlike behavior.

Conclusion

Sports can be an effective medium for teaching moral behavior because moral decisions are frequently forced upon the young athlete. But sports themselves are no escape from evil and immorality. Instead, through sensitive adult leadership, our children can be taught how to live morally in a world that is less than moral.

Children, and adults as well, sometimes misconstrue good sportsmanship as compromising their pursuit of excellence. They mistakenly think that playing intensely and aggressively in the pursuit of victory is unsportsmanlike. Michael Novak in a provocative book called *The Joy of Sports* comments on this point:

> It is "good sportsmanship" to see to it that the basic structure and procedures of the contest are fair. A good contest, by its nature, requires fairness. The outcome should hang uncertainly between evenly matched opponents, playing under similar rules. A false conception of good sportsmanship, however, prevents many players from giving themselves fully to the competition. Instead of concentrating on the excellence of their own performance, many amateurs, in particular, begin to worry about the psyche of their opponents; they hold back. They lack the instinct for the jugular. They don't want to "humiliate" their opponents. Their condescension toward the frail ego (as they imagine it) of their opponents prevents them from playing as well as they might. They "let up." When they do, commitment and fire leave the contest. The true morality of sport is absent.[3]

We certainly do not want our children to develop a false conception of sportsmanship as Novak describes. While I have repeatedly condemned the overemphasis on winning in children's sports, it does not mean that winning is unimportant. It is a significant and immediate goal of any competitive sport.

We want youngsters to learn that giving maximum effort to achieve excellence is a worthy objective. Yet we also want them to learn that they must sometimes make decisions between achieving this success by approved behavior or disapproved behavior. In other words, there are times in every youngster's involvement in sports when he or she must deal with the conflict between adopting a success strategy or a moral strategy. Perhaps moral development is nurtured more when moral decisions come into conflict with winning. Walter Kroll made this point well:

> Perhaps we need to inspect the notion that noteworthy acts of sportsmanship seem always to involve sacrifices of success strategy in favor of a decision guided by moral criteria. Success is not easily relinquished when it is so highly esteemed, but the conduct prescribed by a code of moral behavior can—and often does—compel the individual to forego the rewards of success. . . . Unless winning is important, putting success in jeopardy in favor of conduct compatible with a moral code fails to qualify as a noteworthy event. Such a proposition really needs to be considered by those harsh and outspoken critics of athletics who lambast the emphasis upon winning, who urge that cooperation replace competition.[4]

In conclusion, it is clear that the benefits of sport do not come with mere participation.

> Just as play, games, and sport have the capacity for positive socialization, they also may breed deceit, hatred, and violence. Thus it is not the game, the play, or the sport that automatically determines the worth of these activities for the child; it is the nature of the experiences within these activities. It is the interactions with parents, teammates, and coaches that determine if sports help the child develop morally or immorally.[5]

References

1. Kistler, J. W. Attitudes expressed about behavior demonstrated in certain specific situations occurring in sports. *National College Physical Education Association for Men Proceedings*, 1957, *60*, 55-58.

2. McAfee, R. A. Sportsmanship attitudes of sixth, seventh, and eighth grade boys. *Research Quarterly*, 1955, *26*, 120.
3. Novak, M. *The joy of sports*. New York: Basic Books, Inc., 1976, pp. 312-313.
4. Kroll, W. *Psychology of sportsmanship*. Paper presented at the Sports Psychology meeting, National Association for Sport and Physical Education, AAHPER National Convention, March 1975, Atlantic City, N.J., p. 22.
5. Martens, R. Kid sports: A den of iniquity or land of promise. *National College Physical Education Association for Men Proceedings*, 1976, *79*, 104.

PART FOUR

Bellwethers of Children's Sports

There are little eyes upon you,
And they're watching night and day;
There are little ears that quickly
Take in every word you say;
There are little hands all eager
To do anything you do;
And a little boy who's dreaming
Of the day he'll be like you.

You're the little fellow's idol;
You're the wisest of the wise,
In his little mind about you,
No suspicions ever rise;
He believes in you devoutly,
Holds that all you can and do,
He will say and do, in your way
When he's a grown-up like you.

There's a wide-eyed little fellow,
Who believes you're always right,
And his ears are always open,
And he watches day and night;
You are setting an example
Every day in all you do,
For the little boy who's waiting
To grow up to be like you.
— Author Unknown

Adults know that whether or not sports bring joy or sadness to children is a direct consequence of what adults do. And what adults do is usually a consequence of the goals they have for children's sports. Unfortunately these goals are not always the same goals the children have for participating in sports.

Too many adults have winning as the only goal. Even though they may deny it verbally, their behavior reflects a winning-is-everything attitude. Uncontaminated by adult influence, children far more often have fun as their first goal and winning as their second goal. Watching children play sports without adult intervention make the goals of their play self-evident. For example, when kids were asked whether they would prefer to win or to have fun 95% said to have fun. When asked whether they would prefer to be on a winning team but sit on the bench or be on a losing team and play, over 90% chose to *play* on a losing team.[1]

It amazes some adults that joy and sadness are not synonymous with winning and losing in the minds of young athletes— at least not until adults teach them so. In fact, the coach or parent so imbued with the winning-is-everything philosophy often becomes angry when young athletes do not express sadness when losing. The creed among win-blinded adults seems to be that it is downright unAmerican to show any joy for at least 24 hours after defeat.

I recall an incident in pee wee baseball that illustrates this point. My 8-year-old neighbor Kevin was playing in his very first game on a local pee wee team. The first time he came to bat the much maturer pitcher of the opposing team threw three strikes past Kevin before he had time to get the bat off his shoulder. Kevin walked back to the bench unperturbed by the outcome. The coach, seeing that Kevin was not unhappy with the outcome, concluded that he did not care and gave him a tongue lashing for not putting forth an effort to hit the ball.

Now Kevin was sad. He sat on the bench with his head hanging low as he watched the older members of the team take their turn at the plate. What he saw was that when an older player struck out he threw his bat down, slammed his helmet to the ground, and stalked back to the bench to sulk. The coach would then yell to the players "That's all right, hang in there. You'll get a hit next time."

The next time Kevin came to bat he struck out again, but this time he did swing at the third strike. Now when Kevin walked back to the bench he, too, threw his bat, slammed his helmet, stalked, and sulked. Sure enough, the coach yelled, "That's all right Kevin, you'll do better next time."

Kevin had learned an important lesson in his first game. It wasn't how to hit, throw, or field, but that when you fail you express sadness—that keeps the coach off your back. Of course that is not at all what the coach had intended to teach. He simply did not realize how he was inadvertently reinforcing the wrong behavior.

It is not easy to be a coach or parent of young athletes in a society that defines success synonymously with winning. It is not easy for coaches to resist the influence of a winning-is-everything philosophy when surrounded by college and professional sports programs where winning is indeed everything. It is not easy for parents to help their children keep winning in perspective in a society that seemingly has winning out of perspective. But that is what coaches and parents of young athletes must strive to do.

In Part Four we will examine the important role of the coach (Section A) and the parent (Section B) in determining whether sports are positive or negative experiences for children. The selected articles and comments at the end of each section will consider the outcomes which we wish sports to provide and will then evaluate whether or not certain adult behaviors are appropriate for obtaining those outcomes.

The first two articles in Section A deal with the importance of winning and losing in the eyes of coaches. The tribulations of a rookie coach who becomes caught up in the emotions of competition are humorously described by John Hubbell in *Confessions of a Little League Coach*. Then Erma Bombeck will put a smile on your face with the story of Ralph Corlis who in two seasons compiled the impressive record of 0 wins and 81 losses!

In the next two articles some sound advice for coaches is given first by Thomas Johnson, a psychiatrist, and then by Al Rosen, an ex-major league baseball star. Johnson's *Happiness is Little League* is from a booklet distributed to Little League baseball coaches. Its content will benefit coaches and parents of any sport. Rosen's *The Man in Charge* also contains excellent advice for coaches. Although both of these articles are written about baseball, the message is applicable to coaches of all children's sports.

In Section B we begin with a humorous satire by Donald Kaul on parental involvement in children's sports. Al Rosen then gives fathers some sound advice—and much of what he says is pertinent to mothers. The final two articles in this section advise parents on the importance of children developing realistic success expectancies. Both Thomas Johnson and Pat Van Buskirk show that the greatest rewards from competing in sports are not those obtained from winning, but from making the effort. Be sure to read *A Loser Wins Out* by Van Buskirk; you will see that success is indeed a relative thing.

Reference

1. Orlick, T. D. The athletic dropout—A high price for inefficiency. *Canadian Association for Health, Physical Education and Recreation Journal,* September/October 1974, pp. 21-27.

SECTION A

Coaches—Do They Build Character or "Characters"?

Confessions of a Little League Coach

by **John G. Hubbell,** *freelance writer and associate editor
of* Flight Lines *magazine.*

One night just before my first season as a Little League
coach, I proclaimed my bold approach to the task ahead. I
wasn't going to be like those other Little League fathers. No,
sir! "I've read about those guys," I informed my wife. "Besides
over-organizing everything, they put too much emphasis on
winning. They've taken the game away from the kids, made
emotional wrecks of them."

"You're perfectly right, dear," she agreed. "I think you definitely should get everything disorganized and see that the
boys lose a lot."

"That's not what I meant!" I yelled calmly. "I meant that
when I was a kid we just found ourselves a stick and a ball and
vacant lot. We turned out some pretty good ballplayers, if I
say so myself, and we learned the most important thing of all
—sportsmanship."

That's how I conceived my job: to see that the boys on my team all had a good time and learned sportsmanship—and a little something about baseball. But people continued, in the days ahead, to misunderstand me.

At the coaches' organization meeting, the league president handed out rulebooks and schedules, then asked if there were any questions. I had read a lot about over-competitive coaches who, in their desire to win, cut their least talented players from the squad. I had strong feelings against this practice, and here was an opportunity to express them. "About this business of cutting players," I began.

The president turned lobster-red. "I don't know where *you* have been coaching," he said. "But we don't cut *any* kids in our league. If a boy wants to play, he *plays*—at least half of each game. Let's get that straight right *now!*"

"But that's what I . . ."

"Winning isn't *everything!*" someone hissed.

"Good," I said weakly, sitting down. "That's fine."

Then there was the business with the T-shirts. This was little Little League, sort of a Little League farm league, and my kids were all under eight. When they were issued bright-green T-shirts with white letters proclaiming them the "Cubs," their delight knew no bounds. In a few days my spouse informed me, however, that my shortstop—my pride, my joy, my son—refused to remove his T-shirt for any reason. "He even sleeps in it," she complained. "It's *filthy!* You must speak to him!"

"My mission," I said, "is to see that the boys have a good time and learn sportsmanship. It is their mothers who must keep them sanitary."

But I was misunderstood again. Other mothers with the same problem insisted that *I* had a certain responsibility in this matter of cleanliness. "We're all in this together," they said. Thus it was decided that on Saturday mornings the Cubs would travel en masse to a coin laundry to have their shirts cleaned; and it was "only logical" that the coach, whom the kids "looked up to," should lead these expeditions.

I actually began to enjoy the weekly challenge of keeping 15 half-naked Cubs from tearing up the laundry—but it made the proprietor nervous. "I fast and pray all day on Friday, and go to bed at sundown," he said. "Please take them someplace else."

"Not a chance," I said. "We're all in this together."

Practice was now in progress, and we had some eventful ones. I had got my second baseman, who fielded ground balls well, to think about trying to throw the runner out at first instead of holding the ball high and loudly calling attention to his proficiency. And my first baseman had largely overcome an aversion to covering his post when a runner was bearing down on it. But my son was still playing shortstop sidesaddle. "You've got to get *behind* those grounders," I told him. "It puts you in position to throw."

"What if the ball hops and hits me in the face?" he asked.

"Have you ever seen Zoilo Versalles reach for them like you do?"

"I'm not Versalles," he said. "I'm just a seven-year-old kid trying to learn a little . . ."

"Get behind them!" I explained.

Then came our first game—with the Giants. My lads went to bat first. My lead-off batter, Davy, was 42 inches high and absolutely fearless. To be sure, there was little to fear from the opposing pitcher; his deliveries, which followed a high, lazy arc, had the catcher ambling to all sides of home plate. As the count reached three balls and no strikes, I noticed that Davy was becoming increasingly agitated. "Whyncha throw it somewheres nearda plate, ya jerk?" he inquired.

"Shaddup, ya runt!" the pitcher replied.

As the next pitch headed for the stands, Davy scurried out of the batter's box, pushed the catcher sprawling and timed his swing beautifully. *Pow!* He sent a hot grounder straight at the petrified enemy third baseman. The ball streaked untouched through this worthy's legs and came to rest midway between him and the left fielder, who showed no inclination to involve himself in the situation.

Davy rounded first base and, to the ecstatic shrieks of his teammates, was making for second. But now the catcher had regained his feet and was heading cross-country toward Davy, obviously bent on vengeance. As Davy dived into second, the catcher dived on top of him. They struggled around in a thickening cloud of dust, out of which Davy suddenly appeared running toward third. By this time, the left fielder had been persuaded to pick up the ball, and he now heaved it mightily toward home plate, where there was no one to catch it. Davy bounded home amid much cheering and backpatting by his teammates. "Davy hit a *homer!*" they shrieked.

Above their clamor, the opposing coach was bellowing, *"Illegal! Illegal!"* He danced toward me, waving his finger at Davy. "He can't slug my catcher! What are you *teaching* your kids, anyway?" He turned to the crowd of mothers and fathers behind his bench. "He'd do *anything* to win! He's the one at the coaches' meeting who wanted to *cut* . . ."

"Listen, buddy," I said, sticking my jaw up in his face. My kids were crowding noisily behind me. I heard Davy yell, "Give it to him, coach! Nice guys finish last!"

This unsportsmanlike observation recalled me to my senses, and the umpire, an experienced man with a large voice, restored order. Davy's run was not counted, and he was lectured sternly for his unseemly sentiments.

The rules in our league state that a team shall remain at bat until there are three outs or until nine players have batted. So, when the Giant pitcher walked the eight Cub batters who followed Davy, we took the field for the bottom of the first inning with a comfortable five-run lead. We fattened this as the game progressed; in fact, we went into the bottom of the fifth and final inning with an eight-run bulge—26–18.

This last half-inning proved to be big. My pitcher walked the first two batters and hit the third, loading the bases. Then a husky lad lofted a fly ball to center field. My center fielder got under it, but at the last possible moment he removed himself from harm's way, letting the ball drop and roll to a stop. At this point, he pounced on it and began running with it toward the infield. My shortstop ran to meet him, shouting, "Lemme have it! I'll relay it!"

"*I* wanna relay it!" the center fielder yelled, running past him. The shortstop took after him, leaped on his back and beat him to the ground. Meanwhile, four runs scored.

The next Giant batter grounded one toward my third baseman, who came up with it beautifully—and threw the ball into right field. A series of similar catastrophes followed, and in a few minutes the game ended with the Giants on top, 27–26. Our opponents gave three big cheers for the Cubs. I had some difficulty getting my stalwarts to reciprocate, but finally wrung three weak cheers out of them for the Giants—followed by Davy's departing insult: "You guys really *stink*!"

"We beat you bums!" one of the Giants pointed out.

"Yah, wait'll next time," my shortstop yelled. "We'll *cream-ya*!"

It did seem, as the season progressed, that next time we might cream them. My Cubs took off on a long winning streak. All the parents turned out in support. "Kill the umpire! Get him a seeing-eye dog!" they would shout.

As the season waned, we continued winning. What bothered me, though, was that the opposing coaches kept yelling to the umpires to make sure that I played all my playesr, not just my best nine. ("He's the one at the coaches' meeting who . . .") This began to wear me down. "Listen, buddy!" I would shrill, charging at them. "Well, all *right*," they would say, "you don't need to get so up*set* about it. After all, it's only a *game*."

We won our park championship. Then, in the district championship game, we lost, 16–15. I was gloomy. To my astonishment, the Cubs were not; they had done their best and had no apologies to make to anyone. Without even being told to, they gave three lusty cheers for their conquerors. It made me feel good, and I knew they had learned something big when Davy yelled, "Nice game, you guys. Ya beat us fair 'n' square. But wait'll next year!"

"Yah," I shouted at the opposing coach, "wait till next year! We'll *creamya*!" I could tell from the man's face that I had been understood at last.

The Coach Who Played To Lose

by **Erma Bombeck,** *author of several best-selling books and the syndicated column "At Wit's End."*

In the annals of Little League baseball, there was only one man who made it to the Baseball Hall of Shame five seasons in a row. That was Ralph Corlis.

Ralph was an enigma in suburban sports. He brought his two sons to a housing development two years after his wife died, and together they hacked out a life for themselves. They planted a little garden, built a little racing car in the garage, and on a summer evening would go over to the ballfield and watch the kids play ball under the lights.

It was after the third or fourth game that Ralph began to take note of the thirty or forty kids on the bench who wore the uniform, but who rarely played the game.

"What do those kids do?" Ralph asked his sons.

"They watch the team play ball."

Reprinted from *The Grass Is Always Greener Over the Septic Tank* by Erma Bombeck. Copyright © 1976 by Erma Bombeck. Used with permission of McGraw-Hill Book Company.

"For that they have to get dressed up in full uniform?"

"Oh no," said his son, "they go to all the practices, work out, run, field, catch, pitch, and do everything the team does . . . except play."

Ralph thought a lot about the bench warmers and one day he approached several of them and said, "How would you like to join my team?"

When Ralph was finished, he had enough for five teams and sixteen benches. The first night they met on a piece of farmland donated by a farmer.

"This is first base," said Coach Corlis, dropping his car seat cushion on the ground, "and this is second," he continued, dropping his jacket, "and I see there's already a third base."

"But . . . it's a pile of dung," said one of his players.

"So, don't slide," said Ralph.

"Do you want to see me pitch?" asked a tall, lean, athletic boy.

"No," said Ralph. Then turning to a kid two feet tall who could scarcely hold the ball in his hand, he said, "You pitch today."

At random he assigned a catcher, basemen, infield and outfield, and said, "The rest of you—relax. On this team, everyone plays."

You cannot imagine what an impact a team where "everyone plays" had on the community. Word spread like a brush fire.

One night Coach Corlis answered his door to discover a visit from three other coaches.

"Hey, what a surprise," said Ralph. "Come in."

"What's your game?" asked one of the coaches.

"Baseball," said Ralph.

"You know what we mean," said one of the other men. "What are you trying to prove? Playing every boy who goes out for the team. How many games have you won?"

"I haven't won any," said Ralph. "I didn't think that was very important."

"What are you, some kind of a loonie? Why would you play a game, if not to win?"

"To have a good time," grinned Ralph. "You should have been there the other night when Todd Milhaus slid into third."

"Unfortunately, losers don't draw crowds," smirked the third coach.

"Oh, we don't want crowds," said Ralph. "Adults just mess things up for the kids. I heard at one of your games that a mother threw a pop bottle at her own son."

"And he deserved it," said the first coach. "He should have had his eye on second base. That kid has the brain of a dead sponge."

"He's pitching for me tomorrow," said Ralph.

"Look," said the second coach, "why don't you let the boys go? What do you want with them? They're not even winning."

Ralph thought a minute then said, "It's hard to explain, but kids go all through their lives learning how to win, but no one ever teaches them how to lose."

"Let's get out of here, Bert," said the third coach.

"Wait a minute," said Ralph. "Just think about it. Most kids don't know how to handle defeat. They fall apart. It's important to know how to lose because you do a lot of it when you grow up. You have to have perspective—how to know what is important to lose and what isn't important."

"And that's why you lose?"

"Oh no. We lose because we're too busy having a good time to play good ball."

"You can't talk sense to a man who won't even sell hotdogs at a game and make 13 cents off each dog."

Ralph Corlis's team racked up an 0–38 record the very first season. The next year, it was an even better 0–43. Parents would have given their right arms to watch the team play, but they were not permitted to view a game.

All eighty of the players used to congregate at a drive-in root beer stand and giggle about their contest. When there was criticism it was from themselves. The important thing was that *everyone was sweating.*

In the annals of sandlot baseball, there had never been another team like it. They had lost every game they played and they did it without uniforms, hotdogs, parents, practice, cheerleaders, lighted scoreboards, and press coverage.

Then one afternoon something happened. Ralph had a little nervous bedwetter on the mound who had never played anything but electric football. He wore glasses two inches thick and refused to take the bicycle clamp off his pantleg.

The kid pitched out of his mind, throwing them out at first, catching an infield pop-up and pitching curves like he invented them.

Ralph's team (it had no name) won the game 9–0.

The boys were strangely quiet as they walked slowly off the field. Defeat they could handle—winning was something else. Ralph sat in his car a long time before putting his key into the ignition. He wanted time to think.

"See you next week, Coach," yelled a couple of the boys.

But Ralph Corlis never went near the cornfield or a baseball game again. As he explained to his sons, "I couldn't stand the pressure."

... Happiness is Little League Baseball

by **Thomas P. Johnson**, *former Little League player, coach, and umpire, and now a psychiatrist in San Diego, California.*

A Coach Can Have Worries

It's not unusual for even an experienced coach to approach the season with some uneasiness. How will his team do? How will the players and parents react to him? How will he stack up against the other coaches? How knowledgeable will he appear to the boys?

The danger here lies in the fact that his uneasiness may cause the coach to become tense and overly critical. Or he may become too passive—even try to be a "pal" to the boys. A pal can't set standards for the team that give the boys direction and the confidence that comes from knowing someone is in charge.

A smile that lets the boys know you like them and are looking forward to the season with them will help promote good feelings. Decide early how you will motivate them. Will you make them fear your criticism or seek your approval and praise? (No one can like someone he fears.)

Reprinted with permission of the author.

How will you handle your own mistakes? Bluff? Argue that it wasn't a mistake? Ignore it? Or will you call attention to it yourself, apologize and rectify when possible?

Remember, the most powerful teaching device you have is not what you advise, but what you do.

Think about how you would like your players to handle their mistakes. Then show them by the example you set. It's not necessary to purposely make mistakes in order to teach this—you'll probably make a few during the season anyway. That will be enough to make your point.

How to earn respect. Respect is something a coach can never successfully demand. (It is possible though to be so frightening that the disrespect is kept hidden by scared boys.)

True respect is earned. It comes when the coach respects himself and when he shows respect for all others—his players, their parents, the umpire and the opponents. Abuse any of them and the players will wonder when it will be their turn to be your target. Be less than you ask of the boys and you'll get less.

How to disagree. There will be many situations when you'll disagree with an umpire, an opponent or one of your own players. You can't solve a problem until you get the facts. Start by listening. You can't learn by talking. People will be more willing to consider your views if they feel you've taken the time to understand (not necessarily agree with) their position. Present your question or complaint without sarcasm or insulting remarks. Anyone can show respect when things are going well. The boys need to be shown how to do it when things are tough.

How to get a boy to care. An "I don't care" or "I won't try" attitude may be masking a boy's fear of failing. In Aesop's fable, "The Fox and the Grapes," when the disappointed fox couldn't reach the grapes he wanted, he ended up by saying they were probably sour anyway. This is the kind of defense mechanism you may be dealing with in the "I don't care" boy. Boys feel free to care when they have the self-confidence that makes them believe they have a chance for some satisfaction in the activity. You help a boy care by increasing his confidence.

How to handle praise. Be liberal with praise. Nobody was ever ruined by being overpraised. Praise the little things that others might not notice. Sincerely given, praise doesn't make people rest on their laurels. It gives them the confidence to continue when the going is hard.

How to handle criticism. Be sparing of criticism. Surround it with positive comments. For example: a boy playing the infield lets a ground ball get through. He gets over to it or makes a good try, but he bobbles it and doesn't make the play. Start with a positive comment about something in the play that he did well. You might say, "You got a great jump on that ball, Johnny." Then you can add, "I think if you start out with the other foot first, you'll make the play next time." With each successive try, emphasize and reinforce the part he did right before focusing on the aspect that needs improvement. This approach helps build boys who won't coast when they are ahead. Who won't give up when they are behind. Who won't feel the pressure to go beyond the rules and good sportsmanship to win.

The Day of the Tryout

Don't forget that all boys come to the tryout scared. Some cover the fear of their failure with bravado or clowning. But underneath, each is wondering how he'll do. Will he look bad? Will he be picked? Even last year's star feels the pressure of living up to all that is expected of him. Each boy needs a word of encouragement for the frightened part inside him. Don't forget it's there. Find something positive to say even if it's only that you appreciate his coming to try. Praise the effort, not the result. Then no boy will leave feeling he's failed. That should be your goal in tryouts. Every boy should leave feeling better for having tried.

The team—those who don't make it. Deciding who doesn't make the team can be one of the hardest jobs a coach has. Not every boy can make the majors. Not every boy can start. The coach decides. Sometimes you may feel guilty about the disappointment showing in the face of a boy who doesn't make the team. You may feel responsible for his disappointment or for the anger his parents show. You're not. You had to choose someone. It's part of being a coach. Some people who are made unhappy by a decision need to find reasons why the decision is "bad" or "unfair." Expect it to happen. Don't apologize for doing your job. Don't try to convince them your decision was right. They won't be able to understand just now and an argument won't help anyone. Empathize—don't sympathize. Don't scramble for an explanation that will make everyone happy. There isn't any. Just listen carefully and understand. A decision from someone who understands is easier to take. Not easy. Easier.

How to tell a boy he didn't make the team. Lists are impersonal. The boy deserves to hear it directly from you. It can be difficult to be the bearer of bad news. A boy's sadness or anger may make you feel uncomfortable. It's easier if you remember that this is a normal feeling. You help most by listening and understanding. The boy who takes it glibly may be finding it too painful to let if show. Don't joke with him. That would be "tuning out" the disappointment inside. Allow the defense, but don't join in. Say only, "I appreciate your trying out. I hope you'll try again next year."

How To Set Team Policies

Players follow team rules better if they participate in making them, and understand the reason for them. At an early team meeting discuss the need for rules. Ask the boys for suggestions. Let them know by the way you listen that you value the ideas and feelings of each player. Prove you are a coach who can listen by giving 100% of your attention. Repeat back in your own words what you believe a boy said. If he says, "Yes, that's it" then you both know you have listened and understood.

Players can accept even rules they dislike if they are clear, if the coach believes in the rules and if they apply fairly to all players.

Some Chronic Problems You May Run Into

Some ground rules. Don't try to solve problems in public. Speak to the boy privately. Express your concern. Ask his views on the cause and possible solutions. If he comes up with one that you feel is worth a try, use it. If it doesn't work, offer a solution of your own. Removing him from those situations where the problem comes up may eventually be necessary.

Don't lecture when a player breaks a rule. Don't tell him

that he let you down. Don't tell him how disappointed you are. Casually call it to his attention. If you feel a consequence is in order, select one you feel is appropriate based on your team policies. Don't wave it threateningly over his head. Just do it. Don't make him feel he's in the "dog house." If you've kept things in perspective, dealt with him fairly, and you're comfortable with your decision, he should still feel a valued member of the team.

Don't pick consequences you're going to feel guilty about. If you can't think of an appropriate consequence right away, don't feel on the spot. Tell him you'll think about it and talk with him later.

There may be a boy who "tight rope walks" the line on rules, stepping over now and then. He'll be a few minutes late. Or maybe he'll forget things. Treat the few minutes just as you would an hour or it will get worse. If you permit rule breaking, others may start doing it to get you to take charge.

Being in charge isn't yelling loud or lecturing. It is consistently making your position clear in your actions as well as your words. Players may test the rules periodically. Be prepared to enforce them kindly, firmly, and consistently every time.

The boys will be watching to see if you'll do what you said you would. Will you blow up? Back down? Pretend you didn't notice? Quit liking them? Can they have another chance after they've taken the consequence? Be predictable when the confrontations come.

Swearing. These words may express strong feelings. But that doesn't justify swearing any more than having food in your mouth justifies chewing with your mouth open. But the need to express feelings should be respected. As a coach you have the right to set the standards. Make your expectations clear and follow them yourself. You can help the boys alter the way they express their feelings so they aren't offensive to others. You might suggest they find substitute words. Even invent humorous words for the team. Words that mean "I goofed" or "I'm mad."

In the same way, a coach can be alert in seeing things unique to the team that will help build camaraderie. The best ones aren't manufactured. They happen and are spotted by a sensitive coach as something special for his team. A water container became Minnesota and Michigan's "Little Brown Jug." You might make one of your old hats the team's "hardest worker in practice" award. The value is in what it represents.

Dissension on the team. Dissension is a by-product when players feel unappreciated. While it is more common on losing teams, it can happen to winners, too. So look beyond just the losses for the cause. Ask questions. Perhaps you haven't given enough praise or recognition for what the boys are doing right. Are the goals too high? Is there time for fun on your team? Or has there been too much play? Listen for criticism from your players. Don't take it personally. Try to get things out in the open. Does the critic have a good point? Can you give him credit for the suggestion, or at least for coming to you with it? You must be doing something right if you've created an atmosphere that permits players to come to you with problems.

Back talk. Recognize back talk as the expression of hurt or angry feelings. Accept the feelings. Say something like, "I can understand your being disappointed at not getting to start." Don't get pulled into an argument. Tell him you will talk to him privately later. If he doesn't stop, tell him he has the choice of stopping or being excused from the field.

Quarreling and fighting. Separate the boys early. They can't fight if they're not around each other. A quarrel or a fight stops when the boys are given a choice between stopping themselves or being separated. Don't worry about who's at fault. (It's always the other guy.) Both made a mistake. One started it. The other decided to continue it.

Temper tantrums. If a boy becomes so angry he's losing control of himself, rescue him from the situation with a quick removal. It's kinder to give him that momentary embarrassment than to allow him to further humiliate himself or hurt others.

Temper tantrums are hard work. A boy will give them up when they aren't successful in getting what he wants.

Added thoughts: boys lacking in self-confidence may show their problems in a variety of ways. Each is seeking attention, sometimes without appearing to do so. Often a boy is not consciously aware of why he does it. The coach understands that any kind of attention can encourage behavior. Lecturing the boy who is always late may encourage him to keep it up if that's how he feels he can get the most attention. A casual consequence with minimum attention is a better solution. If you recognize the basic problem of low self esteem, you can avoid being provoked and respond to what's right about the boy— encouraging change and growth.

The Man in Charge

by **Al Rosen,** *former star third baseman for the Cleveland Indians.*

If a boys'-league manager had only two words in which to get his message across to parents, the words probably would be: "Trust me."

If I were to expand on the message, I would say something like this: "You have the boy all the rest of the week, but turn him over to me for a two-hour practice and two ball games. I mean turn him over completely, with no strings attached. Give me your confidence. I am going to be in control of myself at all times. I will expect a lot from your boy, but I can teach him a lot and I am not going to let him down."

The Little League manager must start out with the parents' trust. If he does not have it, he is facing an impossible job. And he should retain that trust through the entire season, unless

Excerpts from pages 25-32 in *Baseball and Your Boy: A Parents' Guide to Little League Baseball* by Al Rosen (Funk and Wagnalls). Copyright © 1967 by Albert Rosen. Reprinted by permission of Thomas Y. Crowell Company, Inc.

his conduct clearly indicates that he is unworthy of his responsibilities. Unworthy, here, does not mean imperfect. All managers, Little League and major league, are imperfect in that they are human and will make mistakes.

The ideal Little League manager would combine the better qualities of Walter Alston and Sigmund Freud. There will not be one in your neighborhood. But there will be men of excellent intentions, of warm interest in boys and baseball, who are going to do the best they can.

To be unworthy of handling boys, a manager would have to be a bad influence on them or guilty of rash and irresponsible conduct. Frankly, I have never seen a manager like that in a boys' league or one who did not deserve the confidence and help of the parents. The nature of his job requires that he be a figure of authority to the boys, and he must be free from parental backbiting and second-guessing.

The youngster will get his lessons in democracy-in-action from other sources. Organized sports are not democratic nor should they be. They teach respect for authority, discipline, and the individual's role in a group activity. The major-league manager who goes to the mound to remove a faltering pitcher does not start out by saying, "You may feel differently but . . ." The manager's job is to make the decisions, and he does not poll an electorate.

The Little League manager should have what is known at officers' training school as command presence. When he sets down the rules, he should act as if it had never occurred to him that they would be questioned or disobeyed. The manager may be benevolent, but he is always the despot.

Discipline is essential in organized athletics. Demands are placed on the athlete that he conform to the standards of his sport. This will be something new to the Little Leaguer. Never before will he have been asked to give so much to anything. He will be told he must devote his full energy to every action on the field. He will be told he must "hustle" even in what will seem small, meaningless ways, such as running back and forth to his position.

Even on the Little League level, the boys should be initiated into the belief that baseball requires all-out effort. But with boys of this age, the manager will not get the desired response merely by being demanding. He must make distinctions, know

when to be forceful and when to be good humored and understanding. He succeeds best when the players give him their
full energies because they want to and because they are enjoying themselves.

Some things a manager should tell his players only once and
then expect compliance. There is nothing to confound the
young mind in being told not to throw bubble-gum wrappers on
the field. If somebody does anyway, the manager must react
briskly. Yet he must explain twenty times how to field a
ground ball correctly and not lose his temper when the boy still
cannot do it properly. A distinction must always be made between lack of effort and lack of skill. The manager should say
nothing about an error but sharply criticize a boy for failing to
run after a missed ball. The unforgivable baseball sin, the
youngster must learn, is not failure, but failure to put forth his
best efforts.

Many professional managers have impressed an audience by
growling, "I treat all my players just the same." It sounds
good. It is good, too, in a limited sense, if what the manager
means is what society would refer to as equality before the
law. In other words, the star player caught tiptoeing in after
curfew should be assessed the same fine as the third-string
catcher. The rules should be for everybody.

However, if the manager is also implying that he treats
every player in the same way, uses the same approach on all
the diverse personalities, either he is kidding somebody or he
is not very good at his job. If a manager is to get the most out
of his players, he must be conscious of their differences and act
accordingly. This is even more important for the manager dealing with youngsters, for he is especially concerned with their
development as humans, as well as athletes. His motto might
be: "Treat them all differently."

It starts out with the physical contrasts that are glaringly
apparent on the first day the manager meets his team. Among
the fifteen youngsters will be the tall and the short, the strong
and the weak, the quick and the slow. What can be expected of
them will be determined largely by their natural capabilities.
The contrast in personalities will be equally sharp, but not so
immediately apparent. The boys sometimes offer misleading
clues to what is going on inside their heads.

The manager may be baffled the first time he runs into the

kind of boy who seems determined to be unhappy in the Little League. He complains constantly. He goes out of his way to provoke his teammates. From the first day of practice, he starts telling his parents that the manager does not like him and will not give him a chance, and that the other players are all against him. The manager comes to realize that, even before he gets a chance, the boy is constructing his excuse, that behind his quarrelsome front he is asking private questions, "Am I really good enough? Can I compete with the others? What if I fail?" A degree in psychiatry is not needed to perceive this boy's problem. And a Little League manager sometimes can help even when he does not fully understand why the youngster acts as he does.

Most groups have at least one extremely aggressive boy. When the tendencies are exaggerated, he becomes the bully. Sports competition often can do a great deal for a youth of this temperament. His high spirits, even his hostility, can be channeled into a socially acceptable expression. Instead of being the neighborhood headache, he can become the hero. Boys of this type often become excellent athletes.

Of course, the manager must start out by putting a harness on the aggressive youth. If the manager is permissive, the boy can be a disruptive influence on the team. The manager holds one powerful weapon that is not available at home or in school. This youngster often wants greatly to compete in baseball and, if he does not follow the rules, the manager can withhold the privilege. The boy will be facing authority backed up by a power he has to respect. A manager who did not put this power to use would not be fair to the boy or the team. The price of making exceptions is too high, even when it means losing an important game. The aggressive boy is easy to identify. For one thing, the manager will always hear him "sounding off." The manager knows he will have to control the boy from the start or there will be trouble.

At the other end of the spectrum is the passive boy. He is easier to overlook because he will be provoking no noisy rows. Yet his hostility may go deeper and be more dangerous merely because he cannot express it. This boy often will pose too difficult a problem for the manager to handle. He is hard to motivate because his pleasure comes from lack of success, from being stepped on. Indeed, this boy finds success itself frightening, and encouragement serves only to push him farther into his retreat. So the manager must proceed carefully. His efforts should be directed toward helping the youngster gain pleasure from positive achievement rather than continued satisfaction from self-denial.

However, few problems will be that difficult. With no help from a textbook on psychiatry, the manager can see that some boys respond to a pat on the back and an encouraging word and that others occasionally need a show of strength. The manager must also be content with small successes. He must try to help a little and not expect to remodel his charges completely.

In dealing with his players as individuals with different needs, the manager runs the risk of showing favoritism. It is an easy error to fall into. Some of the ten-year-olds are very attractive, and the manager may unwittingly give them more than their share of attention. A team of young boys can become very much like a large family group. The manager is looked on as the father. The players can experience jealousies like those among brothers, and the manager will face resentments from those who feel they are being neglected.

If the manager is careful to avoid favoritism, however, he will not have much trouble if his actions are sensible and appropriate. That might be described as doing what the boys can understand, even though they might not always approve. Jimmy is pleased with himself if he hits five straight pitches squarely in batting practice. Yet he may resent it when the manager says, "That's all," and lets Billy step up and take five minutes and a dozen swings to connect once. Jimmy may also resent the manager's spending one minute watching him throw and ten minutes watching and correcting Billy. In such instances, a casual sentence or two can put salve on a wound. The manager can move over beside Jimmy for a moment, ask him how he is doing and then say, "I'm giving Billy extra help with his throwing. He's having some trouble."

What he says is the truth, and Jimmy will realize that it is a compliment to him that he does not need as much help. While he may still resent it a little that he does not get more attention, he will at least understand.

As it is for parents, the key word for the manager is *awareness*, trying to decide what course is appropriate for each of his players. A manager is always forced to do things that will hurt some boys, and he will want to do them in ways that will cause as little pain as possible.

Only a few boys can pitch, and many will want to. Only one can bat fourth, the prestige position in the line-up, and several will think they should. Adroit maneuvering can smooth the sharp edges of some problems. What difference does it make and how much does the team suffer if the best hitter does not always bat fourth? He can be placed third or fifth in some games while another youngster enjoys the distinction of being the clean-up hitter.

But some problems must be met head-on. If for the good of the team the boy who wants to play second base is needed in center field, the manager is obliged to break the news in the best way he knows. With some he must do it very gently and with some very firmly. Yet the sacrifice involved is one of the lessons a young man can learn as an individual taking part in a team sport.

The manager can not afford to be too thin-skinned. In a moment of disappointment, the youngster may turn his anger toward the manager. Still, it usually is not until the boy takes his grievance home that the repercussions come. Most of the time they arrive by telephone. Even while getting an uncomplimentary earful, the manager must try to keep cool and remember how parents suffer along with their children. The manager can expect more trouble from the parents than from the boys, and he should establish definite rules for dealing with both.

My players are under strict orders during games. When they are not on the field, all of them are to be sitting on the bench. They are not to leave the bench without permission. They cannot eat candy or drink pop during a game, and if they chew bubble gum, the wrappers are not to be thrown on the ground. As long as the restrictions are made clear, the boys are not much of a problem.

The parents obviously are more difficult. The manager cannot order them to do anything. All he can do is ask. What I ask of the players' parents is that they stay away from behind the bench during games and that they do not talk to their sons. They are also requested to cheer for all the players and not only for their offspring, and to refrain from saying anything that puts more pressure on a boy. It sounds innocent enough to yell, "Get a hit, Billy!" but I ask them not to do even that. It suggests that a demand is being made of the boy, which puts him under more pressure. "Come on, Billy!" is good enough.

In summing up the role of a Little League manager, it can be said that he need not be a genius in tactics nor a master of child psychology. But he should not take the job unless he will perform it seriously and accept the responsibilities. He has fifteen impressionable children looking up to him. He will make mistakes, and they will still accept him. But he should never do anything that would make him seem unworthy in their eyes.

Comments

I make sure my kids all play, that practices are supervised, that there is no cursing, that I have good volunteer coaches . . . I try for 7-6 games . . . I have not had an injury in four years . . . Frankly, my kids don't hit hard enough to hurt each other . . . I can assure you the future of tomorrow is bright, very bright, because the youth of today are tremendous—just tremendous! That's from someone who knows. Man, I love 'em all.

—Dick Timmerman
Myrtle Beach, S.C.[1]

The Challenge of Coaching

Al Rosen's 10-year-old son Robby announced he was going to try out for baseball. Rosen, of course, was pleased and volunteered to serve as coach. Robby asked if he thought his father had enough experience. "Wouldn't it be better if you started out the first year as an assistant coach?" Rosen, winner of the Most Valuable Player Award in 1954 and who for 5 years had over 100 RBI's, was having his qualifications questioned by his son! Rosen writes, "The funny thing about it, he was right to wonder. I had played the game for 20 years, but I found out that I did not know anything about teaching it to beginners."

Two myths exist about coaching children's sports. One is that the only qualification needed is to have played the sport. The second is that the better a person played, the better coach he or she will be. The ingredients that make a good youth sports coach are much more than simply having been a player in the past. In addition to knowing the sport, a good coach must know something about *kids*. A coach must know about the physical development of youngsters—what they are capable of doing and not doing. A coach must know about differences in personality—that what is right for one youngster is not necessarily right for another, or even for the same youngster in a different situation. A good coach must be an astute teacher, a clever psychologist, a pragmatic philosopher, and a shrewd businessperson.

Another flourishing misconception in our society is that a successful coach is a winning coach. Although at one time this view may have been restricted to the ranks of high school, college, and professional sports, today it is a prevalent attitude in children's sports. For some coaches, the visible end result of any contest—winning—becomes more important than the less visible means—tyranny.

Successful coaches do more, much more, than merely win games. Winning is the immediate, short-term goal of every contest, and both coach and athlete should seek the prize of victory. To do less is to be a dishonest competitor. But truly successful coaches consider winning to be a by-product in the achievement of more important long-term goals. Successful coaches place great importance on teaching well the fundamentals of the sport so that youngsters have the basis for developing their capabilities to the fullest in future years. Successful coaches teach youngsters the satisfaction of striving for excellence, regardless of the outcome. They teach them to enjoy success and to respond to failure with renewed determination. They help children develop positive attitudes toward themselves; and successful coaches help youngsters learn standards of conduct acceptable to society.

The value of sports for each child is dependent so much on the coach's sense of values. The successful coach is one who conveys

The value of time	The power of kindness
The satisfaction of perseverance	The wisdom of honesty
	The influence of example
The meaning of effort	The rewards of cooperation
The dignity of humility	The virture of patience and
The worth of character	The joy of competition.

The challenge for any coach is to make some progress toward conveying these values while striving for victory, and yet not to diminish any of the fun inherent in sports participation. Coaches too often forget that fun is the mortar of a successful sport experience. Without fun, youngsters turn their interests elsewhere or fail to make the commitment to sports which is needed to acquire these values. It is the false importance that coaches give to winning that almost always threatens to obliterate the fun in sports.

The challenge of coaching young athletes is indeed great, but the rewards for meeting this challenge also are great. Good coaches help youngsters acquire a sense of identity and integrity, poor coaches develop feelings of insecurity and debasement. Good coaches strive to build character, poor coaches create "characters."

Who Are America's Volunteer Coaches?

Little information has been available in the past about those adults who give their time and often their money to serve the community as volunteer coaches. But a recent survey of volunteer coaches in the State of Illinois[2] has provided information about their identity, their motives for coaching, and their attitudes toward key issues in sports. The survey consisted of 423 volunteers who were coaching one of the following sports: baseball, softball, basketball, football, gymnastics, ice hockey, soccer, swimming, or wrestling.

The average age of the coaches was 36 years, 92% were males (with the females coaching primarily swimming and gymnastics), and 83% were married. These volunteers spent an average of 11 hours per week coaching during the season, and the average season was 17 weeks long. They averaged 6 years of coaching experience, and their mean educational level was 2 years of college. The education of the coaches was quite high: 26% had earned a high school diploma, 34% had received a bachelor's degree, and 20% had completed some graduate study. Thirty-two per cent were in some profession, another 32% were in some business career, 22% were in skilled or unskilled labor, and 14% were in other types of occupations (including students).

Among these volunteers, 63% had coached their own child in the past, and 47% were now coaching their son or daughter. Over 66% of the coaches indicated they had received no formal training to be a coach, but almost all coaches were interested in receiving some training. Eighty-five per cent indicated they planned to continue coaching for at least 1 more year.

Coaches also completed a scale which assessed their motivation for volunteering to coach in children's sports. Three types of motives were measured—task, affiliation, and self motivation. A coach high in *task motivation* places emphasis on teaching the skills of the sport, on helping children develop physically, and on helping children play as well as they can. A coach high in *affiliation motivation* places emphasis on cooperation and on the social interaction among coach, players, and others involved in the sport. Coaches high in *self motivation* are concerned more with achieving recognition for themselves through their coaching. On a scale from 7 (low) to 21 (high), coaches, on the average, indicated they were more task motivated (16.4) than affiliation motivated (13.9), and least of all self motivated (11.5).

Coaches also were asked to indicate the importance of three objectives of children's sports—socialization, having fun, and winning. The socialization objective refers to helping youngsters develop physically, psychologically, and socially. The coaches rated the socialization objective clearly as the most important (8.1 on a scale from 3 to 9). Winning was rated the lowest (3.9) and fun fell in between (5.8). These attitudes certainly run counter to the criticisms we so often hear about coaches who are obsessed with winning. Perhaps coaches are much less concerned with winning than we have been led to believe. Or perhaps coaches do not always behave in ways consistent with their expressed attitudes—something which needs to be investigated.

The coaches also were asked to express their opinion about a number of key issues by indicating whether they thought a statement was true—both in children's sports in general and in their specific program. The scale permitted coaches to rate each statement from 0% agreement to 100% agreement. Results of four key issues are given below:

Children's sports programs over-emphasize winning.
    In *general* true   73%   In *my program* true   49%

Coaches are poor leaders.
    In *general* true   38%   In *my program* true   27%

Kids are placed under too much stress.

In *general* true   49%   In *my program* true   31%

Parents frequently interfere.

In *general* true   52%   In *my program* true   31%

It is evident that coaches see the problems in children's sports to be greater in programs other than their own. This is as might be expected, particularly with the almost constant negative publicity given to children's sports programs by the media. Except for the over-emphasis-on-winning issue, coaches do not show *high* agreement with most of these prevalent criticisms, especially in their own programs.

Overall, the survey results indicate that most coaches are quite well-educated and are altruistic in their motives. Although the majority lack training as coaches, they would welcome the opportunity to receive such training.

In Praise of Coaches

The United States has one of the most extensive amateur sports programs in the world. Most of these programs are possible only because adults volunteer to become coaches and officials of one type or another. If communities relied entirely on trained, professional leadership to administer and coach, millions of kids would not get to play because the programs would be too expensive. In our quest to improve the quality of children's sports programs, we should not forget the generosity of these adult volunteers.

As so often is the case, a few bad apples can spoil the barrel. It takes only one "bad" coach, and the attention which he or she attracts, to defile the image of a thousand good coaches. It does not nullify, of course, the good work of those coaches, but it certainly taints their image. This is unfortunate, for it must have adverse effects on the efforts of league directors to attract capable adults into coaching. And one wonders how many good coaches quit because they refuse to hassle with the one "bad apple."

Over the past few years I have interviewed and observed hundreds of coaches. My experiences convince me that the vast majority deserve the accolades of the community. We read and hear so much criticism of coaches that we are led to believe that the bad apples predominate. But this is not so.

Most coaches have the well-being of athletes as their primary interest. Certainly coaches make mistakes—just as children's parents and teachers make mistakes. (And sometimes the coach does the right thing, but the kids are at fault!) Yet the intent and effort of most coaches are positive. What is needed, however, is a means for culling out the bad apples and helping the coaches with good intentions do the best coaching they possibly can.

The Need for Coaching Training Programs

Although most volunteer coaches succeed reasonably well without any formal training, most would benefit substantially from such training. It is disconcerting to know that considerable knowledge exists about how to coach effectively, yet there is almost no means for volunteer coaches to obtain this information. The efforts which are being made to improve the quality of coaching in this country are directed exclusively toward those who already have some training and are being paid to coach—namely, the school and college coaches.

Based on current practice, our society apparently believes that the best coaching is needed at the higher levels of competition. It is my contention that these higher levels are the easier at which to coach, and that the coach probably has the least influence on the players and the outcome of the contest at these levels. The best coaching is needed with novices. Good coaching is more important for the beginner because it establishes the basis for future success and satisfaction. Yet, almost always the least qualified coaches are given these most challenging positions. (Considering the behavior of some of our most eminent coaches who have had extensive training, it may be a blessing in disguise that they are not coaching the young beginner!)

Among children's coaches two types of coaching problems prevail. The first occurs among coaches who lack training and therefore make errors simply because they do not have adequate knowledge. The second occurs among coaches who are so caught up with winning that they care about the kids only as long as they are winning. Training programs can help both types of coach, but coaches of the latter type are often more difficult to reach because they usually do not perceive that they need any training. And if they are receptive to any training, the only information they are likely to be interested in is that which will help them win.

Coaches not only need to learn how to teach the specific techniques or skills of a sport, but they also need information about physical conditioning, nutrition, weight control, and injury prevention and treatment. They need information about motor development and principles of skill learning. Coaches need to know about sport psychology—about the causes of competitive stress and the factors influencing motivation. They especially need to understand how to communicate effectively with young athletes.

When suddenly thrust into the role of coach, novices do the obvious. They coach as they were coached or as they see others coach. Novice coaches are particularly likely to imitate the style of some winning college or professional coach because such coaches are likely to receive considerable publicity for their success. Such coaching practices may be appropriate for achieving the goals of professional adult sports, but seldom are they suitable for obtaining the long-term goals of children's sports. And the tragedy is that some novice coaches fail to recognize the difference. Twenty-five years ago it was known that depriving athletes of water during intensive competition is foolish, yet coaches continue to do so. Coaches still teach sit-ups incorrectly, inefficiently organize practices, misunderstand the principles of physical conditioning, give poor or incorrect nutritional advice, and use sarcasm as a substitute for positive instruction. Why? Because their coach did it with them.

Almost every other major sporting nation has a comprehensive training program for coaches at all levels of amateur sports. Although a few isolated examples of training programs can be found in the United States, we have yet to develop a comprehensive system for providing volunteer coaches with an opportunity to improve their coaching effectiveness. Nothing will improve the quality of children's sports more than the development of training programs for coaches. The knowledge exists, the personnel capable of delivering such information are available, and effective delivery systems can be implemented easily. All that is needed is the money.

And speaking of money. . . . Currently the United States Congress is debating a bill which would provide the United

States Olympic Committee with 20 million dollars and eventually would fund the USOC to the tune of 80 million dollars annually. Yet no plan has been proposed for the expenditure of such huge amounts to develop a national training program for novice coaches. Instead, too much of the concern is directed exclusively at developing highly gifted athletes, conducting research only to help these talented few, and providing the best trained coaches for them. At most, 5,000 athletes will benefit from the 80 million dollars per year that is being proposed. But what about the other 16,995,000 youngsters who participate in sports each year? How much will we be willing to spend to help them experience the joy of sports? Six million dollars from an 80 million dollar budget could provide a comprehensive training program for *all* amateur sports coaches. What will our political and sports leaders choose to do? Will they spend 80 million to help 5,000 athletes and not 6 million to help 17 million athletes?

Rewards of Coaching

It is fitting that our major concern is for the benefits youngsters derive from their sports programs, but we should not forget that adult coaches are seeking some rewards for their involvement as well—and rightfully so. What is it in coaching that attracts adults to give hundreds of hours each season to helping children experience sports? Several potential rewards exist.

First, coaches' altruistic behaviors can offer them a great deal of personal satisfaction; the satisfaction of helping youngsters, of providing a community service, and of meeting their own recreational needs. In short, coaching can be fun; the activity is intrinsically rewarding. Second, adults can acquire community recognition for their coaching achievements. Third, coaching provides an excellent opportunity for social interaction not only with young people, but other adults as well. Finally, coaching provides an opportunity for former athletes to continue their involvement in a sport they enjoy. It is a means of extending their participation, of continuing to play vicariously.

When kept in perspective, all of these rewards are deserved by coaches who strive to do their best. But when they coach primarily to achieve community recognition through winning or mainly to vicariously relive their spent youth without regard to the long-term goals of children's sports, then they are *using* children to meet their own needs. Such coaches are not needed, and they should be removed from their coaching positions or educated to accept and work toward the long-term goals of children's sports.

References

1. Beanballs 'n backslaps. *The Christian Athlete*, March 1977, p. 28.
2. Martens, R., & Gould, D. R. Who are America's volunteer coaches. Unpublished manuscript, 1978.

SECTION B

Parents—They Always Know Best

Little League and Charlie

by **Donald Kaul,** *member of the* Des Moines Register *news staff.*

There's only one thing wrong with Little League baseball.
The kids.

Lord knows the adults have done everything in their power to make the Little League a spectacular success; it's the youngsters who keep messing things up.

The pitchers don't throw hard enough, the hitters don't hit often enough and the runners don't run fast enough. It's shameful.

One could argue that the boys play well enough for 10 and 12 years olds, and they do. But this ignores the fact that the adults have provided a setting of sultanic splendor for the Little Leaguers.

These kids not only have leagues and schedules, they have ballparks, scoreboards, bullpens, dugouts, loudspeaker systems, bleachers and uniforms with numbers on them. They have managers, coaches, batboys and cheering sections. They have, in short, facilities that Tom Swift would have traded his Zeppelin for.

And what do the adults get for providing all of this? A game shoddily played by children. They deserve better.

Take the case of Charlie, for example. Charlie sells insurance. When he was a lad, however, he didn't dream of selling insurance; he dreamed of playing centerfield for the New York Yankees just like Joe DiMaggio. To this day Charlie believes that he could have realized his dream had his father but encouraged his ambition, had he but had the proper early training. So, naturally, Charlie is now seeing to it that HIS son, Charlie Junior, gets encouragement and instruction in Little League. The problem is that Charlie Junior not only has his father's best wishes, he has the old man's co-ordination, too. He strikes out when he should be hitting home runs. He waits for grounders he should charge and he charges those that need patience. When Charlie the insurance salesman comes to the games he quite naturally expects his son to be a little Mickey Mantle. After all, the kid's got the instruction, right? He's even got the equipment. Seeing the kid play like a 10-year-old under those conditions upsets old Charlie. He yells at his son, he yells at the opposing players, he yells at the umpire and, at very bad moments, he jumps up and down on his Little League hat. Who can blame him?

It would be bad enough if the failure of the Little League were simply a matter of physical ineptitude but it also involves a failure of the spirit.

The kids don't seem to show any perseverance. Let them get 20 or 30 runs behind and they get discouraged. They stop talking it up in the infield. They tend to show sportsmanship. They don't argue with the umpire when they know he's right; a distinct lack of moxie. Very often they seem more concerned with having a good time than with winning the ball game. Disgraceful.

The younger generation is letting the older generation down.

Advice For Fathers

by **Al Rosen,** *former star third baseman for the Cleveland Indians.*

Little League critics often suggest posting a sign for fathers reading "Keep Out." While such a solution sounds simple, it is highly impractical. To begin with, the manager urgently requires the help of some of the fathers. He needs them as coaches at the games and to help him run the practices. Moreover, most boys do not want their fathers barred from the Little League. Of course, no boy wants his dad embarrassing him by screaming at the umpire or by making a spectacle of himself, but he does want his father to see him play and share in his triumphs. Critics who do not understand this miss something that is essential in the Little League experience. The family is included. The games make the boy the object of some neighborhood attention, one of the reasons why he finds it exciting.

The father-son relationship is at the heart of the Little League experience, and probably no father wants less than the best for his boy. This is true even when a father's conduct seems to send him headlong in the opposite direction. It is not only the boys who need sympathy and understanding. It must be remembered that sometimes the father acts as he does because he cannot stand to see his boy hurt and disappointed. In a rather pathetic way, such a father cannot help himself.

Most fathers have played baseball and are well equipped to help a beginner, but they must avoid a few pitfalls right from the start. Some fathers are overzealous as instructors. They give the boy more advice than he can handle. If such a father keeps up a running stream of critical commentary every time they play catch, the boy soon finds it is not much fun. He wants some instruction to work on, so that he can feel he is improving, but not so much that it defeats him.

When I was starting out in the minor leagues, I got to know another young player whose father had been one of baseball's greatest stars. I was dazzled by his father's reputation, and I tried to talk to him about the older man. He refused to discuss him. From the time he had been a boy, his father had erected impossibly high baseball standards for him. As a result, he had soured on both his father and the game and, although he had some ability, he did not stay in baseball very long.

Most fathers of Little Leaguers will find that their position as baseball authorities will not go unchallenged for long. This is a very interesting development. The image of the Little League manager suddenly intrudes on the father-son relationship. When the father is showing the boy how to throw, the youngster will say, "But Mr. Jones told us . . ." In the following weeks, what Mr. Jones said and what Mr. Jones did will be described across many a dinner table. Unless the father is careful, he will find he is thoroughly resenting Mr. Jones. Until Mr. Jones popped up, the father had been the unquestioned authority on all masculine subjects, the oracle to be consulted for an explanation of the passed ball or the hit-and-run. In addition, he was the most important man, the most impressive man, the boy could imagine.

As the director of the boy's baseball destiny, however, the manager is a formidable rival. He may loom up as a combination of Casey Stengel and the Duke of Wellington in the youth's impressionable eyes. The father may be surprised to find himself leaping into the conversation to debate Mr. Jones' baseball theories and expressing resentments he would never have suspected in himself. If he is discerning enough, he will catch himself, grin, and vow to put up with the boy's new idol.

The manager needs more than the father's mere tolerance. He can use his active cooperation. Much of the boy's progress will depend on what he does outside of practice. Our team has only a two-hour practice each week, which does not offer much opportunity for the youngster to apply what he is learning. The polishing must be done away from practice, in the back yard and corner lot. If there is enough space available, the father can hit grounders or flies. If not, he can toss grounders or short pops. If the boy is a pitcher, the father can get a catcher's mitt and provide the target for an evening session. He can even toss up pitches so the youngster can take a half-swing and learn to improve his hitting.

Without ever stepping on the practice field or saying a word to the manager, the father can find out the lessons his son has been taught and help the boy to absorb them.

However, in many instances the boy will not be taught very much by the manager. When it gets right down to it, many managers are not good instructors. Either they do not know enough about the game's techniques, or they have trouble communicating with beginners, no easy task. After all, most of them are managers only because they like baseball and they like kids and because they know that if they do not volunteer their services, there can be no league.

In the absence of sound teaching, the father has every right to take over the instructor's role and to give his son the individual attention he is not getting at practice. Without undercutting the manager, he can show the boy how the basic things are done, or, if he does not know, he can find out.

Yet even more important than instructing the youngster is the father's attitude toward his son's performance in the boys' league. The key word for the father, it seems to me, should be *awareness*. He should try to be aware of his own emotions and those of his son. A man should realize that his own pride gets mixed up in his feelings about "his son, the Little Leaguer." He should know that one reason he wants the boy to do well is because it reflects on him. In the opposite circumstance, the boy's failure becomes his own. He should realize that the dreams of glory he might have for the young athlete are not completely unselfish.

But if his motives are not untainted, they also are completely human. The father who is aware of his own pride, even capable of being amused by his imperfections, will keep himself well under control. Even the best-intentioned father, however, is not assured of a successful relationship with the Little Leaguer. It is not that simple. Sometimes, a father in trying to meet his son's needs can misjudge what is required of him.

A good player who has struck out three straight times and made a couple of errors does not want to be told, "You did just fine, son." The boy knows how he did, and he is unhappy about it.

A youngster whose error has just lost the game does not want to hear, while his grief is still sharp and fresh, "It really isn't that important." At the moment, it *is* important to the boy. He expects to be permitted the dignity of his unhappiness.

In both instances, the father meant well. He wanted to cheer up his son. But the defect lay in a lack of sincerity and a superficial response. Youngsters seem to have a built-in apparatus for detection of "phony" attitudes, and they resent them deeply. When the father is insincere, the son reduces the value to be placed on his words, and later the boy will be unable to get full satisfaction from praise that may be deserved.

Let us take the youngster whose error lost the game. Suppose the father had instead put an arm around the boy's shoulder, said, "That's tough, Billy, but there will be other days," given him a decent interval for despondency, and then moved on cheerfully to discussing other affairs of the day. The father would not be minimizing his boy's unhappiness, but his response would offer a sense of proportion. He would be indicating that he understands the boy must care and be hurt by the error, and that he sympathizes with his son's feelings, but that this is not a disaster from which recovery is unlikely.

In the beginning especially, the youngster needs a great deal of encouragement. It is not unusual for a boy to go through his first season without getting a hit, even if he has ability. The father who can tell his boy, "Keep swinging, you'll get going," with the appropriately light touch, can make it easier. And the father is not being insincere. From his greater experience, he knows the boy will improve if he does not become discouraged.

Few valid guidelines can be set down for the conduct of Little League fathers. Such a wide variety of father-son relationships are possible that they defy most generalizations. One proud parent must learn to grit his teeth and watch his awkward boy consistently outdone by the neighbors' children but still respond positively to the modest achievements that lie within the boy's ability.

Interference of parents is undoubtedly the biggest problem of the Little League, but even here it is questionable if a rigid rule can be set down against all interference. Parents must guard against the impulse to spring to their son's defense every time they think somebody has wronged him. The most serious consequence is not that the manager will be irritated, which he will be, or that the team will be affected, which it could be, but that oversympathetic and emotional parents can prevent a youth from facing up to reality.

One can imagine an instance in which a boy looked forward with great anticipation to being a pitcher in his final Little League season only to be told that he would be an infielder instead. This might strike him as unjust and a harsh blow. Naturally, he would bring his grievance home, looking for support. He might even want to quit the team. The greatest danger is in the parents' emotional response. Most parents would jump to their boy's defense. Sometimes a father might react strongly the other way, accusing his son of being a quitter. The wisest one would make no immediate judgment at all, siding with neither the boy nor the manager. Instead of leaping to conclusions, he would discuss the problem patiently and try to point out the possibility of viewpoints other than the one his son is taking. Without preaching, he could indicate that a manager has responsibilities to an entire team and that the individual must sometimes give up something for the common good. The father might then let the boy think it over and decide for himself what he wanted to do. The father should then go along with the boy's decision, even if he might not agree with it. Such a course would encourage the youngster to take responsibility, a most worthy objective.

But it is not hard to imagine times at which parents would

feel obliged to make a complaint to the manager. For example, a parent might think there was something very wrong about a boy attending every practice and never getting in a game. I would agree with the parent. Most of the benefits of a boys' league obviously are wiped out if the youngster doesn't get to play. Our league has a rule that every boy must play in each game. Many leagues do. But for those that do not, the parent has reason to protest when winning becomes more important than everybody participating.

Of course, complaints should never be made to the manager when he is surrounded by the team at the field. And second-guessing his strategy is at no time within the limits of fair criticism in a Little League, and especially not right after a ball game.

Here is a checklist a father might consider when his son is starting out in a boys' league. If he can answer yes to all the questions, he will find no trouble ahead.

Can you give him up? That means putting the boy completely in the hands of the manager to make his own way with the team. It means accepting the manager's authority and the fact that the manager may gain some of the boy's admiration that once was directed to you.

Can you admit your shortcomings? When your son asks to be shown the best way to field a grounder, it takes something for a father to admit he does not know. Still, it is the proper response if true. The interested father tells the boy he will find out.

Can you accept his triumphs? It sounds easy, but it is not always so. Some fathers do not realize it, but they are competitive with their sons. If they play catch, they throw the ball too hard for the boy, a way of showing him how much better they are. When the boy recounts something that has impressed him, their impulse is to recall something that was even better. If the boy does well in a baseball game, they bring up something more impressive from memories of their own triumphs.

Can you accept his disappointments? Sometimes being a father means being a target for a child's anger and frustration. It goes along with the job. Accepting his disappointments also means watching him make the error that loses the game and failing while his buddies succeed. Or not being embarrassed into anger when your ten-year-old breaks into tears after losing.

Can you show him self-control? Civilized conduct is basically taught at home and mostly by example. The Little League manager cannot be asked to work instant transformations. The boy's conduct will reflect his home life. But the manager's task becomes immeasurably more difficult if fathers lose control of themselves at the games, shout at the players and the umpires. A manager can hardly be expected to teach sportsmanship and decent restraint to youngsters whose fathers obviously lack these qualities.

Can you give him some time? Some fathers are very busy and this becomes a problem, because they are interested and want to encourage their boys. Probably the best solution is never to promise more than you can deliver. If a father tells a boy he will play with him all evening, the boy will be unhappy if he has to quit after ten minutes. If the father explains he is busy and can spare only ten minutes, the boy is less likely to be dissatisfied.

Can you let him make his own decisions? This is an essential part of the boy's growing up. It is a real challenge to any father. It means offering suggestions and guidance but finally, within reasonable limits, letting the boy go his own way. Every father has ambitions for his son, but he must accept the fact that he cannot mold the boy's life. Baseball offers the father a minor initiation into the major process of letting go.

The development in the father-son relationship can be one of the warm, meaningful aspects of Little League baseball. It can provide both with some years they will always want to remember.

Developing a Realistic Success Expectancy in Young Athletes

by **Thomas P. Johnson,** *former Little League player, coach, and umpire, and now a psychiatrist in San Diego, California.*

A continuing natural psychological task of children is their constant exploring and learning about their world. A critical aspect is the way they evolve a self-concept of their value, how and where they fit into their world. Normally the potential scope and complexity of the world for each child is constantly expanding as still more information floods in each day. Hopefully, it comes at a rate the child can handle. It's important he not be overwhelmed and retreat because it seems "too much." Equally bad is "too little" to make his day exciting, challenging and rewarding as only the sense of progress toward some goal can bring. Adults can help keep the process moving optimally by respecting the individuality and "specialness" of each child within a framework of regard for others, sharing and the varying needs for privacy, special interests and pace of each child.

Abridged from *The Humanistic and Mental Health Aspects of Sports, Exercise and Recreation,* T. T. Craig (Ed.). Chicago: American Medical Association, 1976, pp. 68-70. Reprinted with permission of the author and publisher.

Most people would not quarrel with this basic concept, but the application may often be clouded by the child's great reliance on feedback he reads from the key adults and peers in his life. It is through his perception of their attitudes toward how he measures up that he is guided in his choice of action and feelings about the results. Dangers exist that others, even though well-intentioned, may unwittingly excessively seek satisfaction of their own needs through the life of the child. Also, the child without sensitive adults to tune in to how he might be perceiving things and offer appropriate assistance may be handicapped by misinterpretation of data.

Sports are a normal and potentially beneficial part of each child's life. There should be opportunities for a complete spectrum from unstructured to highly organized, from adult supervised to peers just working things out, from individual to team efforts. Children naturally test against and compare themselves with their own past performances, and with others as a way of locating themselves in relation to others and measuring their progress. To abolish all competition would be not only foolishly eliminating one of the child's key guidelines in his growth, but as impossible as stopping games like "cops and robbers" by banning toy guns. There will always be sticks or fingers to point, and that unique ability of little boys, especially, to make sounds come from somewhere deep in the back of the throat. There will be fences to climb, lines to jump over, repetitions to count. There will be competition. It is unhealthy when it becomes an end in itself—when one's self-image is totally tied to winning or losing. No one lives long or well when self-appraisal is tied totally to being "the fastest gun in the West." Even if we're one of those who make it briefly, it may do more harm than good because we change, the world changes, we grow older, the new challengers keep appearing, and inevitably one day we are not the best when measured on such terms.

How do we help as adults who care? By keeping perspective ourselves. The old, "It isn't whether you've won or lost, it's how you played the game" is really true. Rudyard Kipling, in his poem "IF" had these lines that to me have always meant a great deal in terms of dealing with wins and losses. There's a part that goes, "If you can meet with triumph and disaster and treat those two imposters just the same. . . ." That's what they are—imposters—and the adult who understands that gives a child the best possible kind of experience.

Sports are for children to enjoy. It is when adults let their wishes to succeed become tangled with the achievement of an individual child or a particular team that there is a danger of too much psychological pressure. The adult who is bitter or angry after an error or a loss should consider helping the program in some other way than as a coach. The danger is that he will fill the players with an undue sense of guilt, failure and shame. If you can't walk away from the losses, get into some other role—sell the popcorn or raise the money. Those vicarious needs for success that many of us have in sports as we follow a particular team are better kept with our favorite pro team. If we're unhappy with Johnny Bench or Tom Seaver, it isn't going to bother them too much; but if we're unhappy with a child on our team or our son, there's dangerous pressure.

The key to the psychological impact of sports experience can be set by adults. Place the emphasis on the effort made and not the result. You can praise a child for his faithful attendance at practice, for his attitude and participation. This approach helps build children who keep trying, who don't coast when they are ahead, who won't give up when they are behind or defeated, who won't feel the pressure to go beyond the bounds of the rules and good sportsmanship to win.

All winning could be as harmful as all losing. There is value in a child's experiencing some frustration, tension and anxiety. Properly dosed, it promotes psychological growth. In early childhood development, we find that some frustration promotes the child's will to move about, to communicate and to learn other skills necessary to get along in the world.

The key to frustrations's being helpful is that it not overwhelm the child so that he quits or ends up spinning his wheels with a hopeless feeling. He needs support and guidelines to shift his focus and give him a new sense of direction so that he can finally accomplish some success in the task. The normal grade school age youngster can psychologically handle the disappointment of loss, of personal and team mistakes, if he feels a basic sense of self-worth, if he feels the support of his parents and his coach, and if he feels that his relationship with them isn't changed by his losing, not getting a hit, or dropping the ball.

A Loser Wins Out

by **Pat Van Buskirk,** *mother and freelance writer.*

When my son, Johnny, was in the third grade, he entered
the field of competitive sports. He was ready for the ordeal. I
wasn't. I thought he still looked sort of newly hatched and ter-
ribly vulnerable.

"Today I have to stay after school again and practice track,"
he announced, in a voice surprisingly deep for such a small boy.
"Why don't you come watch me? Lots of mothers are there
sometimes. Why don't you come, too?"

Of course I went to watch. I watched and my heart ached because he was trying so hard with such discouraging results. He
ran with desperation, his thin legs churning furiously. Other
boys ran more easily and went faster.

He wasn't much better at high jumping. He flung himself
through the air, often landing on the bar. He soon became bat-
tered and bruised from repeated all-out attempts.

"I'm not too good at track," he acknowledged after several weeks of this. "I think I'll try out for the Little League. Maybe I'm the kind of boy who's good at baseball."

He wasn't. For one thing, he couldn't see the ball. He was nearsighted, even *with* glasses. He just wasn't baseball material. But he tried—oh, how he tried.

Each evening he returned to me exhausted and discouraged.

One night he seemed even lower than usual. His unruly brown hair stuck out in little sweaty points, and drops of perspiration had made muddy trails through the dust on his forehead.

"I missed every fly that came my way," he said, "and I struck out twice."

"That's too bad," I sympathized. "Maybe you'll do better tomorrow."

He shook his head, doubtfully. I put a comforting hand on his shoulder but he pulled away. Then I noticed several angry-looking red marks on his chest.

"What are these red spots?" I asked. "These marks on your chest? And see, here on your arm, there's another."

He looked down. "Where?"

"Here and here. These round red spots."

"Oh, *those*. That's where the ball hit me."

"My goodness, shouldn't you duck when you're about to get hit?"

His eyes widened, shocked. "You're not supposed to do that. When you're a fielder, you're not ever supposed to duck a ball. You're supposed to catch it."

It isn't easy being a boy, I learned, but there were good moments—like the day I picked him up from practice and he had his new uniform. He ran to the car, the green-and-white uniform slung casually over his shoulder, and the smile on his face could have lit up every baseball field in America.

"I got a uniform," he announced. "Some boys didn't get one. This was the last uniform and the coach gave it to me. He said I earned it."

"Congratulations," I said.

He settled in the seat beside me with a happy sigh and spread the uniform on his lap so the name and number on the back could be read. "Boy, I broke sweat so many times to get this." He paused, then added for my benefit, "'Broke sweat' is what we guys say when we've worked hard."

It was wonderful to see him so happy.

The bench-warming period began after that. One day I took him to baseball practice. He was wearing an orange sweatshirt and cut-off jeans. I left him and drove on to complete the day's errands, then returned to the practice field. I was a block away when I saw a small figure in an orange shirt stretched out on the baseball field, not moving, not moving at all. Everyone was running to gather around him. Somehow I managed to park the car and run across the field.

He wasn't seriously hurt. He had collided with another player. He was stunned and his nose bled alarmingly, but after a bit of first aid he got up and walked unaided to the car. The next day both his eyes were black.

"You'd better not go to the game tonight," I said. "You don't look like you're in very good shape."

"Aw, Mom," he protested, "you don't have to be in very good shape to sit on a bench."

He didn't sit on the bench that night, however. His persistence had finally gotten to the coach. He put him in for part of each game after that. Clearly, he was the kind of coach who cared for things other than winning. Johnny missed balls, threw wild and struck out, and all his mistakes were announced over the loudspeaker. The family's hearts bled as one. Then one night a crucial fly came his way. I saw the coach wince and cover his eyes. The ball sailed into Johnny's glove and stayed.

There was an unmistakable aura of success about him as we drove home.

"Why not stop and get malts for the whole family?" he suggested grandly.

"Why not?" I agreed. After all, success is a relative thing.

Baseball season is ending now and, at this moment, Johnny is alseep. He lies on his back, arms outstretched and limp. There is a football carefully placed beside his pillow. (Oh, Lord, give me strength.) I lean over to kiss the soft curve of his little-boy cheek and an idea occurs to me. I think of other mothers I know, mothers who sit in the stands and cheer sons who hit homers and win medals. It must be great to be the mother of a winner but, I decided it couldn't be half as heartwarming and tender an experience as mothering a gallant little loser.

Comments

Problem Parents

Coaches blame parents and parents blame coaches for the problems in children's sports programs. Meanwhile the kids snicker at the absurdity of the adults who make more out of the contest than they do. For example, I once saw a picture showing an 11-year-old catcher and a 12-year-old batter standing at home plate. Behind them their parents were fighting, and one mother was beating the umpire with an umbrella. The batter quipped to the catcher, "I'd give up this crazy game if my parents didn't enjoy it so much!"

Parental misbehavior at sports contests has become such a problem that in some programs parents are barred from attending games. In Miami a girl's softball league has banned all adults, using teenagers as coaches, umpires, and scorekeepers in an attempt to eliminate the problems which parents so often cause. Other programs have resorted to playing games during the morning or early afternoon hours so that most parents cannot attend.

Banning parents from observing their children's games is a sign of a society which has lost perspective about the meaning of children's sports. Although parental misconduct may be so uncontrollable at times that it is necessary to temporarily bar parents from attending their children's games, this is a poor long-term solution. As Rosen observes, parents are and should be involved in children's sports. It is parents who most often serve as coaches, umpires, scorekeepers, grounds keepers, and fund raisers. Children's sports programs should foster family cohesiveness.

Children want to share their experiences in sports with their parents; they want their support. But just as parents dislike being embarrassed by their children, young athletes dislike being embarrassed by their parents. Hysterical mothers and angry fathers who hurl epithets at opposing players, swear at officials, and bark orders to their children not only embarrass their offspring (and sometimes themselves), but have adverse effects on the entire program. Rather than sports serving as an opportunity for children to learn sportsmanship, they become an arena for parents to display contemptuous and derisive behavior.

Just as coaches, umpires, and players must conform to standards of behavior, so should parents. A few simply lose control of themselves when their children are competing. Such behavior is usually repugnant, and parents must be persuaded to behave appropriately. Occasionally, however, parent behavior can be quite humorous. For example, in a Little League game I saw a mother standing on the sidelines, totally engrossed in her son's batting. When her son hit a ground ball to the shortstop, she ran alongside him to first base. The umpire called her son out, but ruled that the mother had beaten the throw!

Overzealous parents create numerous other problems besides misbehaving as spectators. They are often guilty of pressuring their children into sports and of continuing to push once their children begin participating. Parents impose their own standards of performance on children, expecting them to meet their criteria of excellence rather than helping children to develop their own standards. Parents may prematurely place their children in evaluative situations, not giving them sufficient time to learn the skills before beginning to compete. Parents who push, who constantly evaluate their children's behavior, place great stress on their children. Confronted with these conditions, it is understandable that some children seek to avoid competitive sports. For them, the fruits of sport do not outweigh the risks.

In an article titled "We Live Through Our Children," Bernard Mackler describes how some parents foist their athletic dreams upon their offspring.

It is pathetic to see. Children become objects to be used, to make up for parental deficiencies. Orders are barked out and children are supposed to jump at every command.

In the place of love, we see performance. Children strive to do their best; this is their moment. They want to please, to let Dad know how good they are and perhaps the love and honey that they hunger for will come forward. It never happens. Love is not built upon fleeting moments on a ballfield. The many hours that parents spend ignoring their children are not to be compensated for by these athletic exploits.[1]

Another perennial problem is the behavior of parents after the contest. What parents say to their children after competing is important in helping youngsters understand the significance of winning and losing as well as other events which may have occurred during the contest. Donald McNeil gives an example of the problem in an article "Little Leagues Aren't Big Leagues." He writes:

> One night last season my team lost a close game. I sat the whole team on the bench and congratulated them for trying, for acting like gentlemen. I said I couldn't have been prouder of them if they had won. Most of all, I said, it is as important to be a good loser as a gracious winner. As I talked I could see their spirits lifting. I felt they had learned more than just how to play baseball that night.
>
> But as I mingled with the parents in the stands afterward, I was shocked to hear what they were saying to the boys. The invariable themes was, "Well, what happened to *you* tonight?" One father pulled out a note pad and went over his son's mistakes play by play. Another father dressed down his son for striking out twice. In five minutes the parents had undermined every principle I had set forth.[2]

It is no tragedy, of course, for children to lose a contest, to make an error, or to perform poorly; the tragedy is when parents belittle their children, destroying their self-respect and often their respect for their parents. Some parents seem to think that dealing with their children as athletes is somehow isolated from the rest of child rearing. They become so emotionally engrossed in their children's sports that they forget their child-rearing responsibilities. It is as though parents perceive a reversal of roles. Now they expect their athlete-child to behave as an adult, while they resort to the behavior of an odious child.

But, as with coaches, the number of problem parents are a small minority. Even though they may err occasionally, most parents have the best interests of their children in mind. They try to help, they offer encouragement, they control their emotions, and most importantly, they show their children that they care. When parents err, it is often because they do not know what their responsibilities are with respect to their children's involvement in sports.

Parental Responsibilities

Parents have a number of responsibilities in ensuring that their children's involvement is safe, beneficial, and enjoyable. Parents must realize that sports are not inherently good for every child. And unfortunately, I have seen situations where they are not good for any child. Parents cannot assume that every coach is more worried about the welfare of young athletes than about the outcome of the game.

The first responsibility of parents is to find out what their children want from sports and from them with respect to their sports participation. Most children first want the opportunity to choose whether or not they will participate, and then in which sport and level of competition. In other words, they want to set their own participation goals. They may benefit from parental counsel, especially if they seek it, but they will resent parental dictums.

Parents may push their children into sports without recognizing they are pushing. They may want so much for their children to play, to become stars, to be extensions of their past athletic selves, that they unwittingly convey their expectations in many subtle ways. Youngsters easily sense these expectations, and, if they feel compelled to play, it diminshes their prospects of obtaining the full benefits of sports. The full rewards of sport are only available when children play for intrinsic rewards, not extrinsic rewards such as parental praise or love.

Some parents not only push their children into sports, they also attempt to bribe them to play well. The first year I played Cub Scout baseball I remember the principal of my school paying his son, Jody, 25 cents for hitting a single, 50 cents for a double, 75 cents for a triple, and $2.00 for a home run. That was big money in those days, and while the rest of us were envious in one way, it lessened our respect for Jody's father and for Jody. In fact, we mused with delight when Jody failed to get a hit (as long as we won).

I am sure my former principal thought he was helping his son, or at least saw no harm in offering him money, but research suggests that under certain conditions the use of extrinsic rewards (money, ribbons, and trophies) may undermine the intrinsic motivation to play. Intrinsic motivation refers to an inner desire to do something simply for the sheer satisfaction of doing it. The person acts not for the rewards that others can give but solely for the rewards inherent in the activity. Under the right conditions, extrinsic rewards may help develop intrinsic motivation; but in activities where intrinsic motivation is already high, the introduction of extrinsic rewards may tend to reduce intrinsic motivation.

For most children it is the intrinsic rewards that initially attract them to sports. As we have seen, sports appeal exquisitely to the interest of young people. Sports are active; sports are challenging; sports are fun. But although children begin playing for intrinsic rewards, they soon discover a world of extrinsic rewards awaiting them in adult-organized sports programs. By the time some youngsters are 12 years old, they have won hundreds of trophies, medals, and other expensive prizes. Over a few short years, young athletes are weaned from their intrinsic motives and addicted to the pursuit of gold and silver. By the time they reach their teens they no longer get high on sports alone, they now demand a "medallic upper" as a boost.

And then after addiction to the extrinsic rewards of sports, at the grand old age of 13 or 14 many youngsters discover that the extrinsic rewards are gone. Only the gifted few go on to find increasingly larger rewards. Those who are less gifted must undergo withdrawal.

Some youngsters will rediscover the intrinsic rewards of sports participation, but others will find the withdrawal so painful that they never participate again. And a few are never able to kick the habit. They pursue sports in constant search of the medallic rewards, never able to satisfy their habit. These are society's athletic addicts who never really know the full satisfaction of sports.

While I have urged that parents permit children to determine their own sports involvement, this does not mean that parents should have no part in their children's involvement. Parents should provide a supportive atmosphere that is conducive to their children's participation. Parents ought to be the first to expose their children to the sports of our society. Research has shown that in homes where parents have favorable attitudes toward sports, where parents participate in sports, where they give their children some basic instruction in sports skills, and where they provide the equipment needed to play, children are much more likely to develop an intrinsic interest in sports. What parents must be alert to, however, is the sometimes subtle difference between creating a positive atmosphere for sports participation and pressuring or pushing their children into sports.

Parents also have the responsibility to set limitations on their children's participation in sports, to determine when their children are ready to begin competing, and to insure that the conditions for playing are safe. They have an obligation to learn if their children have any of the disqualifying conditions for participation in collision, contact, and noncontact sports as listed in the table on pages 205-206. And I believe parents have the responsibility to forbid their children to participate in boxing.

Parents also have the responsibility to protect their children from abusive coaches. Parents should know to whom they turn their children over. They should evaluate whether coaches conduct themselves in ways that are beneficial for their children. Parents are not meddling when they inquire why their children never get to play in contests. They are not meddling when they inquire about coaching practices which appear to imperil the health of their children. They are not meddling when they inquire why their children do not seem to enjoy playing the sport. It is the responsibility of parents to know these things; they have the right to ask the coach about them, and, if the answers are unsatisfactory, they have the right to intervene.

One solution of course is for the parents to remove their children from the program. But this is not an easy course of action.

Children often will resent being forced to quit. They fear losing face and may enjoy the sport so much that in spite of a poor coach they want to participate. Parents must use good judgment in such situations, communicating with both the child and the coach to resolve the problem.

Parents have an enormous responsibility to help their children develop realistic expectancies of their capabilities in sports. This, of course, requires that the parents have realistic expectancies about their children, something which parents do not always have. When parents hold excessively high expectancies for their children, they may lead them to believe they are capable of doing more than they actually are. Children with unrealistically high expectancies are often frustrated in sports, for even when they perform near their capabilities, their aspirations remain unfulfilled. Coaches, as well as parents, must help children formulate sensible goals if children are to experience full enjoyment from sports.

Sometimes children hold quite realistic expectancies, even though their parents have unrealistically high expectancies. This situation is equally destructive to children's enjoyment of sports. Regardless of how well children perform, it never seems to be adequate for the parents. This, too, can constantly frustrate children and thwart their motivation to participate. It can also result in children devaluing the worth of the parents' judgment, and hence, the parents themselves.

Parents with excessively high expectancies also frustrate themselves. They find themselves in conflict with the coach who may play their youngster only as a substitute. They demand to know why their child is told to play one position when *they* know he is destined to be a star in another position. They blame the coach when their child fails to bring them vicarious fame. Coaches invariably report that the most frequent cause of coach-parent conflicts is the discrepancy in their opinions about the child's capabilities to play the sport.

Parents are also responsible for helping their children interpret the experiences associated with competitive sports. Parents particularly can help children understand the significance of winning and losing. Psychologists have learned that the causes we assign to the experiences we have (that is, the *attributions* we make) are important in shaping our personality and future behaviors. Parents are especially important in helping children make appropriate attributions about winning and losing.

When children lose or fail some parents are quick to come to their rescue by blaming others—the coach, the other players on the team, the officials. Or the parents attribute their child's failures to bad luck or fate. Never is their child to be faulted for failing to succeed—it is always due to some *external* cause. Parents who express such attributions often unwittingly foster the attitude in their children that they are never responsible for their own behavior. Children begin to view the world as if what happens to them is the result of forces beyond their control. Such a view is unhealthy.

On the other hand, when parents help their children to accurately interpret the causes of events, children develop an attitude that they are responsible for their actions and that they have control over much of their environment. For example, parents can help children distinguish when winning and losing should be attributed to external factors or to internal causes—that is, the child's ability and effort.

Parents also are responsible for disciplining their children. Throughout this book and much of the literature on children's sports, the responsibility for the failure of children's sports programs is placed on the shoulders of adults. This is justifiable, but sometimes children misbehave—they break the rules, are uncooperative, and uncontrollable.

Although tongue-in-cheek, Donald Kaul may not have been entirely wrong when he placed the blame for the failures of children's sports programs on the children. At least sometimes they must accept part of the blame. Children *do* have obligations to their parents and coach when they participate in sports. When children misbehave, the coach has some right and responsibility to discipline them. Ultimately, however, the responsibility for disciplining belongs to the parents, and they must use it wisely.

Certainly some parents care too much about their children's sports participation. They meddle, interfere, and generally become a nuisance. But some parents do not care enough. They let their children participate without any knowledge or interest in what they are doing. Uninterested parents neither meet their obligations to their children nor help other adults who provide the opportunity for the youngsters.

Resolving Parental Problems

Two solutions go hand-in-hand in solving parental problems in sports. The first is to have top-flight leadership in the sports program. Program administrators, coaches, and umpires all must display the leadership qualities discussed previously. Parents who see well-organized, well-run programs are less likely to find reason to complain or interfere. Instead, they will find themselves an active part of their children's participation. When most parents conduct themselves appropriately, the isolated, misbehaving parent is likely to feel quite conspicuous. Through subtle influence, other parents can encourage misbehaving parents to change their ways.

The second solution is to provide parents with an opportunity to receive some education about the sports programs in which their children are involved. I believe every local sports program should have a parent orientation program which is held at the beginning of each season. Such a program serves several purposes:

1. To inform parents of the objectives of the specific league or club.
2. To provide parents with a greater appreciation and understanding of the sport, including its basic rules and the skills required to play the sport. (This may not be so essential in some of the more popular sports, but is most helpful in the lesser known sports.)
3. To inform parents of what the league or club expects of each child and of the parents.
4. To provide parents with an opportunity to become acquainted with the person who will be coaching their child.
5. To help coaches and league officials understand the concerns of parents and to establish clear lines of communication between parents and coaches.

Even though I'm certain most parents want their children to know the joy of sports, today they need more than good intentions to be responsible parents of young athletes. Parent orientation programs, and other means of educating parents, are essential if children are to have safe, beneficial, and enjoyable sports experiences.

References

1. Mackler, B. *We live through our children.* Unpublished manuscript, Hunter College of the City University of New York, p. 6.
2. McNeil, D. R. *Little leagues aren't big leagues. Reader's Digest,* June 1961, p. 142.

PART FIVE

More Joy
and Less Sadness

Thus far, adults have been telling adults what children's sports programs ought to be. In Part Five we conclude by giving the children an opportunity to tell adults what *they* would like their sports programs to be. Young athletes (and former young athletes) tell adults how to put more joy and less sadness into their play. Please listen to the children!

Letter to My Football Coach

by **Larry D. Brooks,** *former young athlete.*

Dear Coach:

You won't remember me. It was just a few years back. I was one of those kids that turn out every year for freshman football without the slightest idea of how to play the game. Think hard. I was the tall, skinny kid, a little slower than the others.

Still don't remember? Well, I remember you. I remember how scared I was of you when you'd slap your hands together and yell "Hit!" I remember how you used to laugh at me and guys like me when we'd miss a tackle or get beat one on one in practice.

You see, you never let me play in a game. Once in a while, when you'd be giving a chalk talk to the first string, I'd get to play a couple of downs of scrimmage.

Letter appeared in *National Federation Press Service*, Volume 36, Number 9, April 1976. Reprinted by permission of the National Federation Press Service.

I really admired you. We all did. But now that I'm a little older and a little wiser, I just wanted to let you know that you blew it. I didn't play football after my freshman year. You convinced me that I didn't have what it took, that I wasn't tough enough.

I remember the first day of practice, when you asked for all the linebackers. I wanted to be a linebacker. The first time I tried to tackle someone I got my helmet ripped off. All I had done was lower my head and hit. No technique. No tackle.

You laughed. You told me I ought to be a quarterback, that I tackled like one. All the guys laughed. You were really funny.

Another time, after I became a guard, I missed a block—in practice. Of course. The guy side-stepped and I wound up with my facemask in the mud.

"C'mon! You hit like a girl" you said. I wanted to hit. I wanted to tell you how much I wanted to hit. But if I had, you'd have flattened me because you were tough and didn't take any backtalk.

We ran the play again, and I hit the same guy a pretty good shot this time. When I looked at you, you were talking to another coach.

I'm the first to admit that I was pretty bad. Even if I had been coached on technique, I still would have been a lousy football player. I was one of those kids who was a couple years behind my peers in physical maturity and strength.

That's where you messed up. I grew up. By the time I was a senior, I stood 6'5" and weighed 220. I couldn't fly, but I could run pretty well. That non-athletic freshman could now throw a baseball harder than anyone in the state. I was drafted and signed by a major league baseball team.

When my strength started to increase about my junior year, the varsity coaches drove me crazy with requests to turn out for football. I told them I didn't like the game.

"But why not? You're a natural!"

"I dunno, Coach, I can't explain it. Football is just not my game."

Looking back I really regret not playing football. It would have been a lot of fun. Maybe I could even have helped the team. But thanks to you, I turned against the game before I ever really got into it. A little coaching, a little encouragement, and who knows? I guess I'll never find out.

You're still out there, I see, coaching the frosh and sounding mean. I wonder how many potentially good athletes, kids that are a year or two behind, that you will discourage this year? How many of them will be the butt of your jokes?

It took me a while to learn that your "toughness" is meaningless. You're just a guy who played a little second string in college. So what have you got to be so tough about?

How sad. You're in a position to do a lot of boys a lot of good. But I doubt that you will. You'll never give up a chance to look "tough" and sound "tough." You think that's what football's all about.

I know better.

Larry D. Brooks

Let the Kids Play

by **Hal Lebovitz,** *sports editor for the* Cleveland Plain Dealer.

After four unforgettable years my son and I have ended our Little League careers, he as a player, I as a spectator. This is my valedictory, written in the hope that other fathers and, yes, even mothers, may see the light.

Frankly, I thought my behavior at the games was exemplary and adult. But recently I decided to interview my son. For years I have been interviewing the Yogi Berras, the Ted Williams, the Jimmy Browns, the Jack Dempseys. Why not Neil Lebovitz, my favorite Little League catcher?

"Are you enjoying Little League ball?" I asked him.

"Yes, dad, a lot."

"Is there anything I could do to help make it more enjoyable?"

"Well, dad, you know a lot about baseball, probably more than most fathers. . . ."

Reprinted from the *Cleveland Plain Dealer*, 1960 with permission of the publisher.

My chest expanded several inches until he said, "But. . . ." This one word punctured the balloon completely.

"But," he continued, "I wish you wouldn't talk to me during the game. You keep yelling to me, 'Get up closer,' and 'Don't step away,' and things like that. I try to listen to you and to the manager and watch the ball all at the same time and I don't feel comfortable. It gets me confused."

"Well, I'm only trying to help."

"I know," he said. "But you asked me, dad, so I'm telling you. If you want to help me improve, I'd like it better if you waited until we got home."

"Is there anything I could say at the game—if I had to say something—that would help you?"

"Well, I like it when my teammates tell me, 'Don't worry, you'll get 'em next time,' after I do something wrong. I like it when you compliment me and encourage me. I don't like it when you tell me what I'm doing wrong at the game."

So ended our interview. Needless to say I was jarred. But I knew he was right. He was saying "Let me play my own game. You can't play it for me." He was reminding me of the truism "Build! Don't belittle," or phrased more commonly, "Boost! Don't knock."

It was no consolation to me to know that I was no different from other fathers. I discussed the matter with George Kell, former major league great who is now broadcasting the Tigers' games. He, too, has a Little League son.

"When my boy takes a third strike it kills me," he confessed. "When he gets a hit I'm reborn. More so than when I experienced those things myself. It's funny how we blow up at our kid's mistakes, forgetting that we made them ourselves. You'd think I never took a third strike or dropped a ball."

The ultimate danger of our actions was revealed by George McKinnon, the baseball coach at Cleveland Heights High. "In our community we have a marvelous Little League program," he said. "You'd think we'd eventually get a lot of talent from it for our high school team. But by the time the boys reach us most of them have turned to other interests. And do you know the reason? Their parents made baseball so frustrating they turned to something in which there was less parental pressure."

Still, I'm delighted my boy played Little League ball. Sports opens doors to friendships as no other endeavor can. I'm especially glad we had that father-son interview, late as it was. During the final weeks of the season he played his own game. I stopped playing it for him. He was a much better player. Clearly, he had more fun.

Surprisingly, so did I.

What's the World Coming To?

by **Nic Pfaffinger,** *young soccer player in Kitchener, Ontario.*

To the Editor:

Although I am only 12 years old I can tell poor sportsmanship when I see it. Not among young people like myself but among adults.

On June 16 our team (Laurentian Acadians) was playing the Rockway team. With four minutes left to play and the score 1–0 in our favor a Rockway boy kicked the ball down the sideline. I and most people thought it went out, and the ref called it that way. Suddenly a Rockway father jumped out on the pitch and started hassling the ref. After a great deal of arguing the man hit the ref. When the ref walked away the man spit at him. After the game the man punched the ref again. He hassled the ref all the way to his car.

We have had many similar experiences and it ruins the game. It must be very frustrating for the referees who are only trying to do their best.

My friends and I play soccer for the fun of it, and we wonder, what is the world coming to?

Nic Pfaffinger
Kitchener

Letter to the Editor which appeared in the *Kitchener-Waterloo Record* June 19, 1976. Reprinted with permission of the publisher.

Dear Mom and Dad

Dear Mom and Dad:

  I hope that you won't get mad at me for writing
this letter, but you always told me never to keep
anything back that ought to be brought out into the
open. So here goes.

  Remember the other morning when my team was
playing and both of you were sitting and watching.
Well, I hope that you won't get mad at me, but *you*
kind of *embarrassed me.* Remember when I went
after the puck in front of the net trying to score and
fell? I could hear you *yelling* at the goalie for
getting in my way and tripping me. It wasn't his
fault, that is what he is supposed to do. Then do you

  Letter appeared in *You and Your Child in Hockey.* Ontario Ministry
of Culture and Recreation and Ontario Hockey Council, 1975. Pp.
27-28. Reprinted with permission of the publisher.

remember *yelling* at me to get on the other side of
the blue line. The coach told me to cover my man,
and I couldn't if I listened to you, and while I tried to
decide they scored against us. Then you *yelled at me*
for being in the wrong place. You shouldn't have
jumped all over the coach for pulling me off the ice.
He is a pretty good coach, and a good guy, and he
knows what he is doing. Besides *he is just a volunteer* coming down at all hours of the day helping us
kids, just because he loves sports. And, then neither
of you spoke to me the whole way home, I guess you
were pretty sore at me for not getting a goal. *I tried*
awfully *hard*, but I guess I am a crummy hockey
player. But, *I love the game*, it is lots of fun being
with the other kids and learning to compete. It is a
good sport, but how can I learn if you don't show me
a good example. And, anyhow I thought I was *playing hockey for fun*, to have a good time, and to learn
good sportsmanship. I didn't know that you were
going to get so upset, because I couldn't become a
star.

Love,

Your son

I Want To Play For Fun

by **Catherine** and **Loren Broadus,** *former coaches and fans for their 3 Little League sons. The authors are now at the Lexington Theological Seminary.*

"It's not fair," my 10-year-old son said. Barry was angry and sounded a little hurt, the way a wife sounds the day after her husband has forgotten her anniversary. "I've been to three practices and the coach hasn't let me practice batting yet."

Barry batted very well the year before and this new coach was not even giving him a chance to show what he could do. Condemned without trial—*my* son! My first impulse was to burn two crossed baseball bats in the front lawn of the coach's house.

Then I had second thoughts about my militant plan. Should I talk to the coach and be an "understanding mother," who was only trying to help by calling this oversight to his attention. After some thought, I realized that this was not a good solution.

Reprinted from *Laughing and Crying with Little League.* New York: Harper and Row, 1972. Reprinted with permission of the authors.

Finally, I suggested to Barry that he tell the coach before practice that he had not batted. He did and the coach told him, at the end of practice—after he had not permitted my son to bat—that he could bat at the next practice.

Now, I felt like burning the bat, ball, glove, suit, and coach on the pitcher's mound at sundown. Four practices and the coach still had not let my son practice batting. Obviously, the coach had his team picked and everyone else was insignificant.

After several games, the expected event occurred. "Mother, I'd like to quit Little League and play minor league for fun." Minor league is baseball for boys who do not make a Little League major division. Barry had made Little League and was entitled to the prestige of wearing the uniform. But he was not playing much ball. I realized that sitting on the bench was a little dull, but thought that the prestige of the uniform might compensate for the boredom.

The next day I asked him if he still wanted to quit Little League.

"Oh, I made up my mind the other day." He was satisfied with his decision. He really wanted to play baseball for fun. He was tired of watching the other dancers at the ball, even though he was dressed for the occasion and listed as an honorable guest. He would rather dance in the honky-tonk than watch at the ballroom.

It was a relief for me. We gathered up the uniform and drove to the coach's house to sever this relationship and let another boy sit out the season dressed in orange and white. The coach was at work so his wife greeted us at the door.

We explained the situation to her.

"But if Barry will just wait and be patient through this season, we will have the best team in the league next year," she pleaded.

"This has nothing to do with winning or losing, Mrs. K. Barry wants to play baseball for fun." This was very confusing to the coach's wife. I could hear the William Tell Overture playing as we rode off into the sunset. I imagined her saying to her husband, "Who was that grinning lady who left this silver bullet (would you believe orange and white uniform with matching socks and belt)?

It was not an easy decision for a 10-year-old boy to make in a competitive world, but he and I cheered inwardly as much as

I cheered when my other son was chosen for the All-Star team.

Seeing your 10-year-old son make a decision against the tide of personal prestige and public opinion ("Nobody quits Little League," people had told him) is a glorious event. It is a great way of winning in Little League.

There is something biblical about turning defeat into victory.

Comments

I believe there always will be children to profit from well designed sports programs; and adults need to become wiser architects of these programs. I believe the way in which a sports program is conducted is more important than the sport itself. I believe children's sports can be more, much more, than merely a means of identifying winners and losers. I believe sports can help nudge this world towards being just a little better place in which to live. I believe the qualities needed to find joy in sports are the qualities needed to find joy in life.

I want young athletes to take sports seriously—seriously enough that they can obtain the full benefits of sports. I want young athletes to strive for excellence, for real joy comes to youngsters who know they have given their best—win or lose—and know their best is appreciated by others.

To know the joy of sports, I want children to have the rights in sports that were given to me, and occasionally denied me. Thus, I am pleased to have played a part in the development of a *Bill of Rights for Young Athletes*. This Bill of Rights is endorsed by many educational, medical, and national youth sports organizations. I urge every parent, coach, and sports administrator to also endorse these rights, and then to uphold these rights for the young athletes of today and tomorrow.

Bill of Rights for Young Athletes

The right to participate in sports.

The right to participate at a level commensurate with each child's developmental level.

The right to have qualified adult leadership.

The right to participate in safe and healthy environments.

The right of children to share in the leadership and decision-making of their sport participation.

The right to play as a child and not as an adult.

The right to proper preparation for participation in sports.

The right to an equal opportunity to strive for success.

The right to be treated with dignity.

The right to have fun in sports.

_____

Reprinted with permission from *Guidelines in Children's Sports*, R. Martens and V. Seefeldt (Eds.). Washington, D.C.: American Alliance for Health, Physical Education, and Recreation, in press.